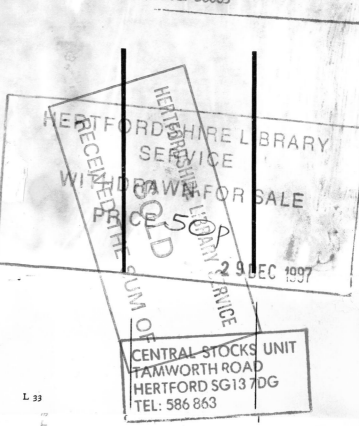

GLUBB PASHA

GLUBB PASHA
A Biography

Lieutenant-General
Sir John Bagot Glubb
Commander of the Arab Legion
1939–1956

JAMES LUNT

HARVILL PRESS
8 Grafton Street, London W1
1984

Harvill Press Limited
is distributed by
William Collins Sons & Company Limited
London · Glasgow · Sydney · Auckland
Toronto · Johannesburg

The author and the publishers would like to thank
copyright holders who gave permission for material
to be reprinted in this book. Full acknowledgements
will be found in the notes at the foot of the
relevant pages.

BRITISH LIBRARY CATALOGUING IN PUBLICATION DATA

Lunt, James
  Glubb Pasha.
  1. Glubb. *Sir*, John Bagot
  2. Jordun—Gays
  I. Title
  355.3'31'0924   DS154.52.G/

ISBN 0-00-272638-6

First published 1984
© Major-General James D. Lunt 1984

Map artwork by Leslie Robinson

Set in Monophoto Plantin Light by Ace Filmsetting Limited
Made and printed in Great Britain by
Robert Hartnoll Ltd., Bodmin

This book is dedicated,
as Glubb Pasha would wish,
to Jordan and its people.

Contents

List of Photographs and Maps *ix*
A Note on the Transliteration of
    Arabic Words and Names into
    English *x*
Glossary *xi*
Foreword *xiii*

1 The Crucible 1
2 An Apprenticeship 17
3 The Brotherhood 31
4 The Young Man
    and the Chariots of Fire 45
5 The Desert Patrol 62
6 A Band of Brothers 74
7 The Golden Years 92
8 Making an Army 108
9 The Intractable Problem 121
10 Backs to the Wall 139
11 The Legion Expands 161
12 The Slide Begins 178
13 The Dismissal 193
14 A State of Shock 210
15 Epilogue 222

Appendix: Glubb Pasha's Orders
    and Decorations 236
Acknowledgements 237
Bibliography 239
Index 243

List of Photographs and Maps

Between pages 112 and 113
Glubb's mother and father
King Abdullah bin Husain
Peake Pasha
Sir Alec Kirkbride
King Talal bin Abdullah
Rainpool in Wadi Gharra beside which Glubb pitched his
tent on his first night in the Transjordan desert in
November 1930
The Desert Patrol marching past
King Husain with General Cooke inspecting a Guard of
Honour
Glubb Pasha in a bedouin tent
Receiving a petition
Rosemary Glubb in Amman with Naomi, one of their
children
King Husain bin Talal at the time of Glubb's dismissal

Maps

The Middle East	xvi
U.N. Partition Plan	127
Jerusalem 1948	143
Rhodes Armistice Demarcation Line	158

A Note on the Transliteration of
Arabic Words and Names into English

Many Arabic words do not lend themselves easily to transliteration into English and it is easy to be pedantic in this context. For example Iraq should properly be transliterated *'Iraq*, or Ibn Saud as *Ibn Sa'ud*. I have preferred to follow the generally accepted form but will be willing to accept criticism for having done so. Wherever, for instance, the name Tawfiq is rendered as Tewfiq, or vice versa, I make no apology; either rendering will do.

I admit to using the word Arab, or Arabs, indiscriminately for the inhabitants of Jordan. It might have been better to have called them Transjordanians prior to 1946 and Jordanians thereafter but here again it has seemed to me pedantic to do so. Likewise with the word bedouin or bedouins; they refer to themselves as *bedu* (pl.) or *bedui* (sing.) but I have used the anglicized version as the most common for the most readers.

The word Arab is employed indiscriminately by many people as a description for races who have little more in common than the Chinese with the Japanese. When I commanded the Federal Regular Army in Aden from 1961–4, I was constantly struck by the difference in character, attitudes and customs of the people of South Arabia from those I had known when serving in Jordan with the bedouins of Central Arabia. Apart from the common religion (Islam) and a common literature, they differed in almost every way.

I have, however, used the word Arab wherever I have wanted to differentiate between the British and Jordanians serving in the Arab Legion, although by no means every Jordanian was of Arab descent; there was for example a considerable Circassian element in the Arab Legion. If I have unintentionally offended by so doing, I apologize.

Glossary

I have done my best to avoid sprinkling the text with Arabic words but sometimes this has been unavoidable.

Abu Father. Traditionally fathers are known by the name of their eldest son. Thus King Talal was known familiarly as *Abu Husain*, and Glubb Pasha as *Abu Faris*.

Aghal or *Agal* The twin black headropes to keep in place the headcloth. The word means 'hobble', since originally the headropes were intended to hobble the camel's forelegs.

Bin or *Ibn* Son of.

Bint Daughter of, or girl.

Bey A Turkish title ranking below Pasha. In the Arab Legion majors and above were usually called *Bey*.

Bayt House. The bedouin tent which was woven from brown or black goats' hair was called *Bayt Shar*.

Al Can mean either the definite article or 'the family of'. *Al Jaysh* would mean 'the army'. *Al Saud* would mean the 'house' or 'clan' of Saud.

Hajj The pilgrimage to Mecca and Medina.

Hadari A dweller in a stone house, used in Jordan to differentiate between the settled Arabs and the Bedouins.

Ikhwan The Brotherhood. The name adopted by the Wahabis who terrorized central Arabia between 1919 and 1930.

Amir Prince.

Jihad Holy War.

Harb War.

Ghazzu Bedouin raids.

Jaysh Army.

Jundi Soldier (pl. *jenud*).

Mutasarrif Civil Governor of a province or large district.

xi

Qyada	Headquarters (of the Arab Legion).
Wadi	Dry water-course.
Jebel	Mountain or hill.
Shareef	Courtesy title for the descendants of the Prophet Mahommed. Shareefs of the Hashimite family ruled Mecca until expelled by Ibn Saud in 1924. King Husain of Jordan still owns property there.
Shamagh	The red and white checkered headcloth of the Arab Legion.
Sidara	Forage cap worn in the Arab Legion by staff officers.
Souq	Market.

Foreword

EARLY IN AUGUST 1952 I was offered a posting to the Arab Legion. At the time I was aged thirty-four and in rank a Major. I had heard only vaguely of the Arab Legion; Glubb Pasha was no more than a name. I spoke no Arabic. However the appointment – to raise and command a Bedouin armoured car regiment – carried with it temporary promotion to Lieutenant-Colonel and offered all the attractions of one's own command. Therefore I required little persuasion to accept. Six weeks later I arrived in Jordan to begin what turned out to be three of the happiest and most rewarding years in all my army service. I fell in love with Jordan and its people and came under the spell of the desert. Time has not weakened that spell – it is with me as I write.

The Arab Legion was only a small army, about 20,000 strong. Alone of the Arab armies it had come out of the Arab–Israeli War of 1948 with credit, and was justly proud of the fact. Most of my officers and soldiers were veterans of that war. Without exception they attributed their success to the man who had transformed the Arab Legion from a gendarmerie to an army and who had inspired it by his own unbreakable resolution during the bitter battles for Jerusalem and Latrun. He was Lieutenant-General John Bagot Glubb Pasha – an Englishman commanding an Arab army in the service of an Arab king. This book is the story of his life.

I can well remember my first meeting with this remarkable man. It was in his office at *Qyada*, as the headquarters of the Arab Legion was usually called. The room was small and unpretentious, its sole decoration portraits of the late King Abdullah and King Talal. Glubb was seated behind a large but shabby desk, his white hair and moustache making him look older than his years. I was immediately struck by his very high-pitched voice which seemed incongruous coming from a man I had always regarded as a desert warrior. After a courteous and rather old-fashioned welcome he told me I should be left alone for the next nine months, after which he would expect my regiment to be fully trained for active operations if required. He told me nothing about the Arab Legion, nor about the Arabs, other than to advise me to learn Arabic if I hoped to get the best out of my soldiers. The interview could not have lasted more than ten minutes.

I doubt if I met the Pasha more than a dozen times during the following three years but his influence permeated the Arab Legion to a remarkable extent. His knowledge of the bedouins was encyclopaedic, his life was dedicated to Jordan and he was completely selfless. He made mistakes because he was only human but he was an inspiring man to serve. Jordan was fortunate to have had a man of his calibre to command the Arab Legion at a time when the country's very existence was at risk.

As I have already said I fell under the spell of Arabia during my service in Jordan. Much of my time was spent in the desert with my bedouin soldiers, who came from as far afield as the Ajman tribe who pasture their camels along the borders of Kuwait. The history of the bedouins, their traditions and customs, fascinated me. I learnt their language, rode their camels and flew their falcons, their saluqis running beside me. It was then that I began to write regularly, often for Blackwoods, and usually about the bedouins. Had I been born fifty years earlier I should almost certainly have chosen to make a career in Arabia, but it was far too late to do so in 1952. Our days as an imperial power were numbered, although the end came sooner in Jordan than I had anticipated. Fortunately I had completed my tour of duty and had left Jordan nine months before Glubb Pasha was dismissed. It was not a happy time in Anglo–Jordanian relations, which have now been restored.

One of Glubb Pasha's most endearing qualities was his modesty. He would not agree that the work he did in Jordan was of any consequence in the Middle East as a whole. Compared with Egypt, Syria and Iraq, Jordan was a small and impoverished country and those who served her were operating on a tiny and insignificant stage. It is doubtful, however, whether most people would agree with the Pasha. He did make a significant contribution to our understanding of the Arabs and he certainly played an important part in the foundation of the modern Kingdom of Jordan.

In a recent television programme Field-Marshal Lord Carver was asked by Bernard Levin whether he considered any of the men he had served under were great men. Carver named only Field-Marshal Lord Harding. Greatness is difficult to define since every man and woman will judge it by their own reckoning. For my part I have no hesitation in saying that in my estimation Glubb Pasha was a great man. Among my closest friends I number many Arabs who would undoubtedly agree with me.

Ardtornish,   JAMES LUNT
Morvern, Argyll,
27 July 1982

Mosul Oil Field

●MOSUL

R. Tigris

Euphrates

R. Diyala

I R A N

N

Ramadi
Habbaniya

Hinaidi
BAGHDAD

I R A Q

R. Tigris

Diwaniya

R. Euphrates

Samawa

Nasiriya

Jaleeba

Abu Ghar●

Shaiba●

BASRA

Busaiya●

Mughaizal●   ● Al Abtiyya

KUWEIT

A R A B I A

NEUTRAL
ZONE

Miles

0   50   100

●RIYADH

The Middle East

Pasha

A Turkish title, derived from the Persian *padshah* (*padishah*) and influenced by the Turkish *bashak*. It was the highest official title of honour in the Ottoman Empire, always used with a proper name, which it followed. It was given to soldiers and high civil officials, not to men of religion, and was purely personal and not hereditary, except in nineteenth-century Egypt . . . On the fall of the Ottoman dynasty *pasha* was reserved only for soldiers but, even after the Turkish Republic finally abandoned its use in 1934, the title survived in former Ottoman possessions; e.g. in Egypt and Iraq . . .

(*Encyclopaedia Britannica* Vol. 17)

Chapter One

The Crucible

'Every man thinks meanly of himself for not having
been a soldier . . .'
SAMUEL JOHNSON, 10 April 1778

JOHN BAGOT GLUBB was born in Preston, Lancashire on 16 April
1897. He was the second child, and only son, of Frederic Manly
and Laetitia Frances Glubb, his sister, Gwenda, being three
years older. Frederic Glubb was a Major in the Royal Engineers
at the time his son was born; he retired from the army in 1920 in
the rank of Major-General, having been knighted in 1914 for his
services at the battle of the Aisne.

Although Jack Glubb, as he was always known in his family,
was to be of the third successive generation of Glubbs to take up
soldiering, his great-grandfather, John Matthew Glubb, had
been a parson, serving first at Dartmouth in Devon and ending
his days as Vicar of Shermanbury in Sussex, where he had also
been Rural Dean. The first record of this predominantly West
Country family was of Henry Glubb, Member of Parliament
for Okehampton in 1313. They were a family who for generation
after generation had provided Devon and Cornwall with country
lawyers, parsons and naval or army officers; respectable middle-
class gentlemen who considered themselves to be pillars of the
Crown and Constitution, which they probably were.

Some of the Glubbs may have been rich but John Matthew's
branch of the family most certainly was not. He had two sons,
both of whom went out to India at the age of fifteen to serve in
the Honourable East India Company's Bengal Native Army.
Jack Glubb's grandfather, Orlando Manly, distinguished him-

I

self during the Indian Mutiny and might have gone far in the Indian Service had he not been struck down by cholera at Meerut in 1861. His widow, who was left virtually penniless, returned from India with her two small children to set up home in the Vicarage at Shermanbury. There, her children enjoyed a happy and secure upbringing, but it was a home in which every penny counted; a country parson's stipend, augmented by the miserable pension of an officer's widow, did not allow for many luxuries.

Fortunately Frederic Manly Glubb was a clever child, winning a scholarship to Wellington College at the age of twelve. It was a condition of these scholarships that the recipients had to enter the army and Frederic Glubb chose to do so in the Royal Engineers. At that time in the British Army's history an officer's commission had to be purchased, and, thereafter, steps in rank. The Royal Engineers were however a 'non-purchase' Corps; nor were its officers expected to possess ample private means as was the case in the Cavalry, Foot Guards and certain Infantry Regiments of the Line. The Royal Engineers, together with the Royal Artillery, took its officers from the Royal Military Academy at Woolwich, known usually as the 'Shop'. Cavalry, Guards and Infantry took their officers from the Royal Military College at Sandhurst.

The Sappers, as the Royal Engineers are always known in the British Army, have long possessed a reputation for professional excellence; an aspiring cadet had to pass out high from the 'Shop' in order to join them. They have provided the army with a succession of generals far out of proportion to the size of the Corps, among them such distinguished officers as Napier of Magdala, 'Chinese' Gordon, Kitchener of Khartoum, and now Glubb Pasha. Frederic Manly Glubb, who was to end his army career as Chief Engineer of the British Army of Occupation in Germany, is also to be numbered among the Sappers' more distinguished sons. He was commissioned into the Corps in 1879.

It was while at the 'Shop' that Frederic Glubb acquired his love for horses, a passion he was later to share with his son. The army in those days was entirely dependent on the horse for land transport and every officer was expected to be a competent horseman. Frederic Glubb was much more than competent and wherever he served he became well known for his skill and courage as a steeplechase rider and in the hunting field. Nowhere was this more in evidence than when serving at the Curragh in Ireland, where he met, wooed and married a high-spirited and very intelligent Anglo-Irish girl, Laetitia Frances Bagot. Her father was the squire of Carranure in County Roscommon and a member of a family who came over with Duke William from Normandy in 1066. The Bagots have their roots deep in both England and Ireland. It was probably from his mother that Jack Glubb inherited the emotional and contemplative side of his character; from his father came the sense of duty and the love for an active life. His deep Christian faith was inherited from both his parents.

Like every army family at that time the Glubbs seldom stayed anywhere for more than three or four years. After Frederic Glubb returned from war service in South Africa, there was a spell in Mauritius where Jack first began to speak French. Mauritius was followed by Aldershot where he began to ride, and where almost every week there was some kind of military parade. 'When we left Aldershot after three years', Jack Glubb was to write seventy years later, 'I had acquired two qualities – I was to be a soldier in heart for the rest of my life, and my chief passion was horses!'

When his father's three years in Aldershot had been completed, he was placed on half pay. This was a device used by the War Office to retain the services of officers for whom no immediate employment could be found. It was accepted as an inevitable consequence of army life but it bore very hard on those officers without private means. Switzerland was then the cheapest country in Europe and Frederic Glubb moved there with his family. Jack was sent to a school at Vevey where he became fluent in French. His father's next posting was to York where Frederic Glubb was able to indulge his passion for fox-hunting, his son riding beside him whenever possible. But boarding school had now claimed Jack, first at a preparatory establishment at Matlock in Derbyshire, and then at Cheltenham College where he won an open scholarship.

The public school system of education in Britain must ever remain a mystery to most foreigners, as well as to many of the natives – but it appears to have a curious capacity for survival. So far as Frederic Glubb was concerned there were no doubts of any kind; a public school education was an essential part of the training to become an officer and gentleman. Cheltenham was one of several schools which specialized in preparing many of their pupils for the army entrance examination; in Cheltenham's case particularly for the Royal Military Academy. Jack Glubb was to be one of the many distinguished Sappers who entered the 'Shop' from Cheltenham, whose War Memorial provides us with some idea of the price the College paid during the First World War. There are 694 names inscribed on the college's war memorial.

Like most other public schools at that time success at Cheltenham was measured by an individual's ability at games. Jack Glubb, small and slight in stature and looking much younger than his years, did not shine on the games-field. Nor did he much care for cricket and football. Lord Hodson, the eminent judge, who was a contemporary of Glubb's, says he was so small as to be insignificant. Another contemporary, the late Sir Maurice Bowra, a former Vice-Chancellor of Oxford University and Warden of Wadham College, has said that Glubb was perfect material for bullying although there is nothing in Glubb's own account of his schooldays to suggest that he was bullied. He was, however, profoundly shocked by the swearing, which came as a surprise to him. He was never gregarious, boy or man, content always with the close companionship of his own family. Throughout his childhood and adolescence he found this companionship in his father and mother, happy to share with them his interests. His mother was deeply religious, and often sent him tracts which he found embarrassing to read in public. However her Irish blood was apparent in her gaiety and delightful sense of humour. The more one reads about Glubb's early life, the more normal it appears to have been, well calculated to give a growing boy that sense of security and balance which was to serve him so well in later years.

When war came in August 1914, Frederic Glubb, now a

Colonel, was serving at Salisbury as Chief Engineer in Southern Command. His war appointment was Chief Engineer of III Corps and in late August his son, Jack, accompanied him to Southampton where he embarked for France. Inevitably, when they were so close, it was a melancholy farewell. Jack, who was in his last year at Cheltenham, wanted to leave school and enlist as a private soldier in the Rifle Brigade, but was dissuaded by his father. He should instead restrain his impatience and take the entrance examination for the 'Shop' at the end of August. This he did, passing in second, which resulted in a letter from his father that throws an interesting light on Frederic Glubb's own character and beliefs, as well as demonstrating the close relationship which existed between father and son.

The letter is dated 'In the Field, 27/10/14', and goes on:

'My dear old boy, You will well know how proud I was when I heard the news of your having passed into the shop second. You are very nearly a commissioned officer and a man now, dear old boy. See that you are also a gentleman, a simple honest English gentleman – you cannot be anything better whatever you are. Never lower your standards, old boy. And remember that now you are a man, work is no longer "beastly swot" but preparation for your duties as an officer.'

There will doubtless be those who can find fault with such sentiments, regarding them as being in some fashion out-of-date, smug or plain sentimental. But they express an honest belief in such virtues as loyalty, duty, courage and selflessness, without which no man can expect to get the best out of those he has been appointed to lead in battle. Certainly, where Jack Glubb was concerned, they were to serve as a precept not only through the four years of war that lay ahead, but also throughout his life.

Jack Glubb's was probably the last generation of his fellow-countrymen to set forth for battle cheerfully and without a backward glance. The horrors of Ypres, Gallipoli, the Somme and Passchendaele were to say 'Goodbye to all That'; but unlike Robert Graves, Siegfried Sassoon, Wilfred Thomas and a whole school of First World War poets and writers, Jack Glubb did not survive four years of war only to nurse a deep sense of disillusionment, cynicism and loathing for the whole bloody

5

business. That he experienced his full share of horrors is clear from the diaries he kept throughout the war, since published as *Into Battle*,[1] but the picture he gives us is always a balanced one. It may have been because he was so young, just twenty-one when the guns stopped firing, or more likely because he was so truly a professional soldier which gave him a balance harder to find among those who were more intellectually inclined. But whatever it was, he survived two years of battle, including being grievously wounded, without losing either faith, courage or belief in the righteousness of his cause. There were doubtless many others like him but we seldom hear of them.

War after so many years of peace had come as a shock. 'I well remember my mother telling me at this time', Glubb has written, 'that she had been married to an army officer for twenty-six years, during which there had been occasional small campaigns . . . But that in all those twenty-six years, it had never occurred to her or to anyone else she knew, that there could ever again be a war between the civilized Powers of Europe.'[2] It is hard to credit, with the advantage of hindsight, that with so many horrors to come, the principal concern of young men like Jack Glubb, as they paraded round the barrack square of the Royal Military Academy in the early months of 1915, was lest they might be too late for the battle. There was, however, a rule at that time, to be discarded later as the casualties mounted, that no one could take his place in the battle line until he had reached the age of eighteen and a half. This meant that Jack Glubb had to kick his heels at the Royal Engineers depot at Chatham until 24 November 1915, although he had been commissioned Second-Lieutenant in the Royal Engineers on 20 April 1915. 'Every day I passed in England seemed like a year', but there was still a lot of battle to come.

He sailed from Southampton for France on 25 November 1915. 'With a stab of nostalgia I saw that the ship was the *Hantonia*. Two years before, I had crossed to France in the same ship with Dad and Mum when we went to spend a summer holiday in Normandy . . . On 27 November, I received orders

[1] J. B. Glubb, *Into Battle: A Soldier's Diary of the Great War* (Cassell, 1978).
[2] J. B. Glubb, *A Short History of the Glubb Family* (privately published, 1983), p. 48.

posting me to the 7th Field Company, R.E. With my pack on my back, and a stout ash stick in my hand, I set out at 7.30 p.m. to walk to the station [at Rouen]. The moment had come! I was going to the war! I trudged along contentedly, repeating to myself:

> *Marlbrouk s'en va-t-en guerre,*
> *Qui sait quant reviendra.*'[3]

His record in France was to be a remarkable one. Apart from short spells of leave, courses of instruction in the back areas, and three periods in hospital after being wounded, Glubb spent all his service in France as a front-line soldier, almost entirely with his beloved 7th Field Company. He was not in the trenches all the time, of course, but in a war in which the casualty rate among junior officers was appalling, he managed somehow or other to survive. The diary he kept of those years is amazingly vivid, as well as being amusingly matter-of-fact:

'4 December. I have been given a little liver chestnut cob called Minx as my charger. I rode her today to see the work going on at La Flancque. We were shelled at lunch time and at 3 p.m. It rained all day. As I was riding back in the evening, the billets were shelled by a six-inch gun.'[4]

Minx was to become the pride of Jack Glubb's life. Whenever his Field Company was out of the line there were horse shows in which to compete, or long, long hacks across the rolling countryside. Although the sound of the guns was always there in the background, it was possible on occasions to forget about the war in the company of a stout-hearted horse. He was fortunate, too, that his father, now Major-General Sir Frederic Glubb, was Chief Engineer of the British Second Army. From time to time he would collect his son, when in a rest area, and the two could ride together again as they had done in happier times.

On 20 December 1915, he was hit in the foot by a shell which had already badly wounded his commanding officer and killed another. This landed him in the Casualty Clearing Station at Hazebrouck for three weeks but he was back with 7th Field Company as soon as he was fit. 'Sappers are never allowed to

[3] J. B. Glubb, *Into Battle*, p. 24.   [4] Ibid., p. 27.

rest,' he noted on 10 March 1916. Night after night they were digging fresh trenches, or repairing the damage caused by the previous day's shelling. Rarely did a night go by without casualties. Yet morale remained remarkably high. There is no suggestion in Glubb's diaries that generals and other senior officers shirked the trenches; there are frequent references to visits by 'Brass-Hats'.

His first nine months of war were spent in Flanders among the ruined villages and battle-scarred fields of the Ypres salient. Here the old Regular Army had fought and died before handing on the torch to the Territorial and 'New Army' Divisions; 7th Field Company formed part of the 50th (Northumbrian) Division, a Territorial formation with a fine fighting record. After the British offensive was launched on the Somme on 1 July 1916, the Division was moved to that sector of the Front in early August. Glubb's diary entry on 23 September provides a horrifying impression of the beastliness of war:

'The area is thickly dotted with specks of black and grey, lying motionless on the ground. When you approach, the black patches rise in a thick buzzing swarm of bluebottles, revealing underneath a bundle of torn and dirty grey or khaki rags, from which protrude a naked shin bone, the skeleton of a human hand, or a human face, dark grey in colour, with black eye holes and an open mouth, showing a line of snarling white teeth, the only touch of white left. When you have passed on again a few yards, the bluebottles settle again, and quickly the bundle looks as if covered by some black fur. The shell-holes contain every débris of battle, rifles, helmets, gas-masks, shovels and picks sticking up out of the mud at all angles.

'One cannot see these ragged and putrid bundles of what once were men without thinking of what they were – their cheerfulness, their courage, their idealism, their love for their dear ones at home. Man is such a marvellous, incredible mixture of soul and nerves and intellect, of bravery, heroism and love – it *cannot* be that it all ends in a bundle of rags covered with flies. These parcels of matter seem to me proof of immortality. This cannot be the end of so much.'[5]

[5] Ibid., pp. 67–8.

8

It has proved hard for later generations to understand how men could endure so much and yet survive, their belief in human nature still strong. Glubb was one of the survivors, his faith still undiminished. The truth is that no one generation can truly understand another. The tendency is to judge from one's own experience and attitudes, so widely at variance with the attitudes and experience of those who have gone before, or who will follow after. We can only marvel that the majority of those who endured such horrors emerged from the end of the tunnel whole men; for those who did not, there can only be pity, and a bitter regret for the futility of it all.

It is important to remember that life was not all horror. There were glimmers of light. In Glubb's case his fortitude was strengthened by 'the comradeship of the Troop', his care for his soldiers and his love for the horses and mules which played such an important part in the efficiency of his unit. When man had to live as he had to live, like an animal, burrowed into the earth, surrounded by corpses, with death a constant companion, the compensation can only be in comradeship and belief in the cause.

On 26 December 1916, General Glubb sent a car to carry away his son for a brief break from the trenches. 'I very much enjoyed the drive, as it was the first time for four months I had seen houses standing, and civilians and women. Doullens was a joy to me. The pavements shining and wet, the people bobbing past with umbrellas, the lighted shop windows, the women wearing smart clothes, paying for their purchases in the shops. It is like paradise waking up in Cassel [Headquarters of Second Army] after four months on the Somme front; hearing from bed a cock crow, the birds singing, and seeing a tree waving in front of the window . . .'[6]

It was in Martinpuich, the skeleton of a village on the Somme, that Jack Glubb experienced one of those glimmers of light which was to remain with him for the rest of his life. It was early in 1917 on a cold, wet and desperately depressing day that he found himself in what was left of Martinpuich. 'The village was merely an area of vast mounds of débris of earth and broken brick . . . The whole countryside was a vast sea of grey mud, over

[6] Ibid., pp. 78–9.

9

which trailed low grey clouds, discharging a persistent drizzle. No words of mine can describe the dreariness and hopeless desolation of the scene, wrapped in mist and rain. I sat down on a heap of broken brick and rubbish for a few minutes rest. A cold gusty wind blows the driving rain in my face. Just behind me, a torn strip of old curtain, caught between two splintered roof-beams, flaps wearily in the icy wind.'[7]

He could see, through the mist and drizzle, the mound of white stone; all that was left of the village church. Beyond were two tanks, camouflaged and waiting. At intervals an eight-inch shell sailed over and burst with 'a loud incisive *Kr-rump*'. A party of infantry, protected from the rain by their waterproof capes, floundered past through the mud, grunting and grumbling as they went.

'Suddenly I feel my whole self overwhelmed by waves of deep and intense joy, which it is impossible to describe. Never before had I experienced such a feeling of deep interior joy, so that I could hardly contain myself. I sat for what must have been several minutes, filled with the passionate joy of Heaven itself – then the feeling slowly faded away. I remembered how St Francis of Assisi once said that perfect joy lay in being cold, hungry, exhausted and repulsed from the doors of every house at which one knocked. It was the depth of cold, misery, weariness and exhaustion of that day in Martinpuich, which had produced in me those waves of spiritual joy. I had given everything to do my duty and had held nothing back.'[8]

Glubb was to comment when he was eighty that he had never forgotten that experience, claiming that the lesson he had drawn from it had remained with him for evermore. 'The knowledge I acquired from it', he said, 'is that real joy can only be won by the abandonment of self and utter dedication to service.'[9] Although he admits that he did not always succeed in following this precept, he never doubted its truth; and it might be added, few men have succeeded as well as he did in making duty his guide.

It would be wrong to assume that the young subaltern was a particularly serious-minded young man. He took his duties more seriously than many of his contemporaries perhaps, but he was

[7]Ibid., p. 86.   [8]Ibid., p. 86.   [9]Ibid., p. 87.

full of fun and thoroughly enjoyed life. His letters home were full of affectionate humour as they recounted day to day events in and out of the line. He was a good correspondent to his 'Darling Mum', if at times a trifle demanding in his requests for razor blades, tins of Mars oil, Ever-Ready Dry Batteries etc. On New Year's Day 1917 he wrote to tell her, 'Dad sent the Rolls Royce to fetch me on Boxing Day and took me back to the "Shattoo" for two days . . . It was simply lovely seeing Dad again last week after such a long time, and I did enjoy my two days with him. The only thing I could possibly have liked more would have been leave [at] home, so as to have you both . . .'

His mother was an equally conscientious correspondent, always writing, 'My dear Diletto'. To his father he was always, 'My dear Old Boy'. Throughout their lives they wrote to each other regularly and with deep affection. Few families could have been more united in their care and love for each other. In later years Glubb Pasha wrote every week to the sister he had seldom seen since she made her home in Greece.

A Field Company, Royal Engineers, was a major's command. It was divided into Sections, the equivalent of Platoons in the Infantry, each commanded by a subaltern. Jack Glubb's every waking minute was devoted to his soldiers; as later, when he became Transport Officer,[10] he gave so much of his time to his horses. He never asked his men to do anything he was not prepared to do himself and he believed in leading them from the front. His pride in them was beyond compare, 'I meet no men of other units so clean and gallant as mine . . .',[11] and received his reward in their respect for his military qualities, and their affection for him as a man. Forty years later, after his dismissal by King Husain, one of his former soldiers, all those many years a civilian, wrote to say how warmly he was still remembered.

In April 1917, 7th Field Company was involved in the bitter fighting of the battle of Arras. During the fortnight the Company was in the line the losses in killed and wounded amounted to one-third of its strength. The divisional commander marked out

[10]A distinguished contemporary, Lord Reith, was also Transport Officer of his battalion during the same war and was to publish his reminiscences under the title *Wearing Spurs.*   [11]J. B. Glubb, *Into Battle*, p. 159.

the Company for special commendation. 'There is no doubt that we have won a great name,' recorded Glubb. 'This is partly due to comradeship and the old company feeling, and partly due to McQueen's untiring work and influence.'[12] Major McQueen was Glubb's commanding officer.

There was the comradeship of the Troop; there was also the comradeship that comes from working with horses. There can be no doubt that working with horses brings men together in an astonishing fashion. Glubb's affection for his animals was not his alone; the men in his Transport Section felt exactly the same about them. From 9 May to 15 June there were halcyon days out of the line. 'I took all the drivers and horses on exercise every day, and rode through the forest, where the dense green foliage forms an arch overhead, and the ground is carpeted with wood anemones.'[13] He goes on to say, 'All this alternated with periods of lying stretched in the long grass, full of rough flowers, dandelions and daisies, the hot sun on one's back, the hum of the insects, and the larks singing overhead. The horses wandered round, munching and switching their tails, rolling with clumsy ponderance, or nipping one another for fun. These were some of the happiest mornings of my life.'[14]

There are two other revealing diary entries during this period of rest. In one he records, 'I was bidden one day to dine at Brigade Headquarters, somewhat to my alarm, as I am so shy in company. However it all went off very well.'[15] In another, 'My Cornish-Irish ancestry, on the other hand, had made me emotional. I really love my soldiers. I enjoy an occasional party, and used especially to revel in our gramophone, which McQueen had dumped before the battle of Arras. McQueen and I, however, although of such different constitutions, were united by our one ruling passion. Both of us were utterly dedicated to our Company.'[16]

These passages demonstrate how truly the boy was father to the man. In later years, although by then a distinguished soldier whose views were sought by other distinguished men, Glubb sometimes appeared uneasy in the company of those he did not

[12] Ibid., p. 147.   [13] Ibid., p. 155.   [14] Ibid., p. 161.
[15] Ibid., p. 156.   [16] Ibid., p. 169.

know well but his dedication to his job, and his absorption with the people with whom he worked, never flagged nor faltered. As for his emotions, they never changed, although a rigid self-discipline buried them far from sight. His self-control seldom lapsed, making him appear much more reserved than was in fact the case.

In July 1917 he was gazetted Lieutenant, having until then been a Second-Lieutenant. Thus, by the age of twenty, he held the acting rank of Captain and that July he commanded the Company during McQueen's absence on leave. They worked mostly at night, repairing trenches and constructing fresh defences. 'The presence of the O.C. on night work in the trenches has a moral object,' he wrote. 'He should not counter-mand the orders of his juniors, or interfere much with them. But the O.C., having given the order for night work, should show that he is not too lazy to share its hardships as well, which may silence a lot of grumbling.'[17]

On 21 August 1917, Jack Glubb's luck ran out. That evening he set out to meet some of his transport wagons, falling in with one of his drivers en route. 'As I spoke to Gowans, I think I heard for a second a distant shell whine, then felt a tremendous explosion almost on top of me. For an instant I appeared to rise slowly into the air and then slowly to fall again . . . I dropped on to the ground and set out at a half run . . . I must have been dazed, for I remembered nothing afterwards . . . Scarcely had I begun to run . . . when the floodgates in my neck seemed to burst, and the blood poured out in torrents. I could actually hear the regular swish of the artery, like a firehose, but coming and going in regular floods and pauses.'[18]

He had been seriously wounded in the face, his jaw smashed almost beyond repair. There followed a long period in hospital. 'I realized vividly now that the real horrors of war were to be seen in the hospitals, not on the battlefield.'[19] Weeks afterwards, while still only semi-conscious and incapable of eating, he still did not realize how badly he had been wounded, writing to his father to use his influence to keep him in France, so that he could return to his Company the quicker. But the doctors knew

[17] Ibid., p. 179.   [18] Ibid., p. 185.   [19] Ibid., p. 186.

better. By hospital train, ship and train again, Jack Glubb arrived at the 3rd London General Hospital at Wandsworth where he was to lie for three months without much medical attention. In November, however, largely through his mother's efforts, he was transferred to a new hospital for face injuries at Sidcup in Kent.

Plastic surgery was then in its infancy, but Gillies was working at Sidcup and set about reuniting the broken fragments of Glubb's jawbone, still hanging loosely in his mouth. He had lost almost all his front teeth and eating was a constant problem. They succeeded, however, in cementing the lower jaw to the upper and discharged him in January 1918 to recuperate. Healing was a slow process and in March it seemed hopeless, but eventually the bones began to unite and life took on a different meaning. By then he was living in London with his mother, a woman of strong character who was determined her son should recover.

'Mum and Dad had been utterly devoted all their married life', their son has written, 'though their temperaments were remarkably different. Before the war, Dad's chief interest had been in horses, in hunting and in rural sports in general. Mum, although, as she used to say, she had grown up in an Irish bog, was completely uninterested in horses, but was intellectually cultured. She had taught herself French, Italian and German and read extensively in all three languages. Her joy in peacetime had been travelling in Europe.'[20]

Although this strong-minded woman was a semi-invalid for most of her life, she lived to the age of ninety-seven. All who knew her speak of her courage, gaiety and insatiable interest in life and learning. Mother and son were remarkably close, in temperament as well as in interests; without her constant support he might well have lost the battle to win back his health.

In June 1918 he succeeded in persuading a medical board to pass him fit for duty. Then he immediately requested a posting order to France. General Glubb, knowing his son, arranged for his posting back to 7th Field Company. When Jack Glubb finally joined the Company near Dieppe on 23 July, there was

[20] Ibid., p. 194.

14

only one other officer he knew. It had suffered severely, with the rest of 50th Division, during the German offensive in March 1918.

While in hospital at Sidcup, Jack Glubb was informed that he had been awarded the Military Cross for his services at Arras. A year later, when training with his Company at Martin-Église, near Dieppe, he was offered the appointment of staff officer to the Chief Engineer of a Corps. 'Of course this would be priceless experience for my career, as it is a very valuable asset to have been a staff officer in wartime. But sentiment and affection for my comrades overcame interest, and I wrote back refusing, saying that I would sooner go up the line again with the boys. I am afraid this will be a blow to Dad, both because he will be thinking of my future advancement, and because he would have preferred me to be at a Corps Headquarters, almost completely out of danger.'[21]

50th Division moved back into the line at the end of September and 7th Field Company found itself fully occupied building bridges and clearing a passage through the desolation of the battlefield as the pursuit of the German army gathered momentum. There were mines and booby-traps to be cleared, demolitions to be filled in; there were never enough Sappers to go round. But the war was now entering its last stages. On 4 November 1918, 7th Field Company fought its last battle with the German rearguards in the Forêt de Mormal, south of Maubeuge on the Belgian frontier. On 11 November the Company had reached Sars Poteries, near Mons, when the guns stopped firing after four and a half years of slaughter. 'Alas, the war is over, at the moment when it was beginning to be exciting and enjoyable after all these years', wrote acting Captain J. B. Glubb, R.E., on 5 December 1918. For him at least the war had been a crusade from beginning to end.

General Glubb rode on to serve as Chief Engineer of the British Army of Occupation in Germany. His son returned instead to England in February 1919, posted to the Royal Engineers Depot at Chatham where he was to be turned into 'a proper soldier'.

[21] Ibid., pp. 202–3.

For those who fought in it, and who survived, the First World War was a traumatic experience. Few were the same men by the end as they had been in the beginning; they had seen too many horrors, survived too many dangers. Many were scarred for life, mentally or physically, or both; many lost their illusions, many their faith. Some lost all contact with reality; some burned with bitterness and hate for the waste of it all for the rest of their lives; but not Jack Glubb. He had sailed for France as a boy; he returned as a man, bearing scars which would remain until he died. But his spirit was unquenched. He was too intelligent, too emotional in temperament, not to be affected by his experience; but his upbringing had given him the balance to see it in the round. From beginning to end he had sought no more than to do his duty; it was this perhaps, more than anything else, which had helped him to survive.

Chapter Two

———◆———

An Apprenticeship

'Arabia is a hard, barren mistress and those who serve
her she pays in weariness, sickness of the body and
distress of the mind.'

LORD BELHAVEN, *The Uneven Road*

JACK GLUBB RETURNED FROM FRANCE early in 1919 to attend a
course at the School of Military Engineering in Chatham. It was
designed to turn him into a peacetime officer. Drilling and being
drilled, building bridges and constructing fortifications, was
dull stuff after four years of battle, but he took it all in his stride.
The problem was how to fill in the ample hours of leisure that
were part and parcel of a regular officer's existence in peacetime.

Four years of war had not altered his basic character. On 19
July 1919 he watched the Victory March through London and
noted afterwards in his diary:

'So much hardship, so much courage, so much heroism –
and now such overwhelming glory. I am only twenty-one, but I
feel that the crisis of my life is past. Anything which happens to
me after this can be no more than an anti-climax!'[1]

From adolescence to manhood he had grown up in the
comradeship of fighting men, which is one of the few redeeming
features of war. There was nothing like it at Chatham. A serious-
minded and upright young man, he drank very little and danced
not at all. Games did not interest him, nor did shooting and
fishing. He still enjoyed riding but had lost his zest for fox-
hunting. Women, apart from his mother and sister, did not
enter into his scheme of things; if they did not repel, they

[1] J. B. Glubb, *Into Battle*, p. 223.

17

certainly did not attract. On arrival at Chatham, he was billeted in a house near the barracks. Returning to his room after mess, he found the daughter of the house in his bedroom. Deeply shocked, he persuaded her to leave. When the performance was repeated the following night, he moved heaven and earth to get a room in the barracks. Many young subalterns would have acted differently.

Like so many of his generation for whom death had been a constant companion for so long, he found peace unsettling. His path was clear enough in 1914 when the enemy was at the gate; but was there any purpose in being a soldier in peacetime? What had he to look forward to? The slow upward climb that had been his father's experience? And what would he do after his course at Chatham had been completed?

The Chatham course ended in June. Less than a month later the Arabs in Mesopotamia rose in rebellion against the British occupying forces; although they had been glad enough to see the backs of the Turks, they had never anticipated merely exchanging them for the British. It soon became necessary to reinforce the garrison with British and Indian troops and there was an urgent requirement for officers to fill a variety of operational and administrative appointments. Three hundred were needed; Jack Glubb was one of those who volunteered.

By the time he arrived in Baghdad at the end of September 1920, the rebellion had been quelled. There was, however, a pressing need for reconstruction since the Arabs in their fury had wrecked irrigation works, railway stations, factories and bridges. Sapper subalterns like Glubb were worth their weight in gold. It was while he was waiting for a posting order that he sat down one Sunday afternoon to review the courses open to him in planning a future career. Fifty years later he was to come across this paper and commented ruefully, 'As an example of logical thought, concisely expressed, it would not have obtained high marks in the Staff College examination!'

He began by quoting a passage in which De Vigny regrets choosing an army career since it had entailed forcing 'into a purely active life, a purely contemplative disposition'. Glubb found that his character also combined the active with the contemplative; he shares De Vigny's 'disgust' with the army whenever he had time to consider the matter, but became so absorbed in his everyday duties that he thoroughly enjoyed them. Whereas one side of him longed to study, to write and one day produce a great book, 'the means of bringing light and virtue to thousands of lives', the other side yearned for distinction in the military profession. He wondered whether his temperament fitted him for high command; he doubted if his conscience would allow him invariably to carry out orders with which he did not agree. Although he considered the military profession to be an honourable one, he believed an author, speaking from his soul, is in a better position to influence people, always provided that he can write. Since he could not answer for the latter, he concluded that he should remain a soldier while taking every opportunity to broaden his mind and improve the spiritual side of his nature.

However inconclusive the result of this self-examination, it illustrated an unusually serious-minded young man, particularly when at the outset he explained that he was 'not the same as other people in my pursuits and pleasure', and for that reason could not decide whether he should take up 'bridge or tennis'.

Iraq, as Mesopotamia soon became, was to be the beginning of Glubb's long love affair with the Arabs. He spent ten years there, the first five of them without any thought of home leave; early in his service in Iraq three things happened which throw an interesting light on his character.

His first posting was to the headworks of the Diyala where the river breaks through the foothills on its way from the Zagros mountains to join the Tigris. There a barrage had been built to divert the river for irrigation purposes, but dams had been wrecked and canals blocked during the rebellion. Glubb was given a gang of Indian coolies to construct and operate a rope ferry. A cable had been erected from bank to bank with a primitive cable car to convey the workmen across the torrent. The river was in full spate one morning when Glubb, breakfasting in the mess tent, heard shouting from the bank. Running out to investigate, he saw the cable car in trouble and one of the coolies being carried away on the flood. Removing his tunic as he ran, he dived into the river and was fast carried downstream.

It was impossible to swim in such conditions. Swept away by the flood, for part of the time beneath the surface, he was tossed and battered for a mile or more until the force of the river slackened. He managed to manoeuvre himself towards an island where, clutching at a branch, he painfully pulled himself to safety. He was seen by a passing Arab, accustomed to crossing the river on inflatable goatskins, and eventually Glubb was rescued, the Arab refusing any reward for his services. The coolie's body was never recovered. Glubb's account of this narrow escape from death eschews all heroics, 'This was not an act of courage, but of sudden emotion, perhaps hysteria, performed without thought.'[2]

Perhaps he was right, but the same cannot be said of the next event. His work on the Diyala completed, he was moved to Ramadi on the Euphrates where a bridge of boats spanned the river. With a gang of Arab labourers he was responsible for keeping the bridge in good condition, particularly when the Euphrates was in spate. A high bund on either bank prevented the river from overflowing its banks. One morning in April 1921 Glubb was walking from his tent to the bridge when he heard shouts from the other side of the bund. At once his mind went back to his previous year's experience. 'For a second I was seized with a wild panic desire to turn and run', he has written. 'Was I now to find myself jumping into the mighty Euphrates to rescue another drowning man? With a desperate effort of self-control, I walked terrified to the river bank. It was a small empty boat which had slipped its moorings, and was being carried away rapidly downstream on the flood!'[3] As an example of moral courage, Glubb's reaction would take a lot of beating.

The third event discloses another side of his character. In March 1921 the British Government, deeply concerned by the increase in its military commitments in the Middle East, convened a conference in Cairo. Winston Churchill, as Colonial Secretary, was in the chair, and every important British official in the Middle East attended. So did Colonel T. E. Lawrence as Churchill's unofficial adviser. Perhaps the most significant out-

[2] J. B. Glubb, *Arabian Adventures: Ten Joyful Years of Service* (Cassell, 1978), pp. 20–1.   [3] Ibid., pp. 21–2.

come was the decision to make the Royal Air Force responsible for the external and internal defence of Britain's newly-acquired territories in the region. This suited Trenchard, the Chief of Air Staff, who was fighting off takeover bids by the Navy and Army, and it was enthusiastically endorsed by Lawrence. A new form of Imperial Policing – Air Control – came into being, and Palestine, Transjordan and Iraq became Air Commands; Aden was to follow suit in 1928. The resultant economies in manpower were immediately apparent. Eight R.A.F. squadrons, with their ground support, and five thousand locally-enlisted Iraq Levies, replaced an army garrison of thirty-three infantry battalions, six cavalry regiments, sixteen artillery batteries and a large number of ancillary troops; an Air Vice-Marshal (Sir John Salmond) with a handful of staff officers took over from a general with all the paraphernalia of an army headquarters.

A priority requirement was the construction of airfields. Glubb, as a Sapper, was moved to Hinaidi, outside Baghdad, to supervise the building of the R.A.F. base. As usual he threw himself whole-heartedly into his work. His labourers were from the Dulaim tribe whom he had already got to know at Ramadi. He had taught himself Arabic and many of the Dulaim had become personal friends. One day a party of gypsies visited the camp. Known as Solubbas, they are common all over Arabia, travelling from encampment to encampment, selling and repairing pots and pans. The men are rascally-looking fellows and their women, who are bold and unveiled, sing and dance and, for a consideration, grant certain favours. No bedouin would dream of marrying them but many are willing enough to accept the favours.

Some of Glubb's workmen responded enthusiastically to these attentions. He was deeply shocked. Gathering them together, he demanded their *aghals*, the twisted black headropes which hold in place the Arab headcloths. These he proceeded to burn in front of their astonished eyes, explaining that by this symbolic action they were forfeiting their manhood because of their conduct with the gypsy women. The Dulaim were more amazed than angry, fortunately for Glubb. Arab tribesmen soon become violent if they believe their faces have been blackened.

21

Glubb could easily have been murdered, but it appears the thought never occurred to him.

'Policing from the skies', as some of its more ardent advocates described Air Control, had much to commend it on the grounds of economy of force. But in those primitive days of flying it suffered from one considerable disadvantage – the difficulty in identifying friend from foe. Iraq consisted principally of mountain, marsh and desert, with tribes constantly on the move and one mountain valley looking much the same as the next. Aeroplanes had poor endurance, maps were poor and a pilot might as easily bomb and machine-gun 'friendlies' as those opposed to the government. Air Headquarters therefore decided to organize a body of ground intelligence officers whose task it would be to familiarize themselves with the topography and tribal politics of their respective areas. They were to be known as Special Service Officers, or S.S.O.s.

This scheme came into operation at a critical moment in Glubb's career. The British army in Iraq was fast running down; Sappers were in great demand elsewhere in the empire. Soon he would be posted to some other part of the world; but he had come to love Iraq and its people. He was now reasonably fluent in Arabic, which he had largely taught himself, and since he was solitary by nature, he did not much mind spending long periods away from his own people with only the Arabs for company. Above all he enjoyed responsibility and the knowledge that the job he was doing was worthwhile. When he was approached by Air Headquarters with the offer of an appointment as S.S.O., he had no difficulty in accepting. He did however stipulate that he was to stay a soldier; he would not exchange his khaki for light blue. However he had seen the last of the Sappers and had chosen instead to make a career with the Arabs. Quoting one of his mother's Irishisms, he wrote that his career as a Royal Engineer had been 'short and sweet like a donkey's gallop'.

Glubb's parish extended for 500 miles down the Euphrates from the Syrian border to just north of Basra; in width it ranged from 40 miles on either bank of the river to 200 miles in the south, where it included Iraq's southern desert. It embraced a vast area of marsh and date palms inhabited by the amphibious

Marsh Arabs. Out in the desert were the true bedouin tribes, Shammar and Dhafir, with their black tents and camels; there were also the shepherd tribes with their goats and sheep, summering along the river but wintering far out in the desert once the winter rains had transformed the wilderness into lush pastures. For a young man aged twenty-five it was a tremendous challenge.

His headquarters was at Nasiriya, the headquarters of the Muntifiq Division, where a few British advisers assisted the Iraqi officials. Iraq was a British Mandate, a word difficult to translate into Arabic, and British motives were suspect. The countryside was still in a very disturbed state, tribe fighting with tribe and all resentful of British attempts to establish an efficient administration based on the Indian model. None of this affected Glubb's enthusiasm for the job; he spent every waking moment touring his bailiwick on horseback, on foot, or by launch and canoe. In the marshes, as in the desert, there was an almost total absence of law and order; the men who dwelt there were murderers many times over but they made Glubb welcome as an honoured guest. He was later to write of them:

'These men were full of humour, simple people adhering to their own codes, hospitable, generous and cheerful . . . the marshman was the Cockney of the Arab world, always ready with a joke or an antic. Always near death, he would disregard it in a tribal fight, or, even more, in seeking revenge in a blood feud . . . I have not lived with them since 1922, but I shall always remember them with affection.'[4]

There could be no set rules for a job like his; always on the move, living among Arabs and speaking Arabic for ninety per cent of the time, he was acquiring an affection for the people, and an understanding of their problems, that soon became all-absorbing. There was no longer any soul-searching over bridge or tennis; the Arabs he met played neither, nor did Glubb. Unlike most of his fellow-countrymen serving in Iraq, his off-duty hours were not spent in the Club pursuing purely British activities. They were spent with Arabs, mostly simple tribesmen and villagers, hearing their complaints and listening to their

[4]Ibid., p. 54.

heroic poems being declaimed far into the night. Only a man who loved the work and sympathized with the people could have endured the primitive conditions, the loneliness and the absence of any kind of privacy. Thirty-three years later a bedouin soldier from the Dhafir tribe, with twenty years' service in the Arab Legion, had this to say about Glubb's early years in Iraq:

'The Pasha, may God bless him, never knew the Arabs before he came to my country. Then he lived with us, and in our fashion. He was not like the usual Englishman. He lived like an Arab. He respected our customs and he was always patient. He listened a lot and spoke very little. At first we thought he was a spy for the government but when we got to know him better we knew he was one of us. There has never been anyone quite like him. May God remember him for good!'[5]

In those early years of flying, communications were in their infancy. The man on the ground could only communicate with the pilot by setting out panels in a prearranged code or by a complicated system of smoke signals. When planes were carrying out a mission to strafe recalcitrant tribesmen they would usually be guided to their target by the ground intelligence officer riding in the flight commander's plane. His was the task of identifying friend from foe, or pointing out the village or encampment which was to be bombed. This demanded an excellent knowledge of the local topography since the maps were virtually useless. Cockpits were open and the planes were vulnerable to rifle fire; in winter it would be freezingly cold, in summer the target might well be obscured by clouds of dust driven by the wind. The R.A.F. would eventually make of Air Control a fine art but in the days before Radio Telegraphy it was very much hit or miss; it was also dangerous.

Glubb barely had time to acquire a knowledge of his area before he was moved to Ramadi at the end of 1922. Britain was at odds with Turkey over the province of Mosul to which Turkey laid claim on the grounds that its population consisted mainly of Kurds, and also because oil was already being extracted by

---

[5]Statement made to the author in 1953 by an Arab soldier (an Iraqi) who had joined the Arab Legion soon after Glubb Pasha established the Desert Patrol in Transjordan.

the Iraq Petroleum Company. There was a very real likelihood of war and Glubb found himself regularly flying on missions over Kurdistan where the tribesmen were in a state of chronic rebellion against the Arabs (as they still are today). It was flying amidst high mountains but apart from the occasional forced landing Glubb came to no harm. The threat of war receded after the signing of the Turkish Peace Treaty in July 1924, before which he was posted back to Nasiriya.

The eight months that Jack Glubb spent at Ramadi were probably the most significant months in his life, for it was during this time that he came under the spell of the desert and first discovered his interest in the bedouins. Many years later Julian Huxley was to write of him:

'If the Middle Eastern countries could arrange to utilize human catalysts like Glubb Pasha in other than military fields, such as public health or education or agriculture, the entire region might acquire a new dynamism.'[6] Glubb did turn out to be a human catalyst where Transjordan's bedouins were concerned and it is for this that he will be longest remembered. It began at Ramadi.

He had virtually no routine duties. His principal task was to familiarize himself with the area and the people. He already knew the Dulaim tribe who were only semi-nomadic; they lived in tents but were primarily cultivators. Farther out in the desert were the true bedouins from tribes like the Shamar and Aneyzeh, two of the biggest tribal confederations in Central Arabia, whose life-style differed little from the Old Testament. Glubb spent every available moment visiting their tents, either by camel or horseback, sipping their bitter bedouin coffee, studying their ways and perfecting his Arabic.

The romantic conception of the bedouins owes much to Lady Hester Stanhope and others of her ilk. It is that of the handsome warrior chieftain, or sheikh, galloping across the sands on his mettlesome steed, white robes billowing out behind him as he rides to rescue some damsel in distress. The true picture is very different. Since most bedouins are miserably poor their clothing is usually in tatters and they smell strongly

[6]Julian Huxley, *From an Antique Land* (Parrish Rogers, 1954, New Portway Reprints, 1972).

of camel and goat. Such horses as they possess are usually unkempt and seldom groomed, albeit kin to the world's blood-
stock. But what is a bedouin? Glubb has provided us with a
definition, which is probably the most accurate:

'The first requisite is that the bedouin must be a nomad who
breeds and keeps camels. Any non-nomad is automatically
ruled out. But there are tens of thousands of nomadic tribesmen
in Syria and Iraq who live in tents and are continually on the
move, but who are not bedouins for they do not primarily breed
camels, but sheep and donkeys. Having decided that a bedouin
must be a nomadic breeder of camels, however, we have not
completed our definition; for he must also be able to trace his
descent from certain recognized pure-bred bedouin tribes. You
and I could never become bedouins. A pure-bred Arab, an
agriculturist in Iraq or Transjordan, could never become a
bedouin unless he could prove pure bedouin descent. We find
therefore that a bedouin, in the strictest sense, is a camel-
breeding nomad of certain specified tribes.'[7]

The bedouin do not refer to themselves as such. They speak
of either *Al Bedu*[8] or *Al Arab*. They do not include the settled
Arabs among *Al Arab* but usually refer to them as *Fellahin*, or
those who cultivate the fields, a form of manual labour no true
bedouin would contemplate. In Jordan the settled Arabs are
often known as *Hadari*, or those who live in stone houses. There
was a time when no true bedouin would dream of living in a
house; the black tents woven of goats' hair were as much symbolic of their breeding as the nobleman's castle in feudal England.
The nomad's fear, suspicion or dislike of the townsman extended
to the very air the latter breathed; bedouins often stuffed their
nostrils with rags to keep out the foul odours of the town before
entering from the desert.

The poorest of them had all the arrogance of the aristocrat.
They called themselves *Asil*, or Noble, reserving the word also
for their pure-bred camels, horses, saluqis and falcons. They
were herdsmen and warriors, never sullying themselves with

[7]J. B. Glubb, *The Bedouins of Northern Iraq* (Journal of the Royal Central Asian
Society Vol. XXII, Part 1, 1935). (Now the Royal Society for Asian Affairs.)
[8]Singular *Bedui*.

manual labour of any kind. Their favourite pursuit was camel-rustling or raiding, which they called *Ghazzu*; it provided a kind of economic balance. Tribe X raided your camels, and in reprisal you raided Tribe Y; when raiding ceased, there was economic disaster. The great chieftains or sheikhs would make war on each other, largely in an attempt to subvert each other's tribes. War was known as *Harb* and had more serious conse-quences than raiding. Much of the code of chivalry brought back to Europe by the returning Crusaders derived from bedouin traditions. They loved poetry of the epic kind, were great boasters and terrific snobs. Slavery persisted in Arabia long after it had been abolished elsewhere and most great bedouin sheikhs had their personal bodyguard of slaves, all of them Moslems and many of them second and third generation dwellers in Arabia. Some of them were of high rank and great wealth but the poorest bedouin would not give his daughter in marriage to any man of slave descent.

The bedouins' tribal structure was much the same as the Highland clans'. This may account for the curious attraction they have long possessed for the British, which James Morris expressed so well. He is writing of Oman in 1957:

'Gone, almost everywhere, were the long star-lit nights beneath Bedouin tents, in which the Englishman pleasantly deluded himself that his friendship with the Arabs was some-thing special, mutual and indestructible, and that there existed some affinity of spirit between the desert and the shires.'[9] That was true when written, but it was not so in 1922, when Glubb first encountered the desert tribes. At that time the internal combustion engine and the discovery of oil had yet to transform ancient Arabia. It was a way of life little changed over thousands of years and Glubb has himself provided us with a lyrical des-cription of it. It is of the Shammar tribe crossing the Euphrates in their flight from Ibn Saud:

'For five days the Shammar flowed in a constant stream across the bridge – five of the most strenuous but absorbing days of my life. Before my eyes passed in review a complete pageant of that nomad life which had not changed in its essentials since

[9]James Morris, *Sultan in Oman* (Faber & Faber, 1967), p. 135.

27

the days of Abraham, but which was so soon to pass away. An almost unending procession of tanned men's faces, framed by long ringlets like those worn by the young ladies of the Victorian age. Horses stepped daintily on to the bridge with fine muzzles, arching necks and tails carried high – the breed from which in the past were drawn the ancestors of the thoroughbreds of the world. On their backs sat riders in dirty cloaks frayed at the edges, their bare feet swinging by the horses' flanks. They looked unkempt and ragged to English eyes, but they managed their horses with unconscious ease, riding only on a pad without stirrups and using a rope or a head-collar in place of bit and reins. Some carried long lances decorated with ostrich feathers, but the majority had rifles slung on their backs. At other times came great camel litters, wooden crescent-shaped frameworks hung all over with carpets, tassels, white shells and blue beads. They seemed to lurch uncomfortably from side to side. Now and then the face of a smiling girl would peer out from behind the curtains.

'The whole pageant was dominated by camels. One by one the great herds would pace slowly up to the bridge-head. There is no shade in the desert for hundreds of miles, and the slow heavy camels would pause or shy ponderously at the un-accustomed shadows of the date palms. On reaching the head of the bridge the whole flock would pause, pushing and jostling against one another. Long necks were stretched out suspiciously, staring eyes gazed vacantly at the swift-flowing Euphrates and the frail wooden bridge. Then from the front of the herd, an old, rather moth-eaten camel would tread slowly forward on to the planks of the bridge. A boy of twelve or fourteen would be lying flat on his stomach along her back, his cotton night-shirt tucked up to his hips. Advancing ten yards along the bridge, the old camel would stop, and look contemptuously at the swift Euphrates twirling and spinning below the frail planks of the bridge. Then the herdsman, in a shrill voice, would give his call: "Way-oh! Way-oh! Way-oh! Hei! Hei! Hei!".

'The jostling herd at the bridge-head would quieten. One long neck after another would rise, the thin head turning slowly to listen. Yes, that was the familiar voice! Then suddenly the

28

whole herd would press forward towards that voice and on to the bridge. In a second the old camel was tearing across the frail planks, the herdboy bouncing on her back. Behind her charged a solid phalanx of enormous animals, the outside ones leaning in at an angle of sixty degrees, pushing their neighbours to prevent themselves being pushed into the stream. The plank decking of the bridge clapped up and down, the pontoons sank to their gunwales as the charge passed over them, and then shot up again as the weight passed on . . . For five days the pageant continued. The lumbering flocks, the cantering horsemen, the swaying litters, the deep voices, the veiled faces of which only the eyes were visible. Then the last flock was over, the last of the swaying litters and lean horsemen disappeared once more into the shimmering mirage of the desert to the east of the river.'[10]

Glubb was deeply moved by the scene. From that moment onwards the desert and its people held him in thrall; so much so that when he came to write the story of the Arab Legion twenty-five years later, the picture of the Shammar crossing the Euphrates was as vivid in his memory as when it had occurred. He was not to know at the time that he was witnessing the passing of an era, the end of an economy based on the camel; there are still black tents in Arabia today but as likely as not there will be pick-up trucks or cadillacs parked alongside them.[11]

Early in 1923 Glubb was posted back to Nasiriya. It was a different world from the desert. One of the tribes in Glubb's area, the Beni Huchaim, was in conflict with the government in Baghdad. Their territory stretched for fifteen miles on either side of the Baghdad–Basra railway line and in return for their good behaviour the government had not taxed them. In 1923 it decided to levy taxes and the Beni Huchaim took up arms. Two of the tribe's sub-sections, the Barkat and Sufran, were particularly obstreperous and it was decided to take air action against them; as a preliminary Glubb was told to find out all he could about the Barkat and Sufran.

The *Qaimaqam* (governor) at Samawa, the nearest adminis-

[10] J. B. Glubb, *The Story of the Arab Legion* (Hodder & Stoughton, 1948), pp. 19–22.
[11] In the course of a visit to Jordan in January 1982 the author counted only a few camels where formerly there would have been thousands.

trative centre, told Glubb he could not possibly visit the tribes since they were in open revolt. Disregarding this, he set out on his horse for the sheikh of the Barkat's village, his uniform concealed under an Arab cloak. Entering the guest-house, he gave the greeting of peace which was returned. Coffee was poured, a meal prepared and Glubb took off his cloak. The Barkat were surprised but remained friendly. Glubb explained the purpose of his visit and hoped the tribes would make peace with the government. After the meal he rode round the tribal area, making his map and warning the tribesmen that they would be bombed if they did not submit. No man raised a hand against him.

Summoning the sheikhs of the two tribes, he told them he was going to Baghdad to lead the planes against them. They were polite and said they understood; but they failed to report to the *Qaimaqam* at Samawa as instructed. The R.A.F. duly arrived, with Glubb in the leading aircraft to point out the targets, and bombs were dropped. They were very small bombs and did little damage (one old woman was killed), but the message was plain. Not only the Barkat and Sufran, but all the sub-sections of the Beni Huchaim made their peace with the government. They appeared to bear Glubb no grudge but the Air Officer Commanding was surprised when he heard how openly Glubb had spied out the land. He recommended him for a decoration but the British government felt it was unwise to advertise the fact that Iraq was still in such an unsettled state.

In Glubb's opinion the government in Baghdad failed to take advantage of this successful little action. Instead of letting the Beni Huchaim go free, they imposed a heavy fine on the Barkat and Sufran who immediately decamped into the marshes. The confidence established by the open way in which Glubb had carried out his mission was destroyed by the government's vindictiveness. Although the action taken against the Beni Huchaim was noted all over southern Iraq with salutory results, the Beni Huchaim felt they had been unfairly punished. Glubb sympathized with them. 'Fight and win, if you must,' he wrote. 'But as soon as you have won, forgive and forget, and make your enemies your closest friends.'[12]

[12]J. B. Glubb, *The Changing Scenes of Life* (Quartet Books, 1983), p. 65.

30

Chapter Three

———————◆———————

The Brotherhood

'The essence of their dogma lay in its refusal to
compromise.'

Robert Lacey on Wahabism[1]

GLUBB PASHA HAS ALWAYS CONTENDED that the Arab intelligentsia have never understood the bedouins, nor have they had
any desire to do so. Neither Greeks nor Romans, Byzantines nor
Turks ever considered the bedouins to be military material; they
were far too wild and undisciplined. It is only within the last
decade that the Egyptians have enlisted them. So long as they
remained in the wilderness, where sensible men seldom ven-
tured, they were free to follow their barbarous pursuits. This
suited the bedouins who considered themselves to be the salt of
the earth.

Every so often, however, the bedouin tribes erupted and
burst out from the desert. The most notable occasion was in
AD 633 under Khalid ibn al Waleed, at the behest of the Khalif
Abu Bekr, when they carried with fire and sword the message of
the Prophet Mahommed to the farthest extremities of the
Byzantine and Persian empires. The bedouins were the har-
bingers of Islam. Again, towards the end of the eighteenth
century (as followers of Mahommed ibn Abdul Wahab, who
preached a puritan revival based on an undeviating return to the
rules laid down in the Koran), they swept out of Nejd to con-
quer the Holy Cities of Mecca and Medina. They were only
driven out after an army was sent from Egypt by Mahommed
Ali in 1813. The Wahabis, as they were known, then retired to

[1]Robert Lacey, *The Kingdom* (Hutchinson, 1981), p. 285.

the desert places to await the arrival of another prophet to lead them against the unrighteous.

The bedouins' life of extremes produced within them a latent fanaticism. In the desert it was blazingly hot or bitterly cold. A man's possessions were limited to those that could be carried on camelback. Nature was at its most violent. So was man, whose every day was a struggle for survival. T. E. Lawrence has written that there were no shades in the desert; it was either black or white. If the rains failed the camels died and the bedouins starved. When the pasture was lush they gorged to repletion. Wealth was measured by the size of the herds. Rich and poor alike lived in tents and slept on the ground.

The bedouins cherished a zany kind of democracy in which all men were equal, only some were more equal than the rest. A sheikh exercised little or no authority, other than that established by his own personality. The constant struggle against the elements resulted in a strange pride. 'I am a bedu, cold won't hurt me,'[2] said Bin Kabina when Wilfred Thesiger asked him why he did not buy a blanket, instead of sleeping on the freezing ground covered only by his loincloth. For such a people any sort of restraint, like that imposed by international boundaries, was intolerable. Bedouins had little sense of nationality; for them the family came first, then the clan or sub-section, and after that the tribe. Lines drawn on maps meant little to a tribe like the Ruwalla who wintered outside Damascus (in Syria) but summered at Jauf, 500 miles away in Saudi-Arabia, and to get there had to pass through Transjordan, and sometimes Iraq. Most tribes had fought against each other at one time or another, either for gain or as part of some tribal confederation. When great Arab princes went to war, their principal aim was to suborn their enemy's tribal allies, as in the wars in India under the Moghuls. Territory as such meant little, until comparatively recently, yet every inch of desert was owned by someone. With the discovery of oil, territory became all-important.

Raiding, or camel-rustling, provided the excitement every bedouin craved. The reason for it has only become obvious since raiding has ceased. 'We had thought the abolition of raiding

[2]Wilfred Thesiger, *Arabian Sands* (Longmans, 1959), p. 186.

would increase the security of desert life', wrote Glubb, 'but we discovered unexpectedly that raiding had not only been a pastime for the chivalry of Arabia but also a social-security system of which our ill-timed intervention had destroyed the balance.'[3] But by then it hardly mattered, because of oil. 'Tribal raiding is a form of gambling,' wrote Sir Alec Kirkbride. 'Like most variations of that amusement, it hardly ever enriched anyone and was a habit which people found most difficult to give up.'[4] In one of the crazier efforts to restrict raiding, the Iraqi government in 1924 required their bedouins to sign in at a police post before leaving on a raid; on their return they were to report the results – so many own side killed, so many enemy, and so many camels looted! The bedouins soon laughed it out of court.

Bedouin warfare was governed by rules handed down over the centuries. Women and children were inviolate and for this reason night attacks were dishonourable; it would be impossible at night to differentiate between male and female. Indiscriminate killing was rare for fear of starting a blood feud; even in the seizure of booty, compassion would often be shown to the losers. There was no shame in retreat in the face of odds; seldom was territorial conquest envisaged. When Kirkbride once commented to a bedouin friend on the lightness of casualties in bedouin warfare, he was told, 'There are not sufficient of us to bear heavy losses. If we all got killed, fighting would have to stop and life would be very dull.'[5]

Wahabism, however, introduced a new dimension into bedouin warfare because all who did not conform were put to the sword. Women were spared, but all males, regardless of age, were slain. Nothing that was not covered in the Hadith (the collected doings and sayings of the Prophet and of his companions) was permissible. The Prophet had forbidden luxuriant moustaches and neatly trimmed beards; Wahabis clipped their moustaches and grew their beards long and unkempt. The Prophet had never worn the black headropes (*aghals*); Wahabis

[3] J. B. Glubb, *The Story of the Arab Legion*, p. 168.
[4] Sir Alec Kirkbride, *A Crackle of Thorns* (John Murray, 1956), p. 77.
[5] Ibid., p. 74.

33

never wore them and shunned every kind of personal adorn-
ment. Smoking, music and alcohol were forbidden. The rules
about prayer five times a day were strictly observed. Wahabis
were a joyless lot, hypocritical and intolerant, harsh and dog-
matic. Yet for some strange reason this highly-disciplined, puri-
tanical revival held out a peculiar attraction for the feckless and
bird-witted bedouins.

Wahabism was revived in Nejd in the early years of this
century. By 1912 several settlements had been established by
the *Ikhwan* (or Brotherhood) as the new-style Wahabis described themselves. The majority were members of the great
bedouin tribes of Mutair, Ateyba and Ajman, whose grazing
districts ranged from the Hejaz in the west to Kuwait in the east.
The Mutair were particularly involved, especially their leading
sheikh, Feisal al Duweesh. At the outset, however, the Ikhwan
were content to follow their religious beliefs peacefully.

The revival of Wahabism early in the twentieth century was
overshadowed by the outbreak of the First World War. The
Hejaz was drawn into that war by Shereef Husain's revolt against
the Turks, but Nejd was little affected by the conflict. Ibn Saud
bided his time to settle old scores with Ibn Rasheed of Hail, who
supported the Turks, meanwhile fostering his links with the
Wahabis. His ambition was to make himself 'Lord of all the
Bedouins'.

Soon after Glubb's arrival in Iraq, Ibn Saud attacked Ibn
Rasheed, driving his tribe, the Shammar, helter-skelter out of
Nejd.[6] On the far side of Arabia Shereef Husain and his sons
were endeavouring to establish their own Hashemite empire. It
was the moment when the British and Arabs were to discover
that promises made in the stress of war were difficult to honour
in the changed conditions of peace. Allenby's capture of Damascus on 1 October 1918 had proved to be the high water mark in
Anglo-Arab relations; sadly, that point was never to be reached
again.

It is difficult to take much pride in Britain's dealings with
the Arabs. Confusion began with the correspondence in 1915

[6]It was this flight by the Shammar which was described by Glubb in *The Story of the
Arab Legion* (pp. 20–2) and which is repeated in this book on pp. 27–9.

between the British High Commissioner in Cairo, Sir Henry McMahon, and Shereef Husain of Mecca. It was confounded by the shocking agreement reached by Sir Richard Sykes with M. Picot of France in 1916. Mr Balfour's declaration of a national home for the Jews in Palestine, made in 1917, added further confusion; and France's eviction of Feisal from Syria in 1920 made things worse. There is little in all this to make an honest British heart feel proud, the story being largely one of muddle, mismanagement, duplicity and, on occasions, downright deceit. The achievements, and there were many, were largely cancelled out by the failures. Therefore it is hardly surprising that from those days to this the situation in the Middle East has been the despair of the world's chancelleries.

It is hard to believe that at the end of 1918 Britain could do no wrong in Arab eyes. British arms had freed the Arabs from Turkish domination. British money had fuelled the Arab Revolt. British influence far exceeded that of the French. Yet, with all the cards in her favour, Britain proceeded to lose trick after trick, possibly because she could never decide which cards were trumps.

Britain's defeat of Turkey had left a power vacuum in Central Arabia. There were three claimants to fill it. To the west in the Hejaz there was Shereef Husain, Guardian of the Holy Places; as head of Al Hashim,[7] Husain was a direct descendant of the Prophet Mahommed. He proclaimed himself King of the Hejaz, but he was a man whose ambitions far outran his abilities. His sons Ali, Abdullah, Feisal and Zeid had played active parts in the Arab Revolt against the Turks.

To the east in Nejd, the bedouin heartland, the Al Rasheed from Hail, the second claimants, were at odds with the Al Saud from Riyadh, the third claimants. The Rasheed were head of the Shammar confederation of tribes whose annual migrations reached beyond the Euphrates. The Al Saud belonged to the equally important Aneyzeh confederation. After nearly a century of adversity their fortunes had been revived by a remarkable man, Abdul Aziz ibn Saud, who would one day make himself King of Saudi Arabia. He took the first step in this

[7]In this context the word *Al* signifies 'The House of . . .'.

35

direction in 1921 when he defeated Ibn Rasheed and proclaimed himself Sultan of Nejd.

In that same year Amir Feisal, who had been thrown out of Syria by the French, was proclaimed King of Iraq. This had been arranged by the British although it had been originally intended that Feisal's elder brother, Abdullah, should be offered the throne of Iraq. The disappointed Abdullah had already launched an expedition to recover the throne of Syria for the Hashemites but he got no farther than Amman before he realized that the task was beyond him. Local support was weak and the French were strong. The British resolved the problem for him by carving out the Principality of Transjordan from the 'lands east of the Jordan' and by proclaiming Abdullah the ruler as Amir (Prince). They also provided him with a subsidy. Britain had been given mandates in Palestine, Transjordan and Iraq by the League of Nations; the French held mandates in Syria and Lebanon. It was all very confusing for the local in-habitants. Mandates were a new idea and were difficult to explain. It seemed to the Arabs that after all they had been led to believe by the Allied Powers between 1915 and 1918, all they had achieved was an exchange of masters – the British and French for the Turks.

Although no fanatic himself, Ibn Saud conceived the idea of utilizing the fanatical Ikhwan as his storm-troopers very early in his career. By 1917 there were no less than two hundred Wahabi settlements dotted throughout Nejd, each one within a day's march of another. By their very nature the Ikhwan were secretive and suspicious of strangers, which accounts for the fact that the world knew little about them until they burst out of Nejd in the early 1920s.

Their tactics were simple. They aimed to confuse and then to terrify. Assembling a thousand men or more with their camels took time and could not be concealed. However their objective was invariably kept secret and was known only to a handful of their leaders. Rumours preceded their advance, leading all those supposing themselves to be in their path to flee in panic. They would often delay deliberately as they moved forward, loitering for days or even weeks to allow the rumours to increase. Then in one swift move, generally overnight, they would cover seventy miles or more, riding their camels and leading their mares, which they mounted only for the final charge. This was usually just before dawn when they would come screaming out of the desert, calling on God's name and slaughtering every male in their path. No quarter was given or asked since every Wahabi killed in battle was assured of paradise. They were a murderous bunch and the chief killer among them was Feisal al Duweesh of the Mutair.

Ibn Saud let them loose on the Hejaz on 4 September 1924, when they sacked Taif. On 3 October they were before Jeddah, whose citizens persuaded King Husain to abdicate in favour of his son, Ali. Husain sailed away in a British ship to Aqaba, shortly followed by Ali. Ibn Saud would soon be King of the Hejaz and Guardian of the Holy Places. Meanwhile the Ikhwan were ranging all over Central Arabia, virtually out of control. In the spring of 1924 one of their raids nearly reached Amman; it was halted at Ziza, fifteen kilometres to the south, by the combined efforts of R.A.F. planes and armoured cars, nobly assisted by the Beni Sakhr tribe. At the same time the Mutair had launched a murderous attack on the Iraqi shepherd tribes. Thousands of sheep and goats were carried off and every tent was looted. The shepherds were in a state of terror.

Glubb was away in Transjordan when the shepherds were attacked. He had spent the previous January exploring Iraq's southern desert and getting to know the Dhafir, the principal bedouin tribe in that area. In March 1924 he took two months' leave and set out for Transjordan on a camel, Ramadi being his starting point; his sole companion was his servant, Ali. 'An impecunious subaltern could not afford an escort of armed followers,' he wrote. 'I took with me only a single servant and we bought two inferior riding camels for £15 each from a tribal encampment near Ramadi. My expenses were limited to the purchase of these two camels and a cheap suit of Arab clothing.'[8]

It was not a journey to be undertaken lightly. Nearly 500 miles of desert separate Iraq from Transjordan and all travellers at that time were fair game for marauding bedouins. Leachman,

[8] J. B. Glubb, *The Story of the Arab Legion*, pp. 37–8.

who travelled the same route in 1912, narrowly escaped with his life only to be murdered near Falluja in 1920. Leachman had disguised himself as an Arab but Glubb made no attempt to conceal his identity; it was for comfort that he wore Arab clothes.

The journey took them four weeks. They visited the tent of the paramount sheikh of the Amarat, an old acquaintance who always addressed Glubb as 'my little lad', and also the encampment of the formidable sheikh of the Ruwalla, Nuri ibn Shalaan, of whom T. E. Lawrence had written, 'All feared and obeyed him.' Nuri was not welcoming, but he did provide Glubb with a *rafiq* (guide) called Qasim to see him across Ruwalla territory. By ancient bedouin tradition a *rafiq* was not merely a travelling companion and guide; he also provided a safe conduct. If a traveller was molested or murdered while in the *rafiq*'s territory, it was the *rafiq*'s solemn duty to avenge him. But Qasim turned out to be a useless rogue; Glubb described him as a 'swarthy villain'. He eventually decamped with Glubb's riding saddle, waterskin and warm gloves. Many years later, when Glubb's was a name to conjure with in the Transjordan desert, Qasim was arrested by the Desert Patrol for some petty crime. 'You don't know who I am,' he boasted to his captors, 'I'm the man who employed *Abu Hunaik* as herdsman for my camel!'[9]

The Beni Sakhr are the principal tribe in northern and central Transjordan. Stopping for the night in one of their tents Glubb asked his host for news, having been out of touch for four weeks. 'I'll tell you,' the sheikh replied. 'We hear the English have broken their promises as usual.'[10] Two days later they rode their camels into Amman, then little more than an overgrown village, where Glubb had his first encounter with the Arab Legion. His camel, frightened by the bustle in the market, shied and upset a tray of vegetables, bringing down on its rider the anger and blows of a policeman. 'God curse the father of all bedouins,' he yelled as Glubb and his party beat a hasty retreat.

Amir Abdullah was at his winter palace in the Jordan valley; with him were his father, Husain, and brother, Ali, both ex-kings of the Hejaz. Glubb went down to Shuneh to pay his respects. When the old Husain heard that Glubb had travelled

[9]Ibid., p. 46. *Abu Hunaik* was the bedouins' nickname for Glubb.   [10]Ibid., p. 49.

from Iraq by camel he took him to his sleeping tent to show him the camel saddle and riding cane that accompanied him wherever he went. Then he led Glubb back to the reception tent (*majlis*) and said to the assembled company, '*Wallahi hadha Bedawi!*' ('By my God, this fellow is a bedouin!').

The Hashemites were much more sophisticated and worldly-wise than Abdul Aziz and the Saudis, but they never lost touch with the bedouins and the desert. Abdullah and his brothers were sent to live with the tribes as part of their education. When King Feisal I was once asked what he considered to be the supreme joy in life he replied, 'Riding in moonlight across the desert with a pure-bred camel beneath me.' For those who have never experienced it the attraction of the Arabian desert is hard to understand, for there can be no harsher environment. Perhaps Wilfred Thesiger, the distinguished traveller, has come closest to explaining it when he wrote:

'I have travelled through some of the most magnificent scenery in the world and lived among interesting and little known tribes, yet no country has moved me as did the deserts of Arabia. No man can live there and emerge unchanged. He will carry, however faint, the imprint of the desert, the brand which marks the nomad; and he will have within him, weak or insistent according to his nature, the yearning to return. For that cruel land can cast a spell no temperate clime can match.'[11]

Glubb Pasha certainly bore the brand of the nomad. During his later years in Jordan when the demands on his time were many, he would whenever it was possible for him visit the far-flung Desert Patrol's forts. It was his way of recharging his batteries.

On his return from Transjordan to Nasiriya he was met by a people in a state of shock. The Iraqi shepherd tribes were not warlike and the Ikhwan had petrified them. They blamed it on the government for conniving at Ibn Saud's activities and not coming to their aid. It was obvious that as a first step their confidence must be regained. Throughout those burning summer months Glubb spent his time visiting encampment after encampment strung out along the Euphrates, listening to the

[11] Wilfred Thesiger, *Desert, Marsh and Mountain* (Collins, 1979), p. 299.

shepherds' complaints and promising to help. He was a patient listener and gradually gained their confidence. Soon they were accepting him as one of themselves. Glubb had the same success with the Dhafir who, as bedouins, looked down on the shepherds.

Glubb had earlier written to Air Headquarters stressing the need for a Special Service Officer to deal solely with the Ikhwan problem. If, however, he were to guide aircraft to attack targets in virtually featureless desert, he would need to know the area intimately, including the shepherds' grazing areas. There was no reply from the R.A.F., so Glubb took it upon himself to do the job. This was just as well because without warning, he was appointed 'S.S.O. Ikhwan Defence' in December 1924 and told to get on with it.

The tribes were already moving out into the desert to take advantage of the winter rains. Glubb went with them. He was accompanied at first by a detachment of R.A.F. armoured cars but their effectiveness was greatly reduced by orders not to venture farther than seventy miles from the Saudi border. This meant that the shepherds were between the armoured cars and the enemy, a droll situation which became droller when the British returned to base for Christmas leave. Glubb was very angry and sent a caustic letter to Air Headquarters that won him no support. Senior officers were unwilling to be criticized by their juniors. This had the unfortunate and lasting effect of depriving Glubb of R.A.F. armoured car support until nearly the end of his service in Iraq's southern desert.

Meanwhile the shepherd tribes had moved farther and farther out into the desert, despite rumours that the Ikhwan were gathering beyond the distant horizon. Glubb was so concerned by the news that, on Christmas Eve, he set out in his car from Nasiriya with the intention of persuading the shepherds to fall back. Leaving his car with the Dhafir who were camped near the railway line, he transferred to a camel and rode on with four companions until far into the night. At dawn on Christmas Day they rode on at speed, scanning the horizon for any sign of approaching camelmen.

They had been riding for several hours when they came to the crest of a low ridge. The depression ahead of them was crowded with groups of people frantically running in their direction, driving their sheep and goats before them. 'A whole shepherd nation seemed to be moving northwards,' wrote Glubb, 'the entire face of the desert being covered as if by swarms of ants.' Their pursuers were clearly visible in the distance and from time to time a rifle shot winged over the heads of Glubb and his companions. 'Oh Allah! Oh Mohammed! Oh Ali! Oh Allah protect us!' cried the shepherds as they stumbled on, frightened out of their wits.[12]

There was little Glubb could do and his companions were in any case plainly in a hurry to be gone. Scribbling a hasty message calling for air support, Glubb sent the uneasiest of his companions off to the nearest railway station, Jaleeba, with instructions to the station master to telegraph the message to the R.A.F. Then, as the Ikhwan drew nearer, he decided to ride back himself in search of help as his party was virtually unarmed. Flogging their camels into a canter they rode all that afternoon and early evening until they came to some Dhafir tents. By then Glubb's camel was foundering from exhaustion and he borrowed a horse. Now with just one companion he galloped through the night towards Jaleeba and its vital telegraph office. The going was rough, the night pitch-black, and towards midnight it began to rain in torrents. Glubb was riding without stirrups on a pad as a saddle, with a headrope to guide his mount. Only an Arab horse could have carried him in such conditions. Losing the way at one stage it was dawn before they reached the railway, and later still Jaleeba. There Glubb found that his earlier messenger had failed to arrive.

The R.A.F. reacted slowly – it was Boxing Day. Not until 27 December did a frustrated and angry Glubb, flying in the lead aircraft of three from Shaiba, see far below him the Ikhwan making off with their loot. He had the satisfaction of scattering them with bombs but there were too few planes to do much damage. By the following day, when the whole of 84 Squadron was available, the raiders were across the frontier and immune from attack.

It was clear to Glubb, if not to Air Headquarters, that the

[12]J. B. Glubb, *War in the Desert* (Hodder & Stoughton, 1960), p. 126.

Ikhwan would win every time unless a proper ground organization was established to work with the pilots. But in those early years of its independent existence, the R.A.F. was obsessed by the flexibility and mobility of air power, believing that everything could be achieved from the air. It was to take many years, many disappointments and some appalling failures before senior R.A.F. officers were persuaded that aircraft alone could not ensure air control. It was men like Glubb who were the forerunners of the remarkably efficient ground intelligence organization eventually established by the R.A.F. throughout the Arabian Peninsula.

Nothing like that seemed possible early in 1925. The Ikhwan were terrorizing the tribes. Moreover that winter was unusually cold and the sheep and goats were dying in their thousands. The British and Iraqi governments made formal protests to Ibn Saud who sent bland replies. The truth was that the officials in London and Baghdad cared little about the shepherd tribes. Their attitude infuriated Glubb who had identified himself emotionally with the shepherds; they were *his* people and he would fight to the death in their service.

The picture we have of him from his contemporaries is one of a man of great enthusiasms, completely absorbed by his work, impatient of authority but totally loyal. This loyalty spread in many directions. He was as hard as nails and inured to discomfort, being largely indifferent to the squalor and dirt of a bedouin encampment. His high principles were unaffected by his environment: if anything they were strengthened. He cared as little for worldly possessions as the bedouins who were limited to those they could carry by camel. Despite the scars of war, he looked younger than his age, burnt a pinkish-brown by the desert sun. He read as widely as conditions permitted, but his was essentially an active life. Until the Ikhwan problem had been resolved there was no time for relaxation.

This was the time when he acquired the nickname by which he became known throughout Central Arabia. The bedouins delight in the use of diminutives for nicknames. Glubb's half shot-away jaw became known as the 'little jaw' and he was known as *Abu Hunaik,* or 'the father of the little jaw'. For many years

the dimmest bedouin camel-herd would know whom you
meant if you referred to *Abu Hunaik*. 'Ah,' he would probably
reply, slightly amazed by the thought, 'he lives like one of us,
you know!'[13]

As a result of Glubb's persistent pressure, the Iraqi government established a small post at Abu Ghar, thirty miles south-
west of Nasiriya in the southern desert. A landing ground was
cleared and a Wireless Telegraphy station established. Glubb
camped there for several weeks hoping that this would encourage the shepherd tribes to venture back into the desert;
however they had been too shaken to rely upon government
help. Glubb used the breathing space to set up an intelligence
system which would provide early warning of Ikhwan concen-
trations across the border. The system was simplicity itself. In
the desert the first question asked of every passing traveller is,
'The news? What is the news?' Glubb set up a guest tent which
was a regular port of call for passing bedouins. By careful
questioning he was able to establish what was happening across
the Saudi border. A temporary lull in the tension helped; Ibn
Saud and the Ikhwan were deeply involved in the Hejaz. But
sooner or later they would be back.

Iraq's southern desert is like Transjordan's desert – rolling,
flint-covered plains intersected by deep, dry, winding, water-
courses known as *wadis*; during the winter rains they became
raging torrents for a few hours. Belts of sand, often blown into
high dunes, provided obstacles, but most of the desert was
motorable. Glubb had a T-model Ford in which he visited
encampment after encampment, listening, sympathizing and
advising. It was all part of a carefully worked-out plan to regain
the confidence of the shepherds, whose faith in the government
had been shattered.

Glubb was careful to observe the local conventions. This
meant keeping the Great Fast, or Ramadan, which fell in the
hottest part of that year. 'I did not do this from directly religious
motives,' he says, 'but on the principle which constrains an

[13]It was as *Abu Hunaik* that Glubb was best known during the early years in
Transjordan. By 1945, however, he was better known as *Al Pasha*. There were many
Pashas in Jordan but only one of them was known as *The* Pasha!

officer to limit his kit to the same weight as that of the men under his command . . . When fasting, Muslims were woken at dawn to take a last meal, or at least a long final drink, before facing the weary hours which divided them from sunset. I can still vividly remember being woken, when lying in the sand dunes near Shagra, and seeing leaning over me the lined old face and straggly beard of my host of the night . . . "Sit up, sit up," he was saying, shaking me by the shoulder. "Here is your *sahoor*," holding in his hand an enormous bowl of frothy camel's milk. "Sit up, dawn will soon appear." '[14]

It was lonely in the desert but Glubb, absorbed by his work, barely noticed it. The warmth of the greetings, wherever he went, provided a powerful stimulus. He felt he was fighting a lone crusade on behalf of his Arab friends against the bureaucrats far away in Baghdad. They, for their part, may be forgiven if they sometimes lost patience with their importunate subordinate. 'He seemed to be utterly obsessed with the Arabs,' complained one R.A.F. officer serving at Air Headquarters. 'He bombarded us with signals and memoranda as if we had nothing else to do than to attend to him.'[15]

The Ikhwan and their querulous master, Ibn Saud, were only one of many problems requiring the attention of the Iraqi government and their British advisers. The Kurds were a continual nuisance and the Assyrians were fast becoming the same. The Turks were still grumbling over Mosul. The Iraqis themselves were growing restive under the Mandate. Not unnaturally Glubb felt he was out of sight and out of mind. His superior officers, however, equally felt that he expected an inordinate amount of their attention. It must have come as a great relief when he went on home leave that summer. He had been away for exactly five years.

[14] J. B. Glubb, *War in the Desert*, p. 146. *Sahoor* is the last food or drink taken before dawn.
[15] Statement to author by one of the R.A.F. officers serving at Air Headquarters at the time.

Chapter Four

———◆———

The Young Man
and the Chariots of Fire

'If you choose godly honest men to be captains,
honest men will follow them.'

OLIVER CROMWELL[1]

IBN SAUD'S WAR IN THE HEJAZ took the pressure off the Iraqi
tribes for most of 1925 and early 1926. There was however an
Ikhwan raid against the Dhafir in June which led to counter-
raiding by the Dhafir. These raids resulted in a meeting in
November 1925 at Bahra, near Jeddah, between Ibn Saud and
Sir Gilbert Clayton, representing the British and Iraqi governments. There it was agreed to prohibit raiding and to discourage each other's tribes from changing sides; but this did
not prevent a substantial number of the Dhafir going over to
Ibn Saud in 1927.

When November came the Iraqi shepherds began to move
timidly out into the desert; but they went no farther than Abu
Ghar where the Iraqis had re-established their police post. The
flocks soon began to die for lack of pasture. Glubb was at his
wits' end to encourage them to move farther out until he hit
upon a rather clever idea.

In the desert the tents, which are woven from goat or camel
hair, are all black or brown, but Glubb's was an army issue and
was therefore white and conspicuous. When he camped alongside the Dhafir, who were more venturesome than the shepherds,
passers-by would inquire, 'Whose is that tent?' 'It is the

---

[1] From a letter to Colonel Robert Hammond dated 25 November 1648, quoted by
Thomas Carlyle in Volume I of *His Letters and Speeches*, 1846, p. 148.

45

government's,' would be the answer. Reassured, the shepherds gradually moved farther out. But Glubb could not spend all his time in the desert; he had to return to Nasiriya frequently. Someone would have to represent him during his absences and by a stroke of luck he chanced upon Hamed el Billal, 'who had more wit and character than many senior officials I have encountered'.[2] This became the answer to his problem.

By descent Hamed was a slave. He had been a man of property in Hail until the Ikhwan came and forced him to leave because he smoked a pipe. He fled to Iraq with his mother and two sisters but got no farther than Abu Ghar, where his camel foundered. There he met Glubb who engaged him as a camel-herd for two pounds a month plus his keep. Hamed adopted Glubb completely and followed him through thick and thin for many years. Whenever Glubb was away, visitors would find Hamed smoking his pipe in Glubb's tent. 'He'll be back soon,' was his invariable reply to all inquiries about his master, and as the Dhafir moved farther out to better pastures, Hamed went with them. The shepherds would then follow. The white tent became their guide.

But it was a chancy business. The desert was alive with rumours. Feisal al Duweesh was back from the Hejaz, where he had fallen out with Ibn Saud, and was reportedly planning more raids. Glubb bore a heavy weight of responsibility, for the shepherds were only there because he was. No one back in Baghdad showed the slightest interest. R.A.F. planes came and went in the skies but that was the limit of Air Headquarters' concern.

'I never, I think, felt as afraid during the First World War as I did in the desert,' wrote Glubb. 'In the Great War I had been surrounded by comrades, my own company first, and then millions of others beyond, all doing the same thing. So many had already passed on ahead of us; we were still alive, at least for the moment, but death seemed less terrible when it meant joining the comrades who had gone before us. But out here I was alone, and moreover the decision rested solely upon me. The tribe said they would follow me in whatever I decided.'[3]

[2]J. B. Glubb, *War in the Desert*, p. 171.　　　[3]Ibid., p. 178.

Fortune favoured the brave that spring and in April the flocks were driven back to the summer pastures along the Euphrates. The shepherds sang the praises of *Abu Hunaik*. 'The Year of the Tent', as it came to be called, was a year to be remembered, for the dreaded Ikhwan had never come. It also turned out to be a year of decision for Glubb personally, since it was the year he resigned his commission in the British Army. During the summer the War Office reminded him that it was five years since he had last served with British troops and that it was time he returned. Glubb was so immersed in his work that the thought had never occurred to him. When faced with the choice, he decided to remain in Iraq, resigning his commission in September 1926, to his father's concern. As a captain with only ten years' service, he was not eligible for a pension.

On the face of it he had made a foolish decision. The British Mandate in Iraq had only two years to run and the Iraqis were unlikely to retain many of their British advisers. But Glubb was offered a ten years' contract with the Iraqi government as an Administrative Inspector and eagerly snapped it up. In November he was posted to Diwaniya and for the next twelve months turned his back on the desert.

They were not happy months. For the first time Glubb came into contact with Arab politics. Most Iraqi officials were fervently nationalist with a profound suspicion of the British; some of them had taken up arms during the rebellion in 1920. Latif Bey, *mutasarrif* of Diwaniya, with whom Glubb had to work, was one of them. He shocked Glubb by his blatantly political approach to every administrative problem. Since Glubb was principally concerned with Land Settlement, in connection with taxation, almost every administrative problem had a political connotation. Time after time Latif Bey overruled him on political grounds. This left Glubb with a profound distaste for politics which in later years amounted almost to an obsession. But he did not allow this to interfere with his duties. Within only a few months he had walked or ridden all over the province and had soon become a familiar figure. One day he was driving his car towards Diwaniya when he chanced upon two Arabs walking in his direction. He stopped and told them to jump in.

47

Arriving at Diwaniya, he inquired where they wanted to be dropped. 'Nowhere here,' they replied, 'we never wanted to come to Diwaniya.' Why then had they got in the car? asked Glubb. 'Because you told us to do so,' they said![4]

Events in the desert cut short Glubb's stay in Diwaniya. In the summer of 1927 half the Dhafir went over to Ibn Saud. In November the Ikhwan killed some workmen building a fort by the wells at Busaiya, eighty miles out in the desert. Glubb had recommended the building of a fort there but Ibn Saud had lodged a protest as soon as the work began. He wanted no forts to interfere with his sovereignty over the bedouins. However, the government pressed on with the building, undeterred by the Ikhwan; R.A.F. armoured cars were sent to protect the workmen. In November and December the Ikhwan raided the shepherd tribes; in January 1928 Al Duweesh took the field in person. He was throwing down the gauntlet to his master, Ibn Saud. The latter had expressly forbidden raiding, but seemed powerless to control the Ikhwan. They struck again in February and there was consternation in Baghdad where it had been assumed that raiding was a thing of the past. Glubb, who knew of Ibn Saud's problems, had warned against over-optimism, but without effect.

For once the government acted promptly. Busaiya was occupied by the Iraqi army and the R.A.F. set up a forward headquarters at Ur. The Iraqi tribes were told to withdraw to four days' march from the frontier or risk being attacked from the air. Air patrols were increased. But despite this evident increased activity, Al Duweesh attacked again on 19 February, cocking a snook at Ibn Saud who was now facing an outright rebellion by the Mutair, Ateyba and Ajman. This seriously alarmed H.M.G. who had no wish to see Ibn Saud overthrown by the fanatical Ikhwan. On 2 March 1928 Glubb was summoned to Baghdad where he was informed he had been appointed Administrative Inspector of the Southern Desert.

It was a grandiloquent title for an appointment that had not existed twenty-four hours beforehand. There had never been any administration in the southern desert where the tribes were

[4]Told by Mrs McLeod whose husband was Civil Surgeon at the time.

a law unto themselves. Glubb was given a handful of camel police to help him, a car and a driver. His plan was to teach the tribes to defend themselves instead of relying on the R.A.F., but his proposals met with scant support at Air Headquarters. The R.A.F. wanted the desert to be swept clean of 'friendlies' in order that they could attack anything that moved; this completely overlooked the tribesmen's need for grazing.

Throughout that March an uneasy peace prevailed. Ibn Saud did not want civil war with his tribes and continued to temporize. Aware of his difficulties, H.M.G. arranged yet another meeting with him. On 12 April Glubb was ordered to join the British delegation, again headed by Sir Gilbert Clayton. The meeting was to be at Jeddah, where Ibn Saud made a profound impression on Glubb: he was 'a tremendous personality. He would have ended up as Prime Minister in any country in the world.'[5] The king was still a bedouin in his attitudes and tastes; his manner frank and open, his hospitality princely. Glubb was not so impressed by the king's counsellors who were Syrians, Egyptians and Palestinians. How much influence they exerted was debatable, but their approach to every problem was legalistic.

At the root of every disagreement was Ibn Saud's distrust of King Feisal who had undoubtedly been meddling in tribal politics. 'Why do you people in Iraq want to control bedouin tribes?' Ibn Saud asked Glubb. 'Town Arabs do not understand anything about them. Ibn Saud is the king of all nomads.' It was for this reason that he was so opposed to the construction of forts in the desert. Glubb sympathized with him and would have favoured meeting him half-way by abandoning the fort at Busaiya, but this was rejected by the Iraqis.

'I have rarely been so miserable as in the last two days,' wrote Glubb on 17 May. 'Yesterday we again met Ibn Saud. His manner was much changed since our first meetings, and he seemed depressed and bitter. To Clayton he said, "When the English first came to Iraq, I congratulated my people. They were surprised and asked me why. I had always abused the Turks as unbelievers, they said, yet here were people who were even

[5] Comment by Glubb to author, October 1980.

49

worse, because they were not Muslims at all. I told them the English were honest and my friends. Now I must admit that we have despaired of the English and their hair-splitting . . ." It was pathetic to hear such a speech, so obviously sincere, and Clayton's vague reply to the effect that he was sure friendship would always continue between His Majesty and Britain . . .'[6]

The delegation returned to Baghdad with little to show for its efforts. However it had become clear to Glubb that Ibn Saud could not guarantee control over the Ikhwan. In less than six months the raiding season would begin and there was little enough time to prepare for it.

He had already sent an outline plan to Baghdad in which he emphasized the ineffectiveness of air reconnaissance in a featureless desert as large as England with only a handful of planes; some form of ground reconnaissance force was therefore essential; and this needed to have a fighting capability. Since the shepherd tribes would starve if they could not move into the desert for the winter grazing, they needed to be supported by mobile detachments of police, specially recruited for the purpose, some in armed cars and some on camels. It would be a great advantage if they were bedouins.

His proposals were considered ridiculous. The Inspector-General of Police, who was British, minuted: 'I will have nothing to do with such catch-'em-aliveos.'[7] The Air Officer Commanding rejected Glubb's request for an issue of Vickers machine-guns. 'I do not agree. I do not want the police to fight.'[8] The very idea of recruiting bedouins as policemen was laughable. Everyone knew that bedouins were untameable and untrainable. The fact that until that moment no one had ever tried to tame and train them escaped their notice.

It was very disheartening, but Glubb was resilient by nature. He continued to battle on until the authorities gave in. He was authorized to raise a force of a hundred bedouin police, seventy of them mounted on camels, thirty in trucks. He was provided with four new Ford trucks on which Vickers machine-guns could be mounted, and two wireless vans. Unfortunately

---

[6] J. B. Glubb, *War in the Desert*, p. 214.   [7] Ibid., p. 225.
[8] J. B. Glubb, *Arabian Adventures*, p. 177.

the radio sets which had to be ordered from England took a year to arrive and Glubb was unable to borrow any sets meanwhile. The force was given the title of the Southern Desert Camel Corps.

There was little enough time to train them. Simple tactics had to be devised for men who were almost all illiterate. It was also necessary to work out some simple system for co-operation with the R.A.F. pilots. In the past there had been many failures, as one of Glubb's letters makes clear. He was replying to a note from C. J. Edmonds, a British official working in the Ministry of the Interior, who had written to congratulate him on the success of his efforts. ' "Fear not for they that be with us are more than they that be with them," ' wrote Edmonds. ' "And the Lord opened the eyes of the young man and he saw: and behold, the mountain was full of horses and chariots of fire round about" (Elisha).'

'You may be right about the heavens being full of horses and chariots of fire,' replied Glubb, 'but the young man seems to experience some difficulty in obtaining their assistance. It took five days at about six cypher wires a day to produce one chariot of fire, and that arrived two hours after the battle was over!'[9]

We are so used to 'instant' communications today that we forget how rudimentary they were fifty years ago. Indeed, it was not until after the Second World War that ground to air communications became a fine art. Glubb's problem was further complicated by the fact that the pilots only understood English and his desert police only Arabic. When he moved out into the desert with them in October 1928 he knew that the odds were weighted against him, but he did not allow this to depress him. He had confidence in his men, and they in him. What did worry him, however, was the lack of understanding in Air Headquarters.

They had their problems, too. 'The trouble about Glubb,' one R.A.F. staff officer has commented, 'was the fact that he knew a lot more about the problem than we did. But he was always in too much of a hurry to take time off to tell us about it. You couldn't help admiring him but most of us thought him a

[9]Glubb's correspondence.

little odd.'[10] Many years later Glubb admitted there might be some truth in this.

Although their normal tactics were essentially offensive, the bedouins had developed a form of defence against the wild Arab charge. Glubb decided to adopt these tactics against the Ikhwan. They consisted of pitching the tents in a long line with the tent ropes overlapping, and the camels hobbled tightly behind in a solid mass. This was known as *manakh*, or couching, and it presented an impenetrable obstacle to men charging on horses or camels. Its disadvantage was that it could only be maintained for three days, after which the camels had to be released for watering. It was therefore essential to have accurate information of the enemy's movements if the tactics of 'couch and hobble' were to be adopted. Glubb already had spies with the Ikhwan, as they had with him, but a more mobile form of ground reconnaissance would be helpful. He asked for the loan of some R.A.F. armoured cars but was refused. The R.A.F. had little faith in Glubb's proposed tactics.

In November reports were received that the Mutair, Ateyba and Ajman had unfurled their war banners and were riding out for the killings. Plainly they were ignoring Ibn Saud's orders. Glubb flew immediately to Baghdad where the Iraqi army agreed to garrison three desert posts; they also provided Glubb with some mobile machine-gunners. The R.A.F. increased their reconnaissance sorties, but that was as far as they would go. It was better than nothing and Glubb returned to Samawa where he had summoned the tribes to meet him. He explained his plan and all agreed to carry out his orders. Then he drove out to Mughaizal, on the edge of the neutral zone which lay between Iraq and Kuwait and Saudi-Arabia; the tribes followed him. The grazing was good and soon the desert was dotted with black tents.

Unfortunately the R.A.F. pilots were forbidden to fly within twenty miles of the frontier lest their appearance should annoy Ibn Saud; their reconnaissance was therefore being carried out *behind* the Iraqi tribes. The machine-gun company of the Iraqi army was similarly restricted but they did lend Glubb

[10]Comment to author.

four guns. When he protested at these restrictions he was told he could always fall back, if pressed, on the fort at Busaiya. There was no answer when he inquired how he could be expected to do this with a mass of men, women, children, camels, donkeys, sheep and goats.

'Meanwhile I had decided,' he wrote, 'that if the Duweesh came my little force would unship their machine guns and dig in, forming a central redoubt . . . The camels would be couched and hobbled so that they could not move, the sheep and donkeys packed between the tents.'[11] The place he chose for this defensive battle was just north of Mughaizal, on a low ridge behind which there were rainwater pools for the animals. It was called Al Abtiyya.

News was received on 15 February that the Ikhwan were within four days' march. At once the tribes were summoned to Al Abtiyya, some of them having to march for thirty-six hours non-stop to get there. On arrival, Glubb's men marshalled them into some kind of order, after which there was nothing to do but wait. He had meanwhile signalled Baghdad reporting that he expected to be attacked at dawn on the 20th, and again requesting the loan of some armoured cars. There was no reply. To keep up their spirits the tribesmen held war dances.

These were noted by the Ikhwan spies, as was the fact that a plane landed at Al Abtiyya on 19 February to convey Glubb to Baghdad. He intended to make a final plea to Air Headquarters for more ground support but he wasted his time. The staff officer to whom he explained the position told him it was impossible to provide him with armoured cars so close to the frontier; Ibn Saud would be furious. When Glubb asked hotly how he could be expected to make an orderly retreat to Busaiya with the hordes of humans and animals dependent upon him for protection, the staff officer replied, 'We thought that if you were as frightened as your telegrams seemed to indicate, you had better run away!'[12] Seething with fury, Glubb grabbed his cap and stormed out of the office.

Throughout the night of his return to Al Abtiyya, and for the

[11]J. B. Glubb, *Arabian Adventures*, p. 181.
[12]J. B. Glubb, *War in the Desert*, p. 261.

next three nights, they 'stood-to' waiting for the Ikhwan. But they never came. Al Duweesh's spies had convinced him that the game was not worth the candle. The Iraqis were ready and spoiling for a fight, so instead, he went looting and killing in Kuwait, and Glubb had won a bloodless victory. Ibn Saud also profited from it. While Al Duweesh was pillaging in Kuwait with the Mutair, their confederates, the Ateyba, fell upon some Shammar in northern Nejd and slaughtered them. The Shammar were Saud's subjects and there was a wave of indignation against the Ikhwan. Ibn Saud took the field and a bitter battle was fought at Sibilla on 29 March. The result was inconclusive but Al Duweesh was wounded and the Ateyba went home in a huff. It would now only be a matter of time before Ibn Saud brought the Ikhwan to heel.

Al Abtiyya marked Glubb's coming of age as a desert warrior. The name of *Abu Hunaik* was on every man's lips and the story of how he had outfaced the dreaded Duweesh lost nothing in the telling. His plan to recruit bedouins into his Camel Corps had also been proved successful. His faith in the bedouin's potential as a soldier, provided he was well trained and led by those who understood him, had been abundantly justified. In July and August 1929, when the Mutair again went raiding into Kuwait, they were intercepted by Glubb's mobile patrols and scattered; all their loot was recovered.

Glubb had good reason to feel pleased with himself. 'Never before had any attempts been made to train or discipline bedouins,' he wrote. 'All the Arab governments I knew had accepted as an axiom that bedouin were militarily useless. Yet when our men were sent to be trained in Baghdad as machine-gunners, their instructors pronounced them to be above the average of Iraqi recruits in keenness and intelligence.'[13]

His success with them was fast becoming common gossip throughout Central Arabia. The bedouin has his own *panache* as a soldier, being by nature a flamboyant individual, and Glubb's Camel Corps was no exception. They called themselves *Al Aujan*, translated by Glubb as 'The Crooks'; they would drive into battle in their battered old trucks, waving their headcloths,

[13]Ibid., p. 227.

54

firing their rifles, and shouting to each other, *Wain al Aujan!
Wain al Nishama!* – Where are the Crooks! Where are the
Gallants! News of their prowess reached as far as Amman where
the Amir Abdullah was having his share of trouble with the
bedouins.

At the beginning of the 1929 grazing season Glubb again
moved out into the Southern Desert. With him went the shepherd tribes; but this time they were joined by sections of the
Shammar and other bedouin tribes. It was a complete reversal
of the earlier situation and a personal triumph for Glubb. This
was even more the case in December when a deputation from the
Mutair came to his tent to beg asylum. They said that Ibn Saud
had announced his determination to settle with Al Duweesh and
they therefore begged for sanctuary in Iraq. Glubb had to
refuse since with his small force he could not hope to control a
tribe as large and as unruly as the Mutair. To make this clear he
drew up his tribes in the same formation as at Al Abtiyya. If Al
Duweesh wanted to enter Iraq, he would have to fight; but
again he never came.

The biters were being truly bit. After a decade of terrorizing
the 'unbelievers', the Ikhwan were being squeezed by the
borders of Iraq and Kuwait and the steady advance of Ibn Saud
from Riyadh, with a tribal army amounting to several thousands.
Most of them were mounted on camels and mares, with a hard
core of Ibn Saud's own slaves travelling by an assortment of
transport, ranging from Buick sedans to Dodge trucks. If the
panic-struck Mutair and Ajman were to flee into Iraq, Glubb
and his handful of desert police would be overwhelmed.

At this critical juncture Air Commodore Burnett flew out,
on 21 December, to examine the situation on the spot. He was
Senior Air Staff Officer at Air Headquarters and this was the
first time in five years that a senior R.A.F. officer had visited
Glubb in the southern desert. It seems incredible that this
should have been so, given that the R.A.F. attached such importance to Air Control, but sadly it is the case. As soon as
Burnett realized the problem, co-operation was assured, although the implementation was not so easy. The British and
Iraqi governments had promised Ibn Saud that the rebels

55

would not be given sanctuary in Iraq but they could hardly be prevented from entry by bombing and machine-gunning. Fortunately they chose to enter Kuwait territory instead. Glubb and Burnett then worked out terms which permitted the Mutair and Ajman to remain in Kuwait until negotiations could take place with Ibn Saud.

On 1 January 1930 the principal sheikhs of the two tribes, among them the dreaded Feisal al Duweesh, came as suppliants to Glubb's tent. 'Feisal al Duweesh was a horrible looking man,' according to Glubb. 'Small and wizened, his face was foxy and his eyes shifty. He looked thoroughly evil.' They were given twelve hours' grace to consider the terms and promised to return with their answer. They never did, which is not surprising considering that the terms required the two tribes to give up their weapons.

Glubb had no jurisdiction in Kuwait, which was under British protection; he was allowed to enter Kuwait but not to spend the night there. Returning from a visit to the Mutair, he found Ibn Saud's army camped only a few miles away. Whereupon he was bombarded by protests from emissaries of the King, claiming that the British were giving sanctuary to the King's enemies. The fact that Glubb was a servant of the Iraqi government, not the British, made no difference; he was held responsible, and hot words were exchanged. However, in typically bedouin fashion, after so much bad temper and complaint, Ibn Saud changed his tune and asked Glubb to provide petrol for his cars and trucks. If he had insufficient petrol to do this, the crews and their transport would be left with Glubb, as his 'guests', until petrol could be brought out from Basra. Meanwhile Ibn Saud intended to move off to the south-east where there was water for his animals. Fortunately Glubb was able to provide the petrol and Ibn Saud disappeared over the horizon with his horde.

The final negotiations were conducted directly between the British and Ibn Saud; Glubb was not involved. The Mutair and Ajman were permitted to return to their allegiance in exchange for giving up the rebel leaders who were flown to Riyadh and put in prison. The Ikhwan never raided Iraq again. Glubb pleaded that the Mutair should be made to return the camels they had raided from Iraq, as well as other booty which Ibn Saud had promised to return, but nothing came of this. He did manage to seize the camels of those Mutair who had managed to enter Iraq, but these were less than a tenth of the whole.

The British government did not wish to put pressure on Ibn Saud with whom its relations were temporarily excellent. Hoping to capitalize on this, they persuaded King Feisal and King Ibn Saud to meet, although the two men bitterly distrusted each other. The meeting took place on 21 February 1930 on board a British sloop, H.M.S. *Lupin*, anchored in the Gulf out of sight of land. The two delegations were taken to the rendezvous in separate vessels, but there was a difficult problem of protocol to be resolved. Which king should board the warship first? It was explained to Feisal that naval custom prescribed that the senior man was the last to board; Ibn Saud was told the contrary. Each monarch concluded that he had been given the precedence and therefore everyone was happy. The two kings concluded a *bon voisinage* agreement that has lasted until this day; it was a minor triumph for British diplomacy since neither Feisal nor Ibn Saud would willingly have met of their own accord.

Glubb accompanied the Iraqi delegation as a tribal expert. There is a photograph of the two kings and their delegations taken on the sloop's quarterdeck. Glubb is in the background in civilian clothes; he is smiling happily, and with good reason. It had been largely due to his efforts that the meeting had come about. If Al Duweesh had triumphed, it is unlikely that Ibn Saud could have survived. This would have meant the continuance of Ikhwan raids on Iraq which might have had incalculable consequences. As it was the shepherd tribes could graze the southern desert in peace, which they have been doing ever since.

During the confrontation on the border with Ibn Saud, Glubb was unwittingly involved in an incident which could have had serious consequences. A fugitive from Ibn Saud's justice entered one of the three tents occupied by Glubb and his police. There he immediately claimed the ancient bedouin right of sanctuary; this not only meant that he could remain for three days and nights but also that the owner of the tent must defend him with his life, if need be. This placed Glubb in a difficult position since the Iraqi government had pledged itself to offer no sanctuary for the rebels; but here was its only official on the border doing just that. His policemen, bedouins to a man, were horrified at the thought of handing over the fugitive; it would be *aib* (shameful), but meanwhile peremptory demands were received for the handing over of the fugitive. Glubb immediately sent a personal message to Ibn Saud, explaining the situation and asking the King to grant him the right of sanctuary. He heard no more of the incident. Later it was reported that two sheikhs of the Mutair had burst into the King's tent in similar fashion and had been pardoned.

His work in the Southern Desert accomplished, Glubb moved north with his Desert Police to Rutba, near the Syrian and Transjordan frontiers on the overland desert route between Damascus and Baghdad. There was an Iraqi fort there and the immediate problem was the Ruwalla, part of the Aneyzeh confederation of tribes. Fawaz ibn Shalaan, grandson of the aged sheikh Nuri, was a dashing and feckless young man with a taste for Damascus night life and fast cars. He and his bully-boys, most of them ex-slaves, were having an enjoyable time rounding up the camels of neighbouring tribes by conducting great sweeps across the desert in their Cadillacs and Buicks. The herdsmen were powerless to stop them and Fawaz had acquired a vast number of camels which he intended to drive across the Syrian border.

Glubb's arrival with his police in trucks mounting machine-guns took the Ruwalla by surprise; but Fawaz, in true bedouin fashion, prevaricated. Although Glubb's little party were greatly outnumbered, they set about separating the stolen camels from the Ruwalla animals, jeered at while they did so by the lookers-on. This so exasperated Glubb that he lined his cars up in the same formation used in the Southern Desert and proceeded to drive the camels before them into the open desert. Fawaz and his men followed on their camels and horses, firing their rifles and yelling their war cries, but Glubb was not to be deflected. This was child's play after the Ikhwan. Eventually the camels were shepherded to Rutba where the astonished garrison could hardly believe their eyes. No one had ever before acted in such a high-handed fashion with the Ruwalla. The looted camels were separated from those belonging to the Ruwalla (every camel had its tribal brand mark), and the Ruwalla were taught a lesson they were unlikely to forget. Glubb's prestige among the bedouins was further increased.

Since Rutba was so close to the Transjordan frontier, Glubb decided on the spur of the moment to visit Amman with some of his Desert Police. The reason was to inquire about, and if possible recover, camels which had been stolen from the Iraqi tribes. Leaving Rutba on 26 March 1930, they arrived in Amman two days later. It was a visit that was to have a profound effect on Glubb's future.

He was received by the Amir Abdullah's adviser for bedouin affairs, the Amir Shareef Shakir bin Zeid, a cousin of Abdullah's. He and Glubb established an instant rapport. Glubb was very impressed and wrote later: 'Rarely in my life have I met with more courtesy, humour and sympathy than I received from the Amir Shakir . . . He possessed the impalpable but magnetic quality of being a gentleman, so rare in the world today. He was always at ease himself and never failed to put his guest at ease. His humour was vivacious but quiet and dignified.'[14] It was the beginning of a friendship that was to last without a single disagreement until Shakir's all-too-early death.[15]

Glubb also made a considerable impression on the British Resident, Colonel (later Sir) Henry Cox. When he paraded his men in their armed cars in the Roman amphitheatre in Amman, the Amir Shakir and Cox inspected them. At the time the Arab Legion enlisted no bedouin nor was it deployed in the desert; that was the preserve of the Transjordan Frontier Force, an 'imperial' unit. The appearance of Glubb's men and the reputation they had earned in conflict with the dreaded Ikhwan greatly impressed Shakir and Cox.

Glubb's reputation stood high in Iraqi government circles, and also among the tribes, but the same was not true among the

[14]J. B. Glubb, *Arabian Adventures*, p. 208.
[15]Lieutenant-General Shareef Zeid bin Shakir, Commander-in-Chief of the Jordan Armed Forces, is the son of Amir Shareef Shakir bin Zeid. He has all his father's presence and courtesy.

urban intelligentsia. They suspected his motives, as the news-paper *Al Istaqlal* reported on 16 November 1928:

'If it is said that Abu Hunaik is come they are seized with trembling and they swoon to the ground. Abu Hunaik is a nick-name given by the bedouin to Mr Glubb on account of a slight injury to his jaw . . . Mr Glubb is the modern Leachman,[16] but the difference is that while Leachman was loud and violent, Glubb is soft and gentle. Their ends are however the same. There is another difference too. Leachman served the English cause with English money while Glubb serves it with the money of Iraq.'

This is typical of the biased reporting common to the Middle Eastern press. As Glubb has written:

'I have spent the greater part of my life amongst Arabs, often, as during the winter of 1929, without any other English-man near me. I have made innumerable Arab friends, some as dear, as intimate and as trusted as any of my own countrymen. But all over the Arab countries I have, from time to time, en-countered this maddening tendency to attribute some treacher-ous and sinister motive to my most sincere efforts to serve them . . .'[17]

The Anglo–Iraqi Treaty which terminated the British man-date in Iraq was signed on 30 June 1930. The Iraqis had made no secret of their intention to dispense with their British advisers as soon as could be contrived; not surprisingly Glubb was con-cerned about his future, as was his father who was busy pulling strings at home to find him employment. Perhaps the time had come to try his hand as a writer? Before he could decide one way or the other there came an offer from an entirely unexpected quarter. The government of Transjordan was being sorely vexed by the behaviour of its bedouin tribes and required them to be brought to heel. Would Glubb undertake the task? He accepted immediately.

But he left Iraq with regret. There he had served his novitiate with the Arabs. He loved the country and the people. He had

[16]Lieutenant-Colonel G. E. Leachman (1880–1920) was a soldier, explorer, traveller and administrator in Mesopotamia where he was murdered near Falluja (by Ramadi) on 12 August 1920. He travelled among the bedouins in disguise.
[17]J. B. Glubb, *War in the Desert*, p. 275.

brought peace to the desert and had made many friends. Many years later, at a grand reception in Baghdad, one of those friends came up to him and embraced him warmly in front of the assembled diplomats. He had been Prime Minister since Glubb had met him last. King Feisal received him before his departure and decorated him with the Order of Rafidain (Two Rivers). He also gave Glubb some advice on dealing with the bedouins, doubtless remembering the lavish distribution of gold and arms to the bedouins by Lawrence during the Arab Revolt against the Turks. Glubb was never to forget it.[18]

Perhaps the nicest tribute to his work was paid by Lady Mary Humphreys, wife of Sir Francis Humphreys, British High Commissioner in Iraq. Writing to him in Amman, she said:

'Dear Captain Glubb, We were so glad to have news of you . . . You will be terribly missed here and it is sad that Iraq should lose you. You have done such splendid work for this country and I am thankful for my own inner conviction that no good work is ever wasted. Anyhow, the name you leave behind you does good and honour to your country . . .'

[18]In 1954 Glubb Pasha, accompanying the young King Husain (who was still under training at Sandhurst), visited the author's regiment then deployed in the Jordan valley in anticipation of an Israeli armoured attack down the valley from Galilee. When it was mentioned to the Pasha that it was very much a 'thin red line' against what were likely to be overwhelming odds, he smiled sweetly and said, 'You must appeal to your soldiers' honour and you will find they will fight to the death!' Fortunately the attack never came, but *sharf* (honour) is a word to conjure with among the bedouins.

Chapter Five

The Desert Patrol

'Bedouins can be roused to do anything for honour.
But once you give them money, the whole moral tone
of your relations with them is lowered.'

King Feisal I to Captain Glubb, November 1930

TRANSJORDAN WAS a small, remote and very poor country in
1930. Britain had infuriated the Zionists by separating Transjordan from Palestine, which had in turn, delighted the Arabs
of course. Transjordan was entirely dependent upon an annual
British subsidy for its continued existence. There was no industry and very little prospect of finding oil. The annual income
of the ruler was little more than £1000. Yet despite these economic disadvantages Transjordan was an oasis of contentment in a
region racked with dissension and dispute.

Much of the credit for this state of affairs was owed to the
ruler, the Amir Abdullah bin Husain. His impulsive and emotional temperament had been tempered by experience and a
certain amount of adversity, so that by 1930 he was beginning
to show signs of the statesmanship he was to manifest later. He
had a largeness of mind and a political wisdom unusual in Arabs,
who too often permit their hearts to rule their heads. There were
two issues, however, over which he refused to compromise –
Palestine and the Hashemite feud with Ibn Saud. Abdullah
hoped that one day he might be King of Greater Syria and that
the Hashemites would once again be the Guardians of the Holy
Places.

Sir Alec Kirkbride describes Abdullah as 'the king with a
twinkle'.[1] He had the ability to evoke a loyalty from those who

[1] Sir Alec Kirkbride, *A Crackle of Thorns*, p. 29.

served him which was based on personal affection; he shared this quality with his brother, Feisal, in Iraq and later with his grandson, Husain. It was invaluable because he could be tetchy and demanding at times and his love of intrigue frequently landed him in trouble. He was well served by his Arab and British advisers and it was an advantage that the latter usually remained long in their posts. Although Amman compared unfavourably with Cairo, Damascus, Beirut and Baghdad to men with ambition, those who served in Transjordan were there because they wanted to be. Since there was only a handful of them, each came to be accepted by the people almost as one of themselves.

Transjordan did not exist on 2 March 1921 when Abdullah arrived in Amman in the course of his madcap adventure to drive the French out of Syria. The Turkish administration had collapsed and the countryside was in chaos. 'Several months before the arrival of Amir Abdullah,' wrote Peake, 'the Palestine government decided to send a few British officers to Transjordan to try to help the local governments – if they could rightly be dignified with such a name – which had been formed in Irbid, Amman and Kerak . . . There were still a few police in the towns . . . They had received little pay for many months, and their uniforms were worn out; their officers had fared no better. They had no authority at all.'[2]

In addition to these demoralized policemen there was a handful of soldiers who had been collected together by a Captain Brunton to form a Mobile Force; they were Arabs who had deserted from the Turkish army and fought under the Amir Feisal. Abdullah had also brought with him from the Hejaz a so-called regiment (*katiba al nizamiyya*) amounting to 200 officers and soldiers. He soon realized that he stood little chance of dealing with the French with such numbers and decided instead to set up a 'private' government in Amman. Winston Churchill, then Colonial Secretary, gave this the British government's blessing when he met with Abdullah in Jerusalem on 28 March 1921. The outcome was the Principality, or Amirate, of Transjordan, with Abdullah as its ruler. On 21 April Abdullah established Transjordan's first administration and

[2] F. G. Peake, *History of Jordan and its Tribes* (Miami, 1958), p. 106.

authorized the formation of a military force to restore order. Command of the force was given to Captain F. G. Peake, a British officer soon to be better known as Peake Pasha.

Peake, born in 1886, joined the Duke of Wellington's Regiment as a regular officer in 1906. He was seconded to the Egyptian army in 1913 and served in Egypt and Arabia during the Great War, commanding an Egyptian Camel Corps detachment during the later stages of the Arab Revolt against the Turks. He joined the provisional administration established in Palestine soon after the Armistice. Beginning that April, he gathered together the motley collection of soldiers and gendarmes he found in Transjordan to form a new Reserve Mobile Force. 'One of the first acts of the Amir on his return [from London in 1923] was to amalgamate the Reserve Force and the Police, and to call it the Arab Legion,' wrote Peake. 'The present writer was appointed to command the Legion, and became responsible to the Amir for public security.'[3]

The Arabic title was *Al Jaysh Al Arabi* – the Arab Army; this was inherited from the force of Arab regulars who served under Feisal. It was Peake who suggested the change of English title from Reserve Mobile Force to Arab Legion. This was readily agreed by the then British Resident in Amman, H. St J. Philby. 'The strange thing is that nobody noticed the change,' commented Peake. It remained the English title until 1956 when it was changed to Jordanian Armed Forces; however, throughout the Arab Legion's existence, it was usually referred to as the 'Jaysh' by Arabs and British alike, as much out of affection as for any other reason.

There were not many British around for a good many years. From 1923 to 1930 there were only one or two, including Peake, who not only founded the Arab Legion on sound lines but who also played an important part in establishing the modern Hashemite Kingdom of Jordan. He was a British officer of the pre-1914 army, a stern disciplinarian and a stickler for military conventions. This well suited his Arab officers, most of whom had served in the Turkish army. 'Slackness, slovenly dress and, above all, lack of respect for a military superior were to them

[3]Ibid., pp. 107–8.

anathema,' Glubb has written. 'Much of that military pride which carried the Arab Legion through the dark days of 1940–1 was derived from the rigid military spirit of the old Turkish Empire.'[4] Peake had the rank of *Feriq* (Lieutenant-General); his deputy was Abdel Qadir al-Jundi.

Peake assumed an Edwardian life-style although he was modern enough to have himself taught to fly while in his fifties. 'The staff officers of the Arab Legion wore at this time a blue patrol jacket, blue overalls and wellingtons. The other officers had a single wide stripe down their overalls, but the Pasha had a triple stripe. Thus clad, and with a high lambskin cap and a stout malacca stick, he could be seen daily striding through the town of Amman to his office. He never failed to change for dinner (he was a bachelor at this time), and dined every night in solitary state.'[5]

Peake Pasha, in common with others of his generation, affected to believe that it paid senior officers to appear angry. His rages were legendary but they caused little rancour because he was at heart one of the kindest of men; when he took to flying himself on tours of inspection, the codeword 'Thundercloud' was flashed from his headquarters in Amman so that all might be warned. Having witnessed the behaviour of tribal levies under Lawrence, Peake had no use for bedouins nor, for that matter, had his Arab officers. These views were shared by the British Resident, Cox, and by his assistant, Kirkbride, until Glubb converted the latter. The Amir and his adviser on tribal affairs, Shareef Shakir, thought differently, but Peake was adamant.

This was significant because the Transjordan government was sorely troubled by tribal problems. Four-fifths of the country was desert, inhabited by about 40,000 bedouins whose entire existence depended on grazing for their camels. The two principal tribes were the Beni Sakhr and the Howeitat. Ibn Saud's efforts to suborn the tribes to his side never ceased and little attempt was made by him to prevent the Ikhwan from raiding into Transjordan. The moment the Transjordan bedouins retaliated, however, Ibn Saud protested loudly to the British government, who passed on the complaint in full

[4] J. B. Glubb, *The Story of the Arab Legion*, p. 199. [5] Ibid.

measure to Amman. The Howeitat, whose grazing areas lay in the south of the country, were particularly badly affected; they were also in Glubb's opinion the wildest and most anarchic of all the bedouin tribes he had met. One of their principal sheikhs, Auda abu Tayeh, who fought under Lawrence, has been immortalized by Eric Kennington, whose portrait of him glowers like a tiger from the pages of *Seven Pillars of Wisdom*.

Peake's plan for dealing with the bedouins was to establish a *cordon sanitaire* along the line of the Hejaz Railway. They were free to behave as they liked east of the railway, but any attempt to cross it for raiding purposes would be resisted. However, if the Arab Legion were to carry out this task, its strength would need to be considerably augmented. The Amir had hoped for an army comprising one infantry division, a cavalry brigade, artillery and other supporting arms. This, to the Amir's disgust, had been turned down by Britain as being too expensive. In 1926 the Arab Legion totalled only 1600 officers and soldiers, but it did include some artillery, signals and machine-gun units.

In that same year came disaster in the shape of Field-Marshal Lord Plumer, the High Commissioner for Palestine and Transjordan. Plumer was a fine soldier, but very conventionally-minded. His concept of a 'native' army was the Indian Army in which British officers commanded Indian soldiers. The Arab Legion did not fit into this pattern in any way. It was altogether too irregular. When Plumer paid his first visit to the Amir Abdullah, the Arab Legion mounted a Guard of Honour. They looked fine when standing solemnly to attention; when ordered to dismiss, the result was a shambles. Glubb believes that it was this incident which decided Plumer that an Arab unit should be raised, based on the Indian Army organization and paid for out of imperial revenues; its officers would be seconded from the British army. The Arab Legion would be reduced in strength to 900 men and converted to a gendarmerie, without any artillery, signals or machine-guns.

'This did not please Jordan or the Amir much,' says Glubb,[6] nor Peake and his officers. Some of the latter joined the new force, which was to be called the Transjordan Frontier Force;

[6] Letter to author.

paradoxically, the Transjordan government was required to pay one-sixth of its cost. The T.J.F.F., as it came to be known, was to be recruited in Palestine and based at Zerqa, a Circassian village fourteen miles north of Amman. The cavalry regiment would also be located there, with detachments in the desert area and in Palestine; a camel company was stationed at Ma'an in the south. The T.J.F.F.'s principal role was to maintain law and order *west* of the Hejaz Railway and to 'operate against enemy raiders or tribes advancing on Transjordan, within the strip of desert fifteen miles east of the railway'. This did not differ much from the task carried out by the Turkish garrisons to protect the Pilgrim traffic to Mecca from marauding bedouns.[7] It was axiomatic in those parts that the bedouins would always raid the settled areas; it was therefore the government's chief responsibility to protect the villagers. No one had ever contemplated the enlistment of bedouins on the principle of 'set a thief to catch a thief'. In the twenty-one years of its existence the T.J.F.F. contained in its ranks representatives of every race in the Middle East, as well as Greeks, Yugoslavs and Germans; but never intentionally did it enlist bedouins.

It says a good deal for both forces that, after some initial heart-searching, relations between them were usually cordial. However Glubb Pasha never agreed with the copying of the Indian Army in the case of the T.J.F.F., believing Arabs and Indians to be different in character and attitudes. Moreover Britain's relations with the Arabs were founded on quite different considerations from her relations with India. Although he was a fervent believer in Britain's influence for good in the world, Glubb was never an old-fashioned type of 'imperialist'. Example meant a good deal more to him than power.

The T.J.F.F. got off to a good start, largely due to the personality and character of its first commanding officer, Lt-Col. F. J. Bewsher. He was able to pick and choose his recruits, many of whom were well educated; at least three of them ended up as Major-Generals in the Jordanian Army. The

---

[7]There are many roads to Mecca. One of the oldest runs from Damascus to the Hejaz, traversing Transjordan from north to south. The Pilgrim Road (*Darb el Haj*), so vividly described by Charles Doughty in *Arabia Deserta*, is still easily identifiable by the tracks made by hundreds of thousands of camels over the centuries.

T.J.F.F. contained a large Circassian element with the force's headdress, the *kalpak*, resembling the astrakhan cap of the Cossacks (which officers in the Arab Legion also wore at one stage). There were several Jews serving in the T.J.F.F., which was truly cosmopolitan, and it soon developed a very special *panache* of its own. Its relations with the R.A.F., who had airfields at Amman and Mafraq, were excellent. The Amir Abdullah was the Honorary Colonel-in-Chief of the T.J.F.F. but the Transjordan government had no control over the force.

Unfortunately the T.J.F.F. was not really suited for operations far out in the desert. It recruited from the settled areas in Palestine and its soldiers were unused to desert conditions. It was also dependent chiefly upon horses for transportation and these were at a disadvantage against bedouins mounted on camels; there was a camel company but the bedouins ran rings round camel troopers recruited in Palestine. Had it been mechanized the story might have been different, but that had to wait until the Palestine rebellion in 1936.

The situation in the Transjordan desert was much the same as that in the southern desert of Iraq two or three years previously. Ibn Saud was encouraging the Ikhwan to raid the Transjordan tribes, partly to further his ambitions, and partly because he had little real control over them. The Amir Abdullah, who had his own reasons for wanting to unseat Ibn Saud, kept the pot boiling by intriguing with Ibn Saud's enemies. Not surprisingly, the two men hated each other.

The victims were the Howeitat tribe, who were being progressively ruined. In one raid early in 1930 they lost 5000 camels, a crippling loss. Since neither the R.A.F. nor the T.J.F.F. had an effective intelligence organization, they sought to establish a no-man's-land about sixty miles deep, west of the frontier with Saudi Arabia. Within this area they could then attack any camelmen they came across on the assumption that they must be hostile. They could also prevent the Howeitat from entering the zone on their way to raid across the frontier. But this deprived the Howeitat of hundreds of square miles of grazing and, as Glubb has pointed out, 'To the bedouin, grazing for his camel is life and soul; he will, and daily does, risk death to secure it.'[8]

'The military forces acted with a thoroughness really remarkable,' Glubb was later to report. 'The camps and grazing grounds were criss-crossed by patrols and reconnaissances. They even went so far as to make nominal rolls of the tribesmen, count all their tents and even attempted to count their camels in order to be able to check at will whether any men were absent on raids or whether their flocks had suddenly been increased by loot. Many men were arrested for raiding, some of them guilty, others innocent, sent into Amman, tried, arrested and sometimes imprisoned or fined. Every step taken in this energetic anti-raiding campaign added to the resentment, hatred and bitterness of the Howeitat. "Why," they asked, "if the government has so many forces to spare and are so determined to prevent raiding did they not prevent Ibn Musa'ad and Al Nashmi[9] raiding us?"' Or, '"Why do they not compel Ibn Saud to return our flocks?"'[10]

The Amir Abdullah and Shareef Shakir were acutely conscious of the problem as deputation after deputation of aggrieved Howeitat came to plead their case. No one knew better than Abdullah that 'Arabs always desire to be on the winning side, and in Arabia a losing cause has no friends.'[11] Inevitably, the Howeitat would change sides unless the situation could be changed. But how? The matter was out of the Amir's hands. The British were running the show.

It was at this juncture that Glubb arrived in Transjordan from Iraq. The British Resident had played an important part in obtaining his services but Peake does not appear to have been consulted; he was on home leave at the time. 'Glubb's appointment was not popular in certain circles,' says Kirkbride. 'The advent of a newcomer to the second highest post in the Arab Legion, not unnaturally, caused some heart-burning amongst the officers of that corps, and the more regular military formations (T.J.F.F.) saw, in the new policy, official recognition of

[8] J. B. Glubb, Monthly Report, July 1932.
[9] Ibn Musa'ad and Al Nashmi were Ikhwan leaders.
[10] J. B. Glubb, Report on Situation, December 1930.
[11] J. B. Glubb, Monthly Report, July 1932.

the fact that their organization and training had not fitted them for the task of controlling elusive nomads.'[12]

Glubb stayed at the Residency with Colonel Cox when he first arrived in Amman in November 1930. He was given no contract, deputy or troops. He had been accompanied from Iraq only by his cook-driver. After discussing the problem with Amir Abdullah, Shareef Shakir, Colonel Cox and the Commanding Officer of the T.J.F.F., Glubb decided to see for himself, purchasing a Buick car for the purpose. Before setting out for the desert he told Cox he would eventually need seventy camelmen and thirty machine-gunners, the latter to be mounted in trucks. They were all to be bedouins. It was Cox's task to extract the money for such a force from H.M.G. Since Glubb's appointment had yet to be confirmed by the Transjordan government, he possessed neither authority nor the right to wear uniform. He wore civilian clothes – European-style, not Arab.[13]

On his return to Amman just before Christmas Glubb was lucky enough to acquire two powerful allies. The first was the Shareef Shakir who as President of the Bedouin Control Board had the Amir's ear on all matters concerning the tribes. Shakir and Glubb liked each other at first sight; as they came to know each other better this liking became a real affection and respect. Shakir was an Arab prince of the old style, at home equally in tent or palace. He had the impeccable manners and complete self-assurance of the true aristocrat and was a staunch friend; he

[12] Sir Alec Kirkbride, *A Crackle of Thorns*, p. 61. Glubb believed that his appointment was made without Peake Pasha's knowledge and chiefly at the urging of Colonel Henry Cox, the British Resident. Cox and Peake did not work closely together and their relations were not particularly cordial. Probably Cox and Amir Shakir between them were responsible for Glubb's appointment.

[13] In February 1953 I retraced Lawrence's famous journey from Bayir, near the Wadi Sirhan, to Aqaba, travelling partly by landrover and partly by camel. On the first day out from Bayir we camped beside the Wadi Gurrah, dry for most of the year but at that season a series of deep pools from which the Howeitat water their camels. Halting on a bluff above one of the pools, my driver drew some water to brew tea. He was a bedouin from the Harb tribe in northern Hejaz and a veteran of the Desert Patrol. 'This is a famous place for the bedu,' he told me. 'It was here that the Pasha, may God bless him, spent his first night when he came to bring peace to the bedouins.' When I gazed at the immensity of the desert from our vantage point, and then thought of the solitary Englishman and his faithful Arab companion with no one else to support them, I realized for the first time what Glubb had accomplished in pacifying the Transjordan bedouin tribes.

could also be a bitter enemy. He fell out with the redoubtable Auda abu Tayeh of the Howeitat and Auda's section of the tribe were in Shakir's bad books, as was their sheikh.

The other ally was Alec Kirkbride. As Assistant Resident he was able to influence not only the British Resident, Cox, but also many Arab officials who had known him for years, and who valued his opinions. Kirkbride had first to be convinced that Glubb was on the right track; he was not predisposed towards bedouins after his experiences under Lawrence. Fortunately the two men forged a firm friendship although they were totally unalike in character and temperament. Their ability to work closely with each other was to stand Transjordan well in the future.

Glubb's message was simple. There could never be peace in the desert unless the tribes agreed willingly to police themselves. An enforced peace, maintained only by the presence of government forces, would never work. The bedouins had looked upon the T.J.F.F. as an unwarranted intrusion on their age-old right to be free. Since this was so, it followed that it was the inalienable right of every tribesman to circumvent the government forces whenever he could get away with it. It was possible to restrict by force the tribes' grazing areas but only at the expense of the animals themselves. Preventing a tribe from raiding would destroy the delicate economic balance of desert life unless that tribe in its turn could be protected from being raided. Glubb had shown in Iraq that the bedouins could police themselves, but first the government forces, which the bedouins regarded as instruments for their oppression, must be withdrawn.

Such advice was hardly likely to be acceptable to rhe T.J.F.F., nor did it make for Glubb's popularity in British circles. There were many Arabs, too, who shared the official British view. However, after much heart-searching, it was agreed to try Glubb's scheme, most people believing it was bound to fail.

For several weeks Glubb travelled from encampment to encampment, listening patiently while the Howeitat voiced their complaints. One of his most valuable qualities was his ability to listen; an oasis of calm amidst violent men arguing violently in full voice, tugging at their beards the while and calling upon Allah to witness that they had been wronged. Why was the government on Ibn Saud's side instead of on theirs? Why should they sit back and do nothing when their camels were lifted from them? What use were the soldiers when all they could do was prevent the Howeitat from taking back their own? Apparently they were incapable of preventing the Saudis from robbing their own people?

Glubb was appalled by their obvious poverty, their bitterness and their conviction that the British were in secret agreement with Ibn Saud to destroy them. In the report he wrote on his return to Amman at the end of December, he said, 'I must confess that, as an Englishman, I was utterly ashamed to discover the complete absence of prestige of Great Britain on both sides of the frontier. This lamentable situation is due to the impression that, in fining and imprisoning their tribes and returning loot to Ibn Saud, while the latter's governor in Jauf is openly urging the Nejd tribes to raid Transjordan, His Majesty's Government is willing to descend to any depths of servility to placate Ibn Saud. I am aware that this is strong language, but it is almost verbatim the language used by the bedouins.'[14]

He goes on to say, 'It is heartbreaking to find the Transjordan government slowly and painfully learning the same lessons which Iraq acquired through ten years of blood and tears, raids and recriminations . . . The key to the situation, both material and moral, is that the Howeitat have been ruined and brought to starvation while under British protection . . . The first step therefore is to help the Howeitat . . .' This could best be done, he suggested, by bringing pressure to bear on Ibn Saud to return the looted camels; failing this (and it did fail), the British government should provide £6000 to enable the Howeitat to repair their losses. Ibn Saud should be required to restrain his governor in Jauf, Al Nashmi, from openly encouraging raids into Transjordan, and an arrangement should be agreed whereby Saudi and Transjordan complaints could be heard by properly appointed officials; in Transjordan's case this would be Glubb. 'I may add,' he concluded, 'that if the

[14]J. B. Glubb, Report on Situation, December 1930.

above proposals can be adopted, and the financial provision for Police and Posts asked for by me, be provided, I have firm hopes that peace, order and good relations can be established at an early date.'[15]

Glubb had his doubts, too. 'It was with mixed feelings', he says, 'that I sat on top of a low hill on the morning of the first of February 1931 and watched the dust of the last British column gradually vanish over the western horizon. Two miles to the east of where I sat lay the frontier of Saudi Arabia and behind it perhaps those dreaded war banners of which we heard so many rumours.'[16]

He had with him only one companion, the faithful Ali. If the Ikhwan did come, both of them would surely die since Glubb would never have abandoned his trust. But there was no time to brood. Now that the soldiers had gone, the Howeitat felt free to go raiding, or so they thought. It was Glubb's task to dissuade them. He moved from encampment to encampment pleading with the bitter and hungry tribesmen. They had seen their herds dwindle almost to nothing and had little faith in the government. And yet Glubb's persuasive arguments had a remarkable effect. A few did slip away, hoping to redress the balance sheet in the way the bedouins had always done; Glubb could not prevent them. But the majority of the Howeitat decided to wait and see what would happen. The government forces had gone, thank God! The Ikhwan were still there over the horizon. What did the fresh-faced young Englishman with the crooked jaw intend to do about them?

[15] Ibid.
[16] J. B. Glubb, *The Story of the Arab Legion*, p. 92.

Chapter Six

———————◆———————

A Band of Brothers

'. . . as herdsmen and wolves, soldiers and Bedouins
may never agree together . . .'

CHARLES M. DOUGHTY, *Arabia Deserta*

THERE WAS NO RUSH to enlist in Glubb's desert police force. As
he waited patiently for Transjordan bedouins to come forward,
two men walked up to his tent one morning. One was from the
Shammar, the other an ex-slave. They were bedouin mercen-
aries selling their swords to whoever would hire them and Glubb
eagerly snapped them up. Soon they were recounting *Abu
Hunaik*'s exploits round the Howeitat coffee hearths, encouraging one Awwadh ibn Hudeiba to offer his services. He
was the first Howeitat tribesman to join Glubb but his service
was short and sweet. An Arab Legion paymaster came out from
Amman to issue uniforms and pay. He insisted that the handful
of recruits should first line up and number before they could
draw their pay. This was too much for Awwadh who threw
down his uniform and returned to his tent in disgust. That night
he rode out on a raid into Saudi Arabia.

He was, fortunately, soon replaced. Three men arrived from
Iraq, having served in the Southern Desert Camel Corps, and
by the end of February the numbers had swelled to twenty,
some of them Howeitat but most from the Beni Sakhr. Four
trucks had been issued and instruction had begun in the
handling of Lewis and Vickers machine-guns. Patience and
perseverance had been rewarded. More surprisingly, there had
been no violence, although most of the Howeitat considered
themselves cruelly wronged and the government their enemy.

74

They were violent men, quick of temper and swift to take revenge, yet Glubb moved among them freely and without fear: 'They all knew about me, you see,' he said. 'In the desert the bedouins may know absolutely nothing about what is going on in Amman or Baghdad, but anything that happens in the desert, even as far afield as the Persian Gulf, soon becomes common gossip round the coffee hearths. They all knew about *Abu Hunaik* long before I arrived in Transjordan. Also it is much easier to get on terms with people who live in tents than with those who dwell in houses. The tent is open to every traveller who passes. I used to drop in and have a gossip and they soon came to know me. The Howeitat never scared me but the thought of the Ikhwan certainly did!'[1]

There were rumours that Al Neshmi was camped not far from the eastern edge of the Wadi Sirhan, waiting for a favourable opportunity to raid the Howeitat with a thousand or more Ikhwan. As the rumours persisted, morale among the Howeitat grew low; their sheikhs wanted to move farther back into Transjordan but the grazing did not compare with the frontier area. Glubb dissuaded them from doing so, insisting that they should move forward to Imshash Hadraj instead, which was almost on the frontier. There he repeated his tactics used at Abtiyya against Feisal al Duweesh with the tents lined up, the camels couched and hobbled (*nowwakh wa aqal*), the four cars in the centre, and the machine-guns unshipped, waiting for the dawn charge. It never came. The Ikhwan never crossed the Wadi Sirhan and Imshash Hadraj became a name to reckon with among Transjordan bedouins.

It also brought the Amir Shakir out from Amman to see what was going on; with him was Kirkbride, the assistant British Resident. Shakir arrived at an inopportune moment for Glubb. A section of the Howeitat had gone raiding despite his orders, and as soon as this was reported their tents were surrounded by Glubb's men and the camels were impounded. Pitching their tents nearby, the Desert Patrol waited patiently for the raiders' return. It was just at this moment that the President of the Bedouin Control Board chose to arrive on the scene. Glubb was

[1] Interview with author, 5 May 1982.

75

acting far beyond his powers in seizing the camels and not unnaturally was anxious about Shakir's reaction. He need not have
worried. 'Not only did he show no resentment,' wrote Glubb,
'but expressed warm approval of my actions and promised me
his support. His help and friendship never failed me until his
death four years later.'[2]

Shakir was anxious to visit the wild Tubaiq mountains on
Transjordan's southern frontier and he, Kirkbride and Glubb
set out with the four cars of the Desert Patrol as escort. High
dunes make entry into Tubaiq difficult but they were lucky
to intercept a party of Howeitat returning from a raid. The
raiders took refuge in the mountains, where they could not be
followed by men in cars, but they abandoned a riding camel in
whose saddle-bags was found a bill from a merchant in Ma'an
and the name of the camel's owner. They were the raiders whose
camels Glubb had impounded. Shakir was delighted. When the
raiders returned, they were confronted by the Amir and Glubb
who only returned the impounded camels on the understanding
that next time the government would retain them. One of the
raiders was Awwadh ibn Hudeiba, the man who refused to
number off for his pay.

It was a minor triumph. The support of Shakir meant that
of the Amir Abdullah in the long run and Kirkbride's the tacit
support of H.M.G. With two such powerful allies in Amman,
Glubb was far better placed than he had been originally in Iraq.
Recruits now started rolling in, among the first an ugly youth
from the Billi tribe in Saudi Arabia whose name was Hamdan al
Biluwi. He was early lamed in the Legion's service and walked
with a limp from then on; Glubb tells the tale graphically in his
Story of the Arab Legion.[3] When asked twenty-five years later
how he accounted for Glubb's success in pacifying Transjordan's
bedouins, Hamdan said:

'Firstly, we bedu were sick and tired of raiding, and being
raided. The Ikhwan were partly responsible for this because
they obeyed no rules. But there were other considerations such
as the aeroplane and modern weapons that changed everything.
Then, of course, there was the Pasha. He was quite different

[2]J. B. Glubb, *The Story of the Arab Legion*, pp. 99–101.   [3]Ibid.

from any other kind of government official. In the first place he lived as we did, in a tent and simply. Secondly, he knew our customs and respected them. Thirdly, he was very patient. He would sit for hours arguing with us round the coffee hearth. He never lost his temper, or only very occasionally, and he never forgot a face or a name. But above all, I think, we knew he was honest; we were so accustomed to being cheated that an honest government official was something remarkable. We trusted him, and without that trust the Pasha could never have succeeded. And later that trust turned to love.'[4]

But it was not all plain sailing. The bureaucracy in Arab Legion headquarters in Amman sorely tried Glubb's patience. In Arabia, as elsewhere in what used to be the British empire, the rules drawn up in Whitehall to guard against corruption and fiddling the books have been so improved upon that no one, or almost no one, can give a decision about anything. Delay, prevarication and resort to the strict letter of the regulations guarantee the answer 'no' to almost every request. Glubb discovered that promotions in his Desert Police could not be agreed because no provision had been made for them. There were similar difficulties over pay. 'The would-be recruits arrive here without a bean, and without food,' he protested to Peake Pasha. 'Every month we send in a car for rations and the men club their money together and send in one or two of their number to buy for them. The new recruits have no money and have to live for two months by scrounging or borrowing from me . . . All this is particularly unfortunate at the moment when the whole success of the enterprise is in the melting pot.' For once exasperation with red tape made him lose his temper. 'I do not know whether Ahid is a fool or Howes very difficult,' he wrote of the two officers concerned, 'but between them they give me more trouble and anxiety at the moment than all the rest of the job put together.'[5]

'Although recruiting for the desert patrol had started slowly,' says Glubb, 'with the Howeitat strange and suspicious, it took us only a few weeks to recruit our ninety men. Very soon we had a long waiting list, and the sons of many leading sheikhs were

---

[4]Interview with author, 1954.   [5]Letter to Peake Pasha, February 1931.

struggling for admission. For the bedouin's chief pleasure in life is to bear arms, and the simultaneous abolition of raiding drove the most gallant and enterprising young men into the service.'[6]

Some years later Glubb was asked whether he had had any difficulty in introducing his wild men of the desert to military discipline. 'At first it was very difficult indeed,' he replied. 'In any case, the discipline must be very different from that used for village and town dwellers. The bedouins are very democratic. For instance, all officers and all men always eat out of the same dish. Also, when on patrol duty, officers and men always have coffee together in the evenings. The men are so proud of belonging to the patrol that an appeal to a man's chivalry, or a threat to take away his arms, or a threat of dismissal from the force, is much more effective than any punishment would be. But again, that zeal for personal distinction leads to a great deal of jealousy, which may make trouble.'[7]

It does indeed, as anyone who has served with Arab tribesmen will agree. Personal jealousy is one of their least attractive characteristics, making promotion by merit extremely hard to achieve.[8] Both in the Desert Patrol and later when he commanded the Arab Legion, Glubb Pasha kept promotion strictly in his own hands, attempting by means of regular promotion examinations to ensure that only those who were fitted for it were promoted. Even so he never entirely eliminated nepotism and fraud, while in later years the Arab Legion far outgrew his ability to control promotion.[9]

Glubb's understanding of the bedouin mentality contributed greatly to the rapid recruitment of the Desert Patrol, and for its subsequent high morale. He did not attempt to base its discipline on either the British or Indian Army's, or for that matter on the village-recruited Arab Legion itself. The same understanding applied to its uniform which was 'cut in the same manner as their ordinary dress, long robes reaching almost to the ground and

[6] J. B. Glubb, *The Story of the Arab Legion*, p. 103.
[7] J. B. Glubb, *Arab Chivalry* (Journal of the Royal Central Asian Society Vol. XXIV, Part 1, 1937). (Now the Royal Society for Asian Affairs.)
[8] The mutiny in the South Arabian Army in June 1967 which complicated the British withdrawal from Aden was due principally to inter-tribal jealousy over promotion.
[9] One of King Husain's chief complaints was that Glubb Pasha kept promotion so strictly within his own hands.

long white sleeves, but the outer garment was khaki in colour. With a red sash, a red revolver lanyard, a belt and bandolier full of ammunition, and a silver dagger in the belt, the effect was impressive. Soon the tribesmen were complaining that the prettiest girls would accept none but our soldiers for their lovers.'[10]

He explained his philosophy in a lecture delivered to the Royal Central Asian Society in 1937:

'What, now, are the essential lessons which Eastern soldiers can learn from Europe? The first is detailed organization, method and discipline. This is ensured by mental and moral training, and does not necessitate the introduction either of *foreign social distinctions or of foreign dress* [author's italics]. The second lesson they require is the use of scientific weapons – motor transport, machine-guns, artillery, wireless and aircraft. I believe it is possible for Arab troops to learn the lessons which Europe can teach in organization, discipline, and scientific weapons, without departing from their hereditary customs, manners and dress.'[11]

The red and white checkered headcloth of the Desert Patrol, known in the Arab Legion as the *shamagh*, soon became famous throughout Arabia and was adopted by two other British-led Arab forces fashioned on Glubb's force – the Trucial Oman Scouts and the Hadhrami Bedouin Legion. At first, however, Glubb ran into trouble over the Arab Legion badge which was pinned to the *aghal*, the twin black headropes holding the *shamagh* in place. To many of his recruits this badge signified a mark of servitude to the government and was accordingly unpinned before entering an encampment or going on leave. Glubb knew this and made no attempt to enforce the wearing of the badge which soon came to be accepted by the wearers as the symbol of an élite organization.

Glubb attached great importance to the moral virtues. 'Serve to Lead', the Sandhurst motto, summed up his feelings on leadership. A policeman's duties did not end with the preser-

[10] J. B. Glubb, *The Story of the Arab Legion*, p. 103.
[11] J. B. Glubb, *Relations between Arab Civilization and Foreign Culture in the Past and Today* (Journal of the Royal Central Asian Society Vol. XXIV, Part 3, 1937). (Now the Royal Society for Asian Affairs.)

vation of law and order; he owed it to the community to set it an example. This may sound a little naïve to those who have experienced the widespread corruption within police forces in the East, but from the very outset Glubb insisted that the Desert Patrol should have a moral as well as a military aim. Every fort built in the desert from 1933 onwards had inscribed in large letters on its inner courtyard wall, 'Example is stronger than orders. Improve the morals of the people by your own good example'; whenever he visited a post, Glubb made a point of conducting a discussion on the subject.

From the outset he was careful to mix the tribes, many of them centuries-old enemies. The Howeitat and Beni Sakhr had fought each other for generations and now men from these tribes made up the majority of the Desert Patrol. At first this demanded careful handling, but in a surprisingly short time Glubb's men accepted each other as comrades. Men came from all over Arabia to join the Desert Patrol, far too many to be accepted. The French in Syria complained that Glubb was recruiting from their tribes, such as the Ruwalla, but in fact there was no inducement to do so. Men would just appear and say, 'I am Fawaz, may God prolong your life, O Pasha! I want to join your army'. Although many came, few were chosen.

If 1931 had been the year of persuasion, 1932 was the year for showing the flag throughout the Transjordan desert. 1933 was the year of consolidation when the forts were built. Wherever there were permanent wells, such as at Azraq and Bayir, or wherever the tribes had to pass on their annual migrations, as at Muddawara on the wrecked Hejaz Railway, Glubb built small forts which contained an officer or senior N.C.O. and ten to twenty men. Each fort was square in construction with walls sufficiently high to deter the fanatical Ikhwan from reaching the parapets by climbing on each other's shoulders. Two towers sited diagonally enabled riflemen and machine-gunners to enfilade the walls. Sleeping and living quarters were sited round a central square, together with the armoury and magazine. There also was the *majlis*, or council chamber, where passing bedouins drank the bitter coffee or milkless over-sweet tea offered to them in exchange for gossip. When not grazing, the camels were couched outside the walls, sometimes being brought in at night if the situation demanded. Each fort was whitewashed and from its main tower flew the Transjordan flag.

The forts controlled the entire desert and became as well-known to travellers as the old posting inns on the road between London and York. Anything that happened within a radius of a hundred miles of each was sure to be reported sooner or later. As soon as money became available each fort was linked by Wireless Telegraphy with Amman, and the bedouins proved themselves to be excellent morse code operators. When Ingrams pacified the Hadhramaut in the early 1940s, he copied Glubb's desert forts, building them along the southern fringe of the Empty Quarter at Thamud, Minwakh and Al Abr. They served the same purpose and achieved the same end – peace where formerly there had been only war.

'It was my pride and joy,' Glubb has written, 'that this new peace and security had been established without the firing of a single shot, or the arrest or imprisonment of a single man.'[12] He quotes Blaise Pascal as saying, 'Win hearts, for men are more important than affairs,' and he certainly made this his guide in his dealings with the bedouins. It was his sympathetic approach *and* his patience which enabled him to achieve as much as he did. Unlike T. E. Lawrence or St John Philby, he never dressed as an Arab, but always wore the uniform of the Arab Legion – usually with the *shamagh* or, often, the *sidara* – the blue and red forage cap of the Legion. He was of course enormously helped by his fluency in Arabic, reading and writing it with equal ease. He was still as fluent at the age of eighty-four. When asked how he remembered it so clearly, he replied, 'For thirty years I wrote and read Arabic more regularly than English; for at least fifteen of them I rarely spoke English except when at headquarters or on leave.'[13]

As O.C. the Desert Area between 1930 and 1939, Glubb spent most of his time in the desert, for much of it the only European in the Desert Patrol. Peake Pasha seldom interfered with him and the two men got on well. Kirkbride was a great

[12] J. B. Glubb, *The Changing Scenes of Life*, p. 106.
[13] Interview with author, 5 May 1982.

ally, often joining Glubb in the desert to revive memories of the days when he rode with Feisal and Lawrence on the long road to Damascus. There is something about the desert that appeals to a certain type of European – possibly those with masochistic tendencies? Although in spring the desert can be wonderfully attractive, the wadis ablaze with wild flowers and the rolling hills a carpet of grass, it is gone in a twinkling and replaced by a wilderness, burning hot by day, often freezing cold at night. Plagues of flies torment and it is alive with vipers, scorpions and huge camel spiders of repellent aspect and poisonous bite; and always in summer it produces a fearful thirst. Seering winds, driving before them clouds of dust, chap faces and lips; in winter they come as from the arctic and make travel a misery. And yet, and yet . . . there is a mystery about the desert, as there is about the sea, that holds those who have experienced it for ever in thrall.

From 1934 onwards Glubb found himself ever more deeply involved with the conflicting ambitions of his master, the Amir Abdullah, and King Ibn Saud. The two rulers disliked and distrusted each other, and with good reason. Abdullah still hankered to be King of Greater Syria; Ibn Saud wanted to be King of *all* the bedouins. These included the Sirhan tribe whose principal grazing areas lay without question well inside Transjordan. Ibn Saud also claimed the whole of the Wadi Sirhan within his territories, whereas the boundary, as drawn, ran down the middle of the broad wadi basin. This led to constant disputes as Transjordan tribes, long accustomed to pasturing their herds in the Wadi Sirhan, found them seized by Ibn Saud's so-called 'soldiers' and taken off to Kaf or Tebuk where they were impounded by the Saudi governors. It required laborious negotiations to obtain their return, usually only after the best animals had been retained by the governors concerned.

These constant disputes were a sore trial to the British government which was anxious to remain on good terms with both rulers. Unfortunately Transjordan had little faith in the British government, believing it to be firmly on Ibn Saud's side, as Glubb makes clear in his Monthly Report for May 1933:

'The facts of the Transjordan deserts are [that] we are afraid.

82

Not only do we suffer from a neighbour five times more powerful than ourselves, but every man in the deserts in Transjordan is haunted by the fear that His Majesty's Government is not really on their side, that, at any time, in pursuit of some remote policy which they cannot understand, His Majesty's Government may find it convenient to hand them, or a further slice of their country, over to Ibn Saud.'

This was written after Glubb's return from Jeddah where he had accompanied a joint British–Transjordanian delegation to conclude a *Bon Voisinage* Treaty between Ibn Saud and Abdullah. The delegation was led by Sir Gilbert Clayton and the mission was accomplished, but Glubb found relations with Ibn Saud very different from 1928, when he had also accompanied Sir Gilbert Clayton to Jeddah. Ibn Saud had then been very approachable. 'No objection was raised to our visiting Ibn Saud personally as individuals, and I have recollections of a tea with him *tête à tête*, on the conclusion of which some of the children were brought in to be introduced. This was in spite of the fact that feelings at that time were running intensely high. On the present occasion conditions are no longer strained, or certainly not in comparison with former days. Yet Ibn Saud, who was only two hours' drive away by car, did not come to Jeddah at all until we had been there for nine days. He then came for two days, but the mission were only given one formal interview of a few minutes, and were not even asked to a meal.'[14]

Things were changing fast in Saudi Arabia, and soon the pace would become frenetic. But despite the altered circumstances, Glubb's admiration for Ibn Saud remained the same. 'Abdul Aziz was a model of common sense. His broad mind and clear intellect was able to grasp the essentials of a situation, even in countries which (it would have been thought) were far beyond the range of his experience. If he encouraged fanaticism it was to use it as an instrument to achieve his object; he was never himself a fanatic.'[15] That this admiration was probably not mutual can be gathered from a comment by Ibn Saud which Glubb tells against himself in the same Report: 'As for Glubb he is a very junior English officer of no importance to anyone'!

[14] J. B. Glubb, Monthly Report, May 1933.   [15] Ibid.

It was probably in an attempt to enhance Glubb's status *vis à vis* the Saudi governors in Kaf and Tebuk, who signed themselves as *Amirs* (Princes), that Glubb was appointed by formal government decree Commandant of the Desert Area in July 1933.

Ibn Saud's disparaging comment notwithstanding, Glubb's reputation among the Transjordanian bedouins continued to increase, bringing with it certain problems:

'A serious and apparently increasing nuisance in the desert is the fashion spreading amongst bedouin fathers of dying and appointing me solemnly as guardian of the child . . . The Arabs allege that a deathbed wish of this kind must be honoured and that there is no honourable means of escape. Naturally these thoughtful fathers always die in very reduced circumstances, if not over their ears in debt. One of my first appointments in this direction dates from 1925, when Hamood as Suwait of the Dhafir tribe of Iraq left an infant son under my charge. This young man paid me a visit last year, from his home in Kuwait, to explain that there was a deficit in the family budget. Were the matter limited to sheikhs, however, it would not be so bad, but in Transjordan every police post in the desert has two or three of my 'wards' attached to it, where they are being taught to read and write. The parents, however, omit to leave them anything in trustee securities, and the cost of clothing and feeding them is a heavy monthly charge.'[16]

Glubb's salary was modest and his reputation for generosity bore heavily upon it. Bedouins attach great importance to generosity and take full advantage of it. There are dozens of men living in Jordan today who owe Glubb an enormous debt. Many were educated at his expense; others were sent to hospital in Jerusalem or Beirut. Glubb paid the bills from his own pocket. Commenting on this, one senior Jordanian officer has remarked, 'The quality I shall always remember longest about the Pasha is his generosity of pocket and spirit. God alone knows how many of us he helped. He sent me to Beirut when I was a lad and I was cured of T.B. It was a long treatment but he paid every penny of the expense.'[17]

[16] J. B. Glubb, Monthly Report, July 1933.   [17] Interview, January 1982.

There would seem to have been no permanency where Glubb's appointment was concerned. He was given no contract, nor did he ask for one. He was so absorbed in his work that he had no time to think about himself. Everything was going so well in the desert that it came as a shock, and a warning, when a minor riot in Amman on 31 October 1933 had repercussions among the tribes. The riot was a manifestation of sympathy for the Arabs of Palestine who were beginning to grow alarmed by the increase in Jewish numbers and influence. A mob collected in the streets and stoned and insulted any European who happened to be passing. Glubb was one of them. He might have been seriously injured had it not been for a man of the Desert Patrol who ran to his side and endeavoured to calm the mob. At a critical moment the Amir Shakir rode up on his horse, accompanied by four of his slaves, and together they kept the mob at bay until Shakir's car arrived. Then he and Glubb drove off unhurt.[18]

Reporting this incident, Glubb wrote, 'The desert has been so very peaceful for the last two years that we had almost come to regard raiding as a thing of the past. It was with something of a shock, therefore, that I received reports of the impression produced among the tribes by these reports. While the majority of the tribesmen are probably fairly satisfied with the present regime . . . a not inconsiderable minority hastened to point the moral that the news meant raiding would again be possible . . . the fact that such remarks were made came as a timely reminder that many bedouins still yearn for the old raiding days, and would seize on any sign of weakness to return to their former habits.'[19]

The Monthly Reports he made to Arab Legion Headquarters make fascinating reading. He was a compulsive writer and everything was grist to his mill. A sample of the subjects discussed includes relations with the French in the Jebel Druse; Bedouin traditional law and the folly of applying a modern legal system to them; the difference between Ottoman tax gathering and Transjordanian; relations with Iraq and King Feisal's in-

[18]It was rumoured in the desert that Glubb had been killed.
[19]J. B. Glubb, Monthly Report, November 1933.

85

trigues; Amir Abdullah's relations with his sons; agriculture in the desert and developing the Azraq oasis; the breeding of camels; and the Arab view of treaties. A paragraph in the Report for March 1933 merits repetition:

'It is rumoured that an oilfield has been discovered in the Hejaz, and that several of the great oil combinations of Europe and America have thought it worth while to approach Ibn Saud for concessions. If this be really true it may indeed mean a transformation in the future history of Arabia. Politically it might even enable the Sauds to hold on to the Hejaz, to the exclusion of the sherifs.' He goes on to point out that Ibn Saud's principal weakness was his dependence on tribal levies to maintain his authority. 'It certainly seems to me that no government can be really stable unless it depends on regular paid forces to maintain order, and such forces are expensive. If, however, the Saudis are going to obtain oil royalties, they really may be able to afford something of the nature of proper paid police and soldiers, and even produce quite a comparatively stable administration, which they cannot be said to possess at the moment.'

It was fortunate that among Glubb's other accomplishments was a fluent command of French. Transjordan's northern border marched with Syria, then a French Mandate, and the French were convinced that the British were subverting the Syrians against them. They constantly complained that Glubb was recruiting their tribesmen and they chose to regard him as some kind of spy. It was true that some of the Ruwalla had joined the Desert Patrol but this was part of Glubb's policy 'that some at least of the police controlling any given tribe must be recruited from that tribe'. The Ruwalla passed through Transjordan every year in the course of their migration from winter to summer pastures and it made sense to recruit a few of them into the Desert Patrol. Matters were improved a little when Kirkbride and Glubb visited the French authorities in the Jebel Druse but relations were never really easy. In view of the Amir Abdullah's known ambition to rule in Damascus, this is hardly surprising.

By 1934 Glubb's duties as Commandant of the Desert Area had become as much diplomatic as military. King Ibn Saud appointed a frontier inspector to deal directly with him over frontier disputes; after initial suspicions and hesitations this arrangement worked well and Glubb succeeded in getting on good terms with his opposite numbers, particularly with the Amir Abdullah as Sudairi, a Saudi *magnifico* who was related to Abdul Aziz himself. The good manners and quiet natural ease of the desert's aristocrats had a particular appeal for Glubb who, in his turn, fitted in well with them. 'He was a natural gentleman,' the Saudi ambassador in New Delhi was to say of him thirty-five years later.[20]

In November 1934 Glubb was joined by another British officer whose appointment had originated at the suggestion of the Iraq Petroleum Company. The company's desert pumping stations at H4, H3 and Mafraq required protection and the Desert Patrol took over this task at I.P.C.'s expense. Additional men were recruited and Norman Oliver Lash joined the Arab Legion from the Palestine Police. Lash was born in 1908 and educated at Tonbridge School and St John's College, Oxford. After a short spell as a schoolmaster he joined the Palestine Police in 1932 as a constable and became rapidly proficient in Arabic, for which language he had something of a gift. Although his precise function in the Legion took a little time to establish, he eventually became O.C. Desert Area under Glubb until 1938, when he left the Legion to join the R.A.F. The Air Ministry released him in May 1939 and he was made a Deputy Superintendent in the Palestine Police and seconded for service with the Arab Legion, with which force he served until 1949 at which point he retired from the Legion (and the Colonial Service). He returned to schoolmastering and died on 9 August 1960.

Lash found his situation anomalous when first he arrived in Transjordan. Glubb was on leave when Peake Pasha decided to inspect the garrisons at the pumping stations. 'The C.O. has inspected H4, H5 and Mafraq,' Lash wrote to Glubb on 16 May 1934, 'accompanied by Omar al Duari. The troops are delighted to see the Pasha but I do not think they care about Omar meddling with their files . . . The C.O. showed signs of

[20]To the author in 1967.

thinking that I was in charge of the area . . . I had no idea I was allowed to inspect anything! I told him that I was not in charge of the area and he said "I know". He has nevertheless come down on me for reports about various subjects of which I know less than nothing . . . This business of being an Important Policeman *vis à vis* the I.P.C., an amiable but insignificant wireless enthusiast *vis à vis* the troops, and a man with an "area" who does not command it *vis à vis* the C.O. is rather wearing and I shall be glad when it is over.'

It was sorted out on Glubb's return from leave and Lash became his deputy for the Desert Area. Although they were not at all alike Glubb and Lash worked well together for many years. Lash never had any pretensions to being a soldier but he was highly intelligent with a flair for getting on with Arabs of all classes. He fitted in easily with the untidy life-style of bedouin soldiers who liked his somewhat donnish approach towards life. However this did not invariably find favour with the more rigid military attitudes of those senior Arab officers who had received their early training in the Turkish army and who regarded Lash as something of an oddity. Glubb seems to have had a tolerant affection for him without much regard for his military qualities.

He was, however, to relieve Glubb of much of the work in the Desert Area. This was as well since Palestine had erupted in rebellion in 1936 and Transjordan was being increasingly used by gangs of Syrian and Iraqi sympathisers as they slipped across the River Jordan to fight the British. More and more British troops were deployed in Palestine as the rebellion gathered impetus and soon the Transjordan Frontier Force was almost wholly employed in the fighting. It was impossible for Transjordan to remain entirely neutral when their compatriots in Palestine were fighting for a cause in which all Arabs believed and for a time relations between British and Arabs in the higher echelons of government became strained. That this was not universal is clear from this account by Glubb:

'In 1936 and 1937 I often rode up the Jordan valley, on the east bank of the river, and was everywhere greeted, not only with kindness but with enthusiasm . . . On the other side of the narrow stream, the Arabs were engaged in active hostilities against the British forces. Few races today, I believe, would have exercised the same personal discrimination as was shown in our favour by the Arabs of Transjordan throughout this bitter struggle.'[21]

Glubb also tells the story of a corporal in the Arab Legion who requested Glubb to enlist the corporal's brother. When asked about his brother's experience, the corporal said he had been engaged in several battles with the English, in one of which he had been wounded. 'But he is well again now, and I am sure he would make a very useful man in the Arab Legion with all his fighting experience'![22]

The Palestine troubles did provide the opportunity to make a modest increase in the Arab Legion which at that time was basically a gendarmerie with only an internal security role. It was about twelve hundred strong, a hundred of whom were bedouins in the Desert Patrol (partly mechanized, partly camel-mounted). The foot police (*Shurta*) operated in the towns, the gendarmerie (*Darak*) in the countryside; the latter provided their own horses. None of the officers had received recent military training and the more senior of them were somewhat elderly. Peake Pasha controlled the force from Qyada in Amman, more a record office than a headquarters, and devolved more and more of the active supervision of operations on Glubb, who had become virtually his Second-in-Command.

If 1938 was an unhappy year in Palestine, it was certainly to prove an eventful one for Glubb personally. It was the year he married Rosemary Forbes – and they did live happily ever after! They were married in the registry office in Tunbridge Wells on 20 August; he was forty-one, she fifteen years younger.

For a man as romantic at heart as Jack Glubb, he had waited a very long time to marry. Throughout his Iraq service he had corresponded regularly with a girl who lived in the same village as his parents. This correspondence was governed by strict rules which seem to have forbidden any overt expression of affection (on her part anyway), but that it continued for so long must surely be evidence of affection on both sides. It came to nothing in the end.

[21]J. B. Glubb, *The Story of the Arab Legion*, pp. 231–2. [22]Ibid., p. 232.

Lady Glubb had wanted someone to speak German with her and Rosemary Forbes had answered her advertisement. As a result, Rosemary met Jack Glubb during his home leave in 1936 and they had corresponded regularly thereafter. General Glubb's death brought him home again in 1938 when they decided to get married. A church wedding was considered unsuitable so soon after the funeral, so they were married in Tunbridge Wells Registry Office. Glubb then returned to Jordan, accompanied by his widowed mother, leaving Rosemary to follow six weeks later, together with her widowed mother. Their marriage was solemnized in the little Anglican church in Beirut. Rosemary was by nature quiet and retiring with little desire to share her husband's limelight. Instead she provided him with the security of a truly Christian home. In a world where privacy was hard to come by, Rosemary Glubb made certain her husband could find it with her. Theirs was indeed a happy partnership.

In Jerusalem, in October 1939, a son was born to the Glubbs and they named him after the first Crusader king, Godfrey de Bouillon. On their way back to Amman the proud parents called on Amir Abdullah in his country house at Shuneh. The Amir believed Godfrey should have an Arab name as well and they settled on *Faris*, which means knight in Arabic. From then on Glubb was usually known, in accordance with Arab custom, as *Abu Faris* (the father of Faris). Several years later the Glubbs adopted three other children, Mary, Naomi and John, to whom they were equally devoted.

There were numerous skirmishes between the Arab Legion and the Arab gangs seeking to cross the Jordan throughout 1938 and early 1939. The bedouins of the Desert Patrol gave as good an account of themselves among the wooded mountains of Ajlun and the precipices of the Yarmouk valley as they were shortly to do in Iraq and Syria. They remained loyal despite every attempt to suborn them, the last action against the guerillas taking place in April 1939. A combined operation of T.J.F.F. and Arab Legion in the vicinity of Ajlun on 11 March resulted in the complete defeat of a powerful gang, but not without loss. Lieutenant Macadam, who had only recently joined the Arab Legion, was killed, and with him a sergeant and three soldiers. Thereafter Glubb was constantly in the field, chasing the gangs as they infiltrated through Transjordan into Palestine. 'It was a pleasure,' he wrote, 'to see the dash of the troops in action and their proficiency with their weapons. The mountains, clothed with deep grass and carpeted with spring flowers, were a constant joy in their silent serenity, a glorious contrast to the activity and the vindictiveness of man. Living in the open on the mountain slopes, surrounded by the fellowship and brotherhood of the troops, those wretched two months had their moments of compensation.'[23]

In the middle of this unpleasant situation Peake Pasha retired. He had commanded the Arab Legion since its inception in 1921 and can rightly be regarded as a founder of the modern kingdom of Jordan. 'His departure,' wrote Glubb, 'marked the end of an epoch for the Arab Legion, and indeed for Transjordan itself.' Peake left the country on 26 March 1939; Glubb took over command of the Arab Legion from him on 21 March. The audience he had with the Amir Abdullah on assuming command is best described in Glubb's own words:

' "You are English," said the Amir, motioning to me to sit down, "and this is an Arab country, and an Arab army. Before you take over command, I want you to pledge me your word, that, as long as you remain in this appointment, you will act always as if you had been born a Transjordanian.

' "I know you would not wish to fight your own countrymen. If it should ever come to fighting between us and the English, I will hold you excused. You may leave us then and stand aside. But if, by God's will, this does not happen, I want you to be one of the people of Transjordan."

' "Sir", I answered, "I give you my word of honour. From now onwards I am a Transjordanian, except under the conditions you mentioned, and which I pray God may never come." '[24]

[23] J. B. Glubb, *The Story of the Arab Legion*, p. 243.
[24] J. B. Glubb, *A Soldier with the Arabs* (Hodder & Stoughton, 1957), p. 19.

Chapter Seven

The Golden Years

'I never knew Jordan existed before I joined the army.'

Comment to author by a bedouin soldier in 1953

JORDAN'S GOLDEN AGE was from 1939 to 1951, according to Glubb Pasha. 'Throughout this period King Abdullah was on the throne, Kirkbride was British representative and I commanded the Arab Legion,' he writes. 'Although we were very different from one another, we made a perfect team. Although the whole of this period was one of endless trouble – World War II, endless disturbances in Palestine and finally the Arab–Israeli war – it was a period of perfect co-operation in the team. I may say also that, until the Palestinians joined us in 1949, it was a period of perfect understanding with the people of Jordan. This is not to say that ignorant bedus took no interest in politics and so we could do as we liked. This was far from being the case. The fact was, however, that nothing succeeds like success. Palestine, Syria and Iraq were in endless chaos and Jordan was always perfectly quiet. The Jordanians soon noticed this and praised their government for it.'[1]

Throughout the period mentioned by Glubb there was hardly an occasion when the Arab Legion was called in to support the civil power. Whatever the rumblings below the surface, and some there must have been, Jordan was not only the safest country in the Middle East; it was one of the safest countries in the world.

Some part of this was due to Glubb's success with the tribes.

[1] Letter to author, 14 February 1966.

92

Sir Alec Kirkbride has written that 'He overcame, by patience and honesty of purpose, the old habit of the tent dweller to regard all governments as enemies who would go to any lengths to prevent the free men of the desert from practising their national sports of camel raiding and highway robbery.'[2] Kirkbride became British Resident in the same year that Glubb took over command of the Arab Legion. They used to meet regularly to exchange views. This gained for the Pasha the ear of the Foreign Office, to which Kirkbride reported, and it meant that Glubb was no longer regarded in London as just a desert warrior, all right with bedouins and camels but not of use for much else.

When war broke out in 1939 Glubb was not only Commander of the Arab Legion; he was also Director of Public Security. This meant frequent access to the Amir Abdullah and the two men struck up a close friendship. Immediately after Britain went to war Abdullah placed the Arab Legion and all the resources of Transjordan at British disposal. This magnificent gesture elicited the reply that for the moment Britain could manage well enough but the offer would be borne in mind. There was therefore little encouragement, and certainly no money, to turn what was basically a police force into an army – much to Abdullah's chagrin.

During 1937, however, as a result of developments in Palestine, the Transjordanian government had authorized the establishment of a mechanized force, to be composed of bedouins and amounting to 350 men. The Desert Patrol provided most of the soldiers, who were then replaced by new recruits, there being more applicants than could be accepted. This raised the bedouin content of the Arab Legion to about thirty per cent. More significantly, the bedouins alone were mechanized; the gendarmerie were still mounted on horses and armed only with rifles.

This is perhaps the time to say something about the policy adopted by Abdullah, Kirkbride and Glubb with regard to the Arab Legion. In later years Glubb was frequently taken to task by Arabs and others for deliberately favouring the bedouins at

[2]Sir Alec Kirkbride, *An Awakening* (University Press of Arabia, 1971), p. 119.

the expense of the *hadari*. It is important to note, however, that it was not a matter of personal preference on Glubb's part alone, but a deliberate policy based on a shared philosophy of all three men.

According to Kirkbride the Arab Legion was intended to be a purely professional force, not a national institution. As Glubb has pointed out:

'According to British ideas . . . armies are intended to defend their countries against foreign attacks, and should not intervene in politics at all. The Jordanian and Moroccan governments defend their employment of tribesmen in the army precisely because they are content to be only professional soldiers, with no political ambitions. Arab armies will not be efficient until they are officered by persons interested in soldiering rather than in politics.'[3]

He also argued that, 'Soldiering requires endurance and hence, in every nation in the world, the best soldiers are those who at home lead hard, difficult and dangerous lives. In every country rural or mountain districts produce the best soldiers and these are likely to be those least interested in politics.'[4]

Although this might be disputed by those who have led Cockneys from the East End of London in battle, it is probably right as a generalization. Glubb is also correct in his criticism of those armies which exist only as an extension of the political arm, as in Latin America and in Syria, although it is by no means certain that he succeeded in keeping the Arab Legion a purely professional army. Indeed, later events would seem to show that he did not.[5]

Nonetheless, during the years 1937–9, Glubb managed to transform the Desert Patrol from a para-military into a military force. This is hardly surprising when one considers the characteristics of the bedouins who composed it and the fact that Glubb himself was a soldier. It would have been difficult, if not

---

[3]Review by J. B. Glubb of *Politics in Uniform: A Study of the Military in the Arab World and Israel* by Riad N. el-Rayyes and Dunia Nahas in *Survival* XV (May–June 1973).   [4]Ibid.

[5]In 1968 a senior Burmese officer told the author that the British view of military power, and the views of many other countries, were diametrically different. 'We need an army to deal with our people,' he said, 'not to fight the Chinese or Indians.'

impossible, to train bedouin tribesmen of that time along the same lines as the Metropolitan Police. However, according to Kirkbride, the British government never intended the Arab Legion to have any role other than internal security (i.e. a gendarmerie), and it was not until 1939 that they suddenly woke up to the fact that Glubb had acted quite differently. But by then, there were sterner problems to be resolved and Transjordan was largely forgotten.

Although Kirkbride approved of Glubb's activities, Peake Pasha clearly did not. He considered that H.M.G. had unduly favoured the bedouins by 'giving them armed cars with machine-guns, wireless sets, forts and other adjuncts to militarism, which had been denied to the old Arab Legion . . . This, however, would not have mattered a great deal if the Desert Force had been kept as police and not trained as an Army unit. The temptation, however, was too great, and gradually we saw the desert nomads being turned into soldiers with modern arms and transport, while the old Arab Legion formed from the dwellers in the town and villages remained for the most part mere police.'[6]

Peake's great fear was lest the British officers should be withdrawn from the Arab Legion, leaving the tribal sheikhs with a military force with which they could dominate the settled areas – the age-old struggle between the desert and the sown – 'and such domination can only lead to poverty and misery'.[7] It seems extraordinary that Glubb could have proceeded along the lines he did in the teeth of what would appear to have been his superior officer's disapproval. We know that he was a very determined man, and he was certainly a master of improvisation, but armed cars, machine-guns and wireless sets cost money, and Peake Pasha and his staff controlled the Legion's budget. Glubb has consistently maintained that his relations with Peake were good, and that Peake was not so anti-bedouin as has sometimes been suggested, but his policy and Peake's seem to be curiously at variance. In his doctoral thesis, *The Bedouin Warrior Ethic*, George S. Dragnich has concluded that

[6]C. S. Jarvis, *Arab Command: The Biography of Lt-Col. F. G. Peake* (Hutchinson, 1942), p. 62.   [7]Ibid.

Glubb got away with it because he militarized the Desert Patrol far out in the desert, where he was safe from prying eyes. But this overlooks the matter of equipment, as well as the fact that Arabs are great talkers; nothing remains a secret for very long. Kirkbride undoubtedly knew, as did Abdullah, whose relations with Peake Pasha were good. It remains a mystery why Peake should have later disclaimed responsibility for Glubb's action.

The Desert Mechanized Force had proved its reliability, and its fighting quality, during March and April 1939, in operations against Arab gangs in the Ajlun mountains and Yarmouk gorge. Although every Arab sympathized with the cause of his compatriots in Palestine, the Desert Mechanized Force had demonstrated that bedouins on the whole were not affected by political considerations. 'Primarily due to Glubb's efforts,' Dragnich has written, 'certain traditional Bedouin warriors had undergone a fundamental change in martial skills and attitudes during the decade 1930–9. Although they still retained many of their old ways and values, they were now dependable, responsive, and disciplined components of a regimented organization serving the central authority . . . But, more importantly, Glubb had changed the centuries-old idea that Bedouins could not become modern soldiers.'[8]

Equally importantly, perhaps, Glubb had made it plain to Abdullah and Kirkbride that the bedouin element in the Arab Legion provided a considerable measure of stability in a force whose members must inevitably be affected by events happening in neighbouring Arab countries. Thus was born the idea of transforming the bedouin element into a kind of praetorian guard whose loyalty would be to its ruler and its commander – and to no one else.

This was further emphasized shortly after Glubb became Commander when six armoured cars were delivered to the Legion. They had been ordered some time previously, as a result of the success the Palestine Police had had with them

[8]George Stephen Dragnich, *The Bedouin Warrior Ethic and the Transformation of Traditional Nomadic Warriors into Modern Soldiers within the Arab Legion, 1931–48* (Georgetown University, U.S.A., May 1975), p. 127.

during the Arab Rebellion; needless to say, they were issued to the Desert Mechanized Force. Glubb appears to have ordered them on his own authority because the Amir Abdullah expressed surprise when told of their arrival by his son, Talal. Glubb was present when Talal told the Amir. 'His Highness was incredulous and looked at me uncertainly,' says Glubb.[9]

While great events were unfolding elsewhere in the world, Transjordan had all the calm of a backwater. There was little money with which to expand the Legion and Glubb was in any case short of expert assistance. His senior Arab officers were basically policemen, and Lash was fully occupied running the Desert Area. The fall of France in June 1940 transformed the situation. General Wavell and Anthony Eden (then War Minister) arrived in Amman to tell Amir Abdullah that from now on every man counted. The Italians were poised to advance in the Western Desert and German officers were beginning to arrive in Syria. Glubb paraded a Troop of the Desert Mechanized Force for Wavell's inspection and it was immediately proposed that the Force should be expanded into a regiment; the British would supply arms and equipment. The Amir offered troops for service in the Western Desert but was asked instead to provide an Infantry Company to guard an important aerodrome in Palestine. Gathering together some one hundred policemen, Glubb turned them by a stroke of the pen into soldiers; they went off to Palestine as the 1st Infantry Company of the Arab Legion. From now on the Arab Legion, and its Commander of course, was in business – as an army, not a police force.

The 1st Desert Mechanized Regiment was the genesis of the Jordanian Army as it exists today and it is important to note that it was chiefly bedouin in composition. There were technicians and clerks who came from the settled areas but the officers and rank and file were all tribesmen, still wearing the uniform of the Desert Patrol, their hair long and in many cases worn in ringlets as was the bedouin fashion. A very high proportion were illiterate; those who could read and write did so with difficulty and very slowly. The provision of officers, then and for many years to come, was to be one of Glubb's greatest problems. There were more than enough men.

[9] J. B. Glubb, *The Story of the Arab Legion*, p. 248.

97

Providing British officers was not, at first, a problem. Glubb and Lash could cope with the training of one regiment and of course their knowledge of both Arabic and the soldiers helped enormously. Hugh Foot (later Lord Caradon), who was Kirkbride's assistant in Amman from 1939–42, has written approvingly of the Arab Legion's efficiency. 'Glubb did not have the opportunities for personal glorification that Lawrence had had,' he wrote. 'Nor did he seek personal publicity. But his knowledge of Arabic and the Arabs was far superior to Lawrence's and the traditions which he built up on the earlier work done by his predecessor, Peake Pasha, have made and will continue to make a vital contribution to the future of Jordan and indeed of Arabia.'[10]

In his monumental history of *The Hashemite Arab Army 1908–1979*, Brigadier S. A. El-Edroos, himself a Pakistani, is very critical of Glubb's apparent favouring of the bedouins over the settled Arabs.[11] He compares Glubb's feelings in this regard with those of British officers who quite arbitrarily divided the peoples of India into martial and non-martial classes. This is unfair to Glubb who was very critical of some Indian Army practices;[12] indeed his main criticism of the Transjordan Frontier Force was that it was modelled too closely on the Indian Army.

It would be foolish to deny that Glubb found himself more at home in tribal society than with the intelligentsia. It is possible too that he attached more virtues to the bedouins than they in fact merit. But he made his views plain in a letter to P. J. Vatikiotis on 25 June 1966:

'The cities and the educated classes were so few that officers chosen from these town dwellers were almost all members of families who also produced politicians and civil officials, or were in some way connected with such families. This has been the ruin of the Syrian army – a country with a much larger popu-

[10] Sir Hugh Foot, *A Start in Freedom* (Hodder & Stoughton, 1966), p. 66.
[11] S. A. El-Edroos, *The Hashemite Arab Army 1908–1979* (Publishing Committee in Amman, 1980), p. 214.
[12] As a result of his experiences in Mesopotamia in 1920–1. The Indian Army was not then at its best after four years of war, particularly where its British officers were concerned.

lation than Jordan. In Arab armies where family loyalties are much stronger than national loyalties, this means that every officer has some connection with a politician or a political party . . . In so small a country as Jordan, it is most important *not* to recruit officers from important or powerful families. This applies as much to the sons of tribal sheikhs as to those of cabinet ministers.'[13]

There is no suggestion here that bedouin fight better than *hadari*, or vice versa. It is a straightforward attempt 'to keep politics out of the army', and also to prevent nepotism. Glubb can hardly be blamed for that, although he might be accused of refusing to face facts. In a country as small as Jordan, where for many years the Arab Legion was virtually the only industry, it was clearly impossible to select officers on their military qualities alone, and then only after they had proved themselves in the ranks. Glubb does seem at times to have attributed his own high-minded sense of duty and devotion to the military profession as an almost universal virtue; whereas, in fact, many men become soldiers for want of anything better to do, or in search of a glamour that fades all too quickly. Those who join from a sense of vocation are probably in a minority.

On 22 December 1940, Amir Abdullah was presented with his pennant as an Honorary Air Commodore in the Royal Air Force. The ceremony took place at the R.A.F. Station in Amman; afterwards the Amir, who was wearing R.A.F. uniform, lunched in the officers' mess. Greatly daring, he was bare headed, the first time he had ever been seen in public without a head covering. Covering the head in those days meant a great deal to Arabs.[14] A tribesman, for example, if surprised scantily clad, would cover his head before all else. 'When His Highness entered the mess without a hat,' wrote Glubb, 'he probably felt as comfortable as an Englishman would feel if he entered a strange ante-room in a pair of bathing drawers. But he faced the ordeal heroically, remarking that for one day he was determined to be a complete Englishman, cost what it might. His Highness

[13]P. J. Vatikiotis, *Politics and the Military in Jordan* (Cassell, 1967), pp. 77–8.
[14]It was noticeable during the author's visit to Jordan in 1982 that this old-fashioned custom has now largely disappeared among the more sophisticated classes.

is, at times, a little trying, especially to members of his Government, but it is impossible to deny the goodness of his heart, and his genuine attachment to the British cause.'[15]

By no means every educated Transjordanian shared his ruler's enthusiasm for the British. Events in Palestine had bitten deep and there must have been some who felt that a German victory would solve the Jewish problem for ever. Others resented their Mandatory status, feeling it demonstrated their dependence on Britain, which, however true, was difficult for a proud people to accept. There was, too, great resentment in Syria over the French, the more so after the capitulation in 1940; therefore most Transjordanians preferred to sit on the fence until choosing sides became unavoidable. The Amir's open espousal of the British cause was not necessarily calculated to add to his popularity.

In the spring of 1941, however, events in Iraq brought the war much closer to Transjordan; and led to the Arab Legion taking an active part in what was essentially a British campaign. Although Iraq is an entirely British creation, there was, and still is, considerable anti-British feeling among educated Iraqis. In Glubb's opinion this was due, as much as anything else, to Britain's foisting on Iraq a constitution copied almost in its entirety from the British. So far from making the Iraqis more democratic it had resulted in a group of self-seeking politicians playing musical chairs when they came to office, enriching themselves in the process at the expense of the ordinary *fellaheen*. Egypt was another example, of course.

In April a gang of ambitious army officers overthrew the government, headed by the Regent, Prince Abdullilah, a blood relation of Amir Abdullah, and placed in power Rasheed Ali al-Gaylani, a politician with pro-Axis leanings. The Commander-in-Chief in the Middle East, General Wavell, was strongly opposed to British involvement in Iraq, arguing that he lacked the troops with which to intervene. However his colleague in India, General Auchinleck, strongly supported by the Viceroy, Lord Linlithgow, was convinced that intervention was essential; so were Churchill and the Chiefs of Staff in

[15]J. B. Glubb, Monthly Report, December 1940.

London. When the Iraq army laid siege to the R.A.F. Station at Habbaniya on 2 May, simultaneously placing the ambassador and his staff in Baghdad under arrest, Wavell was compelled to do something about it; but not before Churchill had minuted the Chiefs of Staff, 'I am deeply disturbed at General Wavell's attitude. He seems to have been taken as much by surprise on his eastern as he was on his western [Libyan] flanks . . . He gives me the impression of being tired out.'[16]

Britain's military situation in early 1941 was grim and the majority of people in Transjordan were convinced that Germany would win the war. It was, therefore, essential that swift action should be taken to restore the situation in Iraq. General Wilson, then commanding in Palestine, was instructed accordingly. He had few troops at his disposal but managed to cobble together some 3000 infantry, mechanized cavalry and artillery, collectively described as HABFORCE. The leading elements, who were to make a swift dash across 400 miles of desert to relieve Habbaniya, were called KINGCOL after their commander, Brigadier Joe Kingstone of the Queen's Bays. Kirkbride had this comment to make on KINGCOL:

'The British units had sufficient transport to move themselves, but nothing over for supply purposes, so resort was had to the requisitioning of civilian lorries in Palestine regardless of their condition. The result was a transport train made up of dozens of different types of cars, with practically no spare parts or tyres, and manned by civilian drivers who were openly rebellious. As a car broke down, and many did, it was pushed into the ditch and abandoned. I saw this amazing piece of improvisation, which was called KINGCOL, leave Mafraq with four hundred miles of desert to cross before it could engage an enemy several times more powerful than itself, and my heart sank.'[17]

Abdullah had placed the Arab Legion at Britain's disposal but it was originally intended that Glubb's services would be utilized to organize subversive activities in Iraq from H4, the Iraq Petroleum Company's pumping station not far from the Iraq–Transjordan frontier. However, after the attack on

[16]W. S. Churchill, *The Second World War Vol III* (Cassell, 1950), pp. 228–9.
[17]Sir Alec Kirkbride, *A Crackle of Thorns*, p. 132.

Habbaniya, Glubb was asked to accompany KINGCOL. He asked if he could take some of his soldiers as escort and then turned up at H4 with no less than 350 of the Desert Mechanized Regiment; the balance of 300 had to be left behind for lack of transport. A mechanized squadron of the Transjordan Frontier Force was also at H4 and they were, of course, 'imperial' troops, but, according to their terms of engagement, they could not be employed outside the borders of Palestine and Transjordan without special proclamation. Such a proclamation was not made, presumably for security reasons, and there already happened to be, for different reasons, some discontent in the squadron. When the Arab Legion and T.J.F.F. were ordered to cross the frontier to attack the Iraqi fort at Rutba, the T.J.F.F. refused to move, leaving the Arab Legion on their own.[18]

In the T.J.F.F.'s absence it fell to Glubb and his ringleted warriors – soon to be christened 'Glubb's Girls' by the British – to attack Rutba with the assistance of the R.A.F. The Iraqi garrison consisted of Desert Police, a bedouin force raised originally by Glubb; one of the defenders had a brother serving in the Desert Patrol. Their morale was unimpaired by the R.A.F.'s machine-gunning and bombing and they repelled the Arab Legion's assault. Glubb withdrew on 9 May to H3, an Iraqi relief column having arrived at Rutba after a sharp engagement with R.A.F. armoured cars. Advancing again on the night of 10 May, this time accompanied by the armoured cars, the Arab Legion found the fort deserted. The way to Habbaniya was now open.

KINGCOL left Rutba on 13 May; Brigadier Kingstone clearly disapproved of Glubb and his bedouins. 'This fellow [Glubb] thinks he is King of Saudi Arabia,' Kingstone told his Intelligence Officer, Somerset de Chair of the Life Guards. 'I am going to get him out of the way as soon as we leave here.'[19] Suiting action to words, he sent Glubb off well ahead of the main column, causing Glubb to comment, 'I was unable to decide whether this post was offered to us in order to guide the column

[18]This unfortunate incident led to the Transjordan Frontier Force being withdrawn from the campaign; however they redeemed themselves in the Syrian campaign which followed soon afterwards. Glubb says their conduct had no effect on his own troops. [19]Somerset de Chair, *The Golden Carpet* (Faber & Faber, 1944), p. 9.

and act as advanced guard, or whether the Brigadier's principal idea was to get us as far away as possible from his column.'[20] It was clearly the latter because once KINGCOL was within striking distance of Habbaniya, Kingstone found an excuse to send Glubb off on a reconnaissance, intending thereby to keep him well out of the way until Habbaniya had been relieved.

However, the British column got stuck in soft sand; when Glubb returned from the reconnaissance he found KINGCOL back at its starting point. He then offered to guide the column, bedouins naturally being experts in their own environment, and two days later, on 18 May, the garrison at Habbaniya was relieved. On the morning of the final advance the Household Cavalry's bivouac area was attacked by three Messerschmidts and the soldiers hastily dived into their slit trenches. At least one bedouin soldier refused to follow suit, saying, 'I was not given this uniform to hide in the earth like a rat.'[21]

Glubb was next given the task of disrupting the road and rail communications between Baghdad and Mosul. These run through the desert between the Euphrates and Tigris, known as the Jezireh. He was also to persuade the local tribes to rise against the Baghdad government, and to cut off Rashid Ali's retreat if he tried to escape north to Mosul where some German aircraft were established. These raids caused great alarm and were highly successful. Glubb comments that '. . . the Iraq army appear to have been hopelessly deficient in transport, and most of their movements were carried out in commandeered vehicles, a process which provoked a good deal of grumbling amongst car owners.'[22]

Major-General George Clark, who had taken over command of HABFORCE, decided on an immediate advance on Baghdad, guided by the Arab Legion. Meanwhile, farther north, plans were made for an attack on the strongly fortified railway station at Meshahida by the Household Cavalry and the Arab Legion. Glubb was with this column, but returned to Habbaniya to collect the necessary stores to defend the station after its capture.

[20]J. B. Glubb, *The Story of the Arab Legion*, p. 269.
[21]Godfrey Lias, *Glubb's Legion* (Evans, 1956), p. 139.
[22]J. B. Glubb, A report on the role played by the Arab Legion in connection with the recent operations in Iraq, 10 June 1941.

That night, however, information was received that Rashid Ali had fled and Glubb accompanied General Clark and Air Vice-Marshal D'Albiac to a prearranged rendezvous with the Iraqis. At 4 a.m. on 31 May the party 'passed through the British front line in the grey dawn, and at a point in No Man's Land, met a car containing two Iraqi officers, bearing a bath towel on a pole. A car was meanwhile sent to fetch Sir Kinahan Cornwallis [the ambassador] from Baghdad. The Iraqis had cut all the canal banks in the vicinity and water was lapping the road ... With water birds flapping overhead the scene was more suggestive of the Norfolk Broads than the City of the Caliphs. The armistice terms were drafted on the back of a telegram form, sitting in the General's car, and were carried back to Baghdad by the British Ambassador. The A.O.C. and G.O.C. returned to Cavalry Brigade Headquarters for breakfast, and the campaign was at an end.'[23]

Freya Stark, the writer and traveller, was one of the many British who had been cooped up in the British Embassy. Describing the arrival of the Arab Legion, she writes, 'Gay, swaggering, dusty, and nonchalant, incredibly cluttered up with garments, these were the second people from the outside world to reach the invested Embassy in Baghdad. The first to arrive in the early dawn of 31 May was an Iraqi car with officers ... to rouse Sir Kinahan Cornwallis and take him across the lines to the signing of the armistice. By the time he came back, the children of the desert in their armoured car were with us. With a fine untidy arrogance of the wilderness they strolled about the decorous but weary purlieus of Chancery, glancing at the pallid and rather deplorable effendis with friendly and tolerant amusement.'[24]

Although by Second World War standards the Iraq campaign was only a minor affair, it was enormously important to Glubb. In the first instance it had demonstrated that his bedouin soldiers could be relied upon, if needs be, to fight against their own co-religionists, which Glubb ascribed to a feeling of military loyalty. Moreover they fought without rancour or hate, chatting cheerfully with the captured Iraqis and even

[23]Ibid.   [24]Freya Stark, *East is West* (John Murray, 1945).

offering them their protection. Secondly it had shown the British army that they were worthwhile allies; '. . . the mere presence of Glubb's desert patrol was a talisman among the bedouin, who would otherwise have molested our straggling supply columns . . . In the event, we had no trouble from the tribes, who remained amicable with so many cousins under our flag . . .'[25] But most importantly, it established Glubb in the eyes of the British army as a 'proper soldier', and not just another 'scallywag' in the T. E. Lawrence image. From then onwards, throughout his service in the Arab Legion, Glubb's views may not always have been agreed, but they were always respected.

In his report on the Arab Legion's role in Iraq he made some interesting observations. He thought the crisis had been entirely artificial as most Iraqis to whom he spoke were in-different to it and indignant with those who had caused it. Many had told him, 'The English made Iraq, and its army. It is they who have taught us civilization. It cannot be right for us to fight them.' He encountered few hostile civilians, other than those imbued with religious fanaticism. His old friends, the Dulaim, around Ramadi, were resentful, but this was due largely to the Arabs' hatred of the Assyrians, who composed a large proportion of the R.A.F. Levies in Habbaniya. The fact that the Iraq police had fought better than the army seemed to Glubb to be due to the fact that they were long-service volun-teers; the soldiers were conscripts. Although the British advisory staff had always been in favour of a small volunteer army, Iraqi politicians insisted on a large conscript army because they thought the British support of a volunteer army stemmed from a desire to keep Iraq weak.

He was very critical of the political system foisted on Iraq by the British. It was both corrupt and undemocratic, in prac-tice if not in theory; '. . . the Arabs are one of the naturally most free and democratic nations in the world. There are no class distinctions in Arabia, and in the armed forces it is common to find a colonel with a brother who is a private soldier. In villages and tribes the ordinary cultivators and tribesmen live on terms

[25]Ibid., p. 194.

of social equality with their sheikhs and leaders. The unfortunate fact must therefore be faced that the Arabs were freer and more democratic before we presented them with a model of the British constitution. The constitution has resulted in a bureaucratic tyranny, wielded by a tiny group of city politicians who play their political games completely divorced from the life of the common people.'[26]

Glubb was equally critical of the way the British Military Missions were staffed in countries like Iraq. He considered it a mistake to base the selection of the officers solely on their up-to-date military knowledge which meant that after three or four years they had to return to the British army lest they became out-of-date. 'It is not necessary for Arab units in the Middle East to be trained according to the very latest European methods,' he wrote; and, 'a three year secondment is not enough to allow an officer to learn Arabic, much less to be familiar with the Arab outlook and mentality, and to mingle with them socially.'[27]

Far worse was the open contempt sometimes expressed by British officers for the very Arabs they were supposed to be training. Glubb would have much preferred to employ those officers who had had long experience with Arabs, although their military knowledge might not have compared with their more up-to-date colleagues. 'But such military knowledge as they possess,' he wrote, 'they are able to impart fluently and with mutual pleasure and profit to themselves and their Arab brother officers. Such officers are infinitely preferable to the smartest young regular officers, primed with the latest ideas, who are ignorant of Arabic and refer to the Arabs as *Wogs*. Such persons breed intense race hatred, far more surely than do more important acts of political injustice . . . Great Britain has treated Iraq with political generosity perhaps unequalled in history. But an unwise choice of tactless British officers has at times produced against her an absolutely undeserved, but not incomprehensible hatred.'[28]

Glubb's contempt for those of his countrymen who behaved as he has described is understandable. Racial snobbery is diffi-

---

[26]J. B. Glubb, A report on the role played by the Arab Legion in connection with the recent operations in Iraq, 10 June 1941.   [27]Ibid.   [28]Ibid.

cult to condone and unfortunately it was common, which most certainly accounted for much of the anti-British feeling. Glubb's long sojourn with the Arabs made him more aware of the ill-effects than might otherwise have been the case. He certainly did not believe that a white skin conferred some kind of superior status over those of darker hue. 'Whatever may be the result of this war in other directions,' he wrote in 1942, 'one thing is certain – "coloured" races are no longer going to accept with resignation a racial status inferior to that of white races.'[29]

[29] J. B. Glubb, Periodic Report, February–May 1942.

Chapter Eight

Making an Army

'*Wei al Nishama!* Where are the gallants!'

Bedouin war-cry

IT WOULD BE WRONG to conclude from Glubb's account of the Arab Legion's part in the Iraq Campaign that it was of enormous consequence. The campaign was predominantly British. There were also those who still had reservations regarding bedouin soldiers. Glubb Pasha took Somerset de Chair to task on this score when sent the draft of de Chair's book *The Golden Carpet* for comment. He felt he had been praised beyond his deserts, his soldiers less than theirs. He can be forgiven for his enthusiastic praise for his soldiers; they had done all – and more – that had been asked of them. General Clark made this very clear in his Dispatches. Glubb was therefore disturbed when the British proceeded to invade Syria on 8 June 1941 without inviting the Arab Legion to participate.

The aim of the campaign was to overthrow the Vichy French regime and deny the Germans use of the Syrian air-fields. Glubb's concern at being left out was set at rest when it was decided to make use of the British 4th Cavalry Brigade, then concentrated at Habbaniya. HABFORCE[1] was to attack Syria from the east, its objective the ancient oasis town of Palmyra. The main British advance in the west was directed on Beirut and Damascus. The Arab Legion was invited to co-operate with HABFORCE. The date for crossing the Syrian frontier was to be 21

[1]Commanded by Major-General George Clark and including the 4th Cavalry Brigade (Brigadier Joe Kingstone).

June and Glubb moved to H3 on the I.P.C. pipeline as a pre-liminary to joining up with the British. The Desert Mechanized Regiment was three hundred and fifty strong, organized into nine Troops; there was also a Troop of home-made armoured cars. Amir Abdullah visited the regiment at Mafraq prior to its moving off and delivered a rousing address.

HABFORCE was organized into three columns, each with an Arab Legion detachment to act as guides and for reconnaissance. Palmyra lies in a flat plain and it was intended to surround it from three sides. The garrison consisted of some Foreign Legion, Camel Corps and a Light Desert Company. Although out-numbered by the British, the French defences were well con-structed; they also had air support which the British lacked. In the open desert the British columns were vulnerable to air attack and it had been hoped to take Palmyra by *coup de main*; th's failed. Meanwhile a party of Howeitat, hearing there was a war in the offing, hastened north to join Glubb. They found the strafing and bombing from the air something of a change from war as they knew it. One of the oldest among them scorned to take shelter in a slit trench but chose instead to position himself on the highest spot available, firing vigorously at the planes as they passed over. He might possibly have hit one; the French certainly never hit him.

An event then occurred which changed the situation dramatically. Although the 3rd Light Desert Company was besieged in Palmyra, the 2nd Light Desert Company was still at large. About fifty miles north of Palmyra was the fort at Sukhna, covering the northern approaches to Palmyra. General Clark decided to use the Arab Legion to capture Sukhna and later he sent a squadron of Household Cavalry to support Glubb. On 27 June the Arab Legion set out, capturing the French post at Seba' Biyar on the way; to the bedouins' disgust it surrendered without firing a shot. Sukhna fell just as easily and Glubb set about preparing defences to cover the approaches from north and east.

Early in the morning of 1 July, as the soldiers were about to have breakfast, a column was seen approaching from the direc-tion of Deir es Zor to the east. It was enemy, consisting of truck-

mounted infantry and armoured cars. The French stopped about
500 yards away and opened fire. Glubb intended to outflank
them and cut off their retreat but the Household Cavalry were
some distance away and unaware of the situation. His own men
and their three armoured cars were positioned on a ridge, firing
on the French, while awaiting further orders. At this critical
moment, while Glubb paused for the Household Cavalry to
join him, three of the Howeitat who had arrived uninvited to
join in the fun could stand the suspense no longer. If the French
would not come to them, they would take the war to the French.
Leaping to their feet, waving their headcloths over their heads,
they dashed down the ridge, calling on the names of their sisters,
and on the gallants! This was too much for Glubb's men who,
in trucks, cars and on foot, swept down on the French in a wild
charge of desert tradition. Although outnumbered by two to
one, the Arab Legion threw the French off balance. Most of
them took to their heels. In all, six armoured cars, four trucks
and eighty men were captured, and when the 3rd Light Desert
Company in Palmyra heard of their comrades' defeat, they too
surrendered.

The tactics hardly conformed with Staff College teaching
but they were traditionally bedouin. The main difficulty in such
circumstances was to halt the pursuit before it lost all cohesion.
The Duke of Wellington's chief complaint about the British
cavalry was that it galloped off out of control once it had scattered
the enemy. At Sukhna, however, the result was a complete victory, as General Wilson signalled to Amir Abdullah:

'The Transjordan Desert Patrol, under Glubb Pasha,
carried out yesterday at SUKHNA, a most successful operation . . .
I offer respectful congratulations on spirited action and fighting
qualities of your troops.'[2]

The intention was to continue the advance to Hama and
Aleppo, reinforced by the 10th Indian Division under Major-
General (later Field-Marshal Viscount) Slim, which had recently
been moved up from Iraq. However the 'Cease Fire' was
ordered on the night of 11–12 July and the campaign was over.
In its immediate aftermath the Arab Legion played an important

[2] J. B. Glubb, *The Story of the Arab Legion*, p. 336.

Glubb's mother and
father: *left*, Major-General
Francis Glubb; *below*,
Lady Glubb

King Abdullah bin Husain

Peake Pasha

Sir Alec Kirkbride

King Talal bin
Abdullah

Rainpool in Wadi
Gharra beside which
Glubb pitched his
tent on his first night
in the Transjordan
desert in November
1930

The Desert Patrol marching past

King Husain with General Cooke inspecting a Guard of Honour

Glubb Pasha in a bedouin tent

Receiving a petition

osemary Glubb in
mman with Naomi,
ne of their children

ROBERT YOUNG

King Husain bin Talal at the time of Glubb's dismissal

part in maintaining law and order in the eastern Syrian desert, around Deir es Zor, but had to be withdrawn as a result of protests by the Free French who were now in control in Damascus. Glubb was awarded the Distinguished Service Order for his leadership in Iraq and Syria. The citation ran:

'During the operations in Iraq, between 12 May and 1 June, Major Glubb, in command of the mechanized portion of the Arab Legion, was an inspiration to all those who worked with him. He led many forays behind the enemy's lines, harassing their communications and destroying railway lines.

'In the Syrian operations, Major Glubb has again been forward in action. On 1 July, his force was attacked by a mechanized enemy column. Despite being under heavy MG fire he at once personally organized a spirited counter attack, which resulted in the capture of about eighty prisoners and much war material. A "bonnie fechter"; his name in the desert is one to conjure with.'[3]

The attitude of the French officials in Syria towards Glubb was interesting. They regarded him with the deepest suspicion. In many ways he represented in the flesh the French conviction of 'perfide Albion'. The French were not particularly good at controlling their bedouin tribes; Glubb happened to be singularly successful. He also recruited members of these Syrian tribes into the Arab Legion for reasons already given but his simple explanation for why he did this held no water in Damascus. It was clear that he was acting as the lieutenant of the Amir Abdullah who would never rest content until the Hashemites ruled again in Syria. The French were obsessed by Glubb. As 'l'espion' in the game of 'L'Attaque' has the power to sweep the board, so Glubb's activities along the southern boundaries of Syria equally disturbed them. The fact that he, and also the British Resident, Kirkbride, spoke excellent French, and rather better Arabic than their French colleagues, only emphasized the differences. Like many clever people, the French sometimes missed the wood for the trees. Glubb bore the uneasy French no ill-will but thought they went about their business in Syria with scant or no regard for the feelings of the people.

[3] *London Gazette*, 21 October 1941.

In his book, *Our Enemies the French,*[4] Anthony Mockler states that after the success at Sukhna, 'Glubb signalled urgently to Jerusalem for £10,000 to distribute to his victorious warriors and to the S'ba and the Ruwalla whom this triumph, backed by gold, might convince to join the side of the angels. It arrived after only forty-eight hours in notes.' Glubb categorically denies having done this, '. . . firstly I would not of course give money to my own troops, the Arab Legion, who were regular soldiers. Nor did I ever give money to bedouins to join our side. Lawrence in World War I set this unfortunate precedent of giving money away, and anyone writing about bedouins since then always assumes that one shovels out cash to win loyalty, which it never does. On the other hand, if one wishes to deal with bedouins one has to conform with their life-style, for example in the matter of hospitality. Wherever we camped we always had a guest tent which was always open to all comers . . .'[5]

Like everyone else in Syria and Transjordan, Glubb was profoundly shocked when it became apparent that the Vichy French regime had merely been replaced by the Free French. 'In the preparatory work undertaken before the invasion of Syria,' he wrote, 'it had been assumed by one and all that French control of Syria was at an end.' He went on, 'The situation gave rise to intense feeling. It was just one more of those misunderstandings – tissues of conflicting promises – which had given us so much trouble in Palestine and the Arab countries after the First World War.'[5] The feeling against the French in Syria was indeed intense and could not have been overlooked by Glubb's Arab soldiers while serving in that country.

Although Glubb spoke French fluently, and had a great love for France, he had little use for French colonial rule in Syria. Prior to the war, as Commander of the Desert Area, he had spent many weary hours negotiating with French officers over border problems of which they had complained. He believed the French had the wrong approach when dealing with Arabs, as a result of which they were hated. As one example of this he

[4]Anthony Mockler, *Our Enemies The French* (Leo Cooper, 1976), p. 175.
[5]Letter to author, 24 November 1982.
[5]J. B. Glubb, *The Story of the Arab Legion*, pp. 344–5.

describes the case of Lieutenant Scott (who had only recently joined the Arab Legion) and three Arab soldiers who were captured by the French immediately before the investment of Palmyra. They had been with a British supply column, all of whom were captured. 'The captives were taken to a prisoner-of-war camp in Northern Syria. The three men of the Arab Legion went into a cage with a large number of British troops. But two evenings later a French N.C.O. entered the camp and took the three Arab Legion away. Asked what he was doing, he said that "natives" were to be confined in a different camp.'[6] On the following morning the British troops refused to turn out or go on parade, insisting that their Arab comrades should be returned. At first the French commandant refused, but faced with such intransigence he gave in. The three Arabs were returned.

During November 1941, Glubb attended a meeting in Damascus with General Collet, the senior Free French commander in Syria and himself an officer of *les troupes coloniales*. 'The principal differences which I noticed between Collet and myself were not so much personal as national,' reported Glubb. 'For example, Collet professed a low opinion of Arabs, Kurds, Muslims in general, and Druzes, even as fighters. He said that by far the best men in the French Levant were the Maronite Christians of the Lebanon. They were equal to five Druzes or to ten Arabs as fighters, let alone their intelligence and progressiveness. Many Maronites not only spoke French, they actually thought in French. This is a very interesting subject, which of course has nothing to do with religion . . . Christians however tend to adapt themselves more quickly to European habits of life than do Muslims. The French favour communities which adopt French manners – the British dislike communities which imitate them, and favour races which adhere to their own customs . . . Wherever the British have penetrated we meet British officers who believe the Bedouins, the Kurds, the Gurkhas, the Sikhs or the Sudanese (whichever they happen to command) to be the most splendid fellows on earth. The French do not share this passionate interest in other races – they only praise individuals or communities insofar as they have

[6] Ibid., p. 320.

become Gallicized. It was remarkable even so to hear Collet, who largely made his name with Circassians, and who now governs Muslim Syria, say that one Christian was worth ten Muslims . . . As a result of this well-known attitude a deep laid and mutual antipathy exists between the French and the Arabs . . . and is quite ineradicable.'[7]

Although the Arab Legion was quite clearly not wanted in Syria – by the French, that is – it seemed in early 1942 that they might well be required to fight there. The Germans were advancing in Russia and were expected to invade Turkey in a drive towards the Suez Canal. If this were to be resisted, the British needed every soldier they could find. Amir Abdullah was therefore requested to expand the Desert Mechanized Regiment into a Mechanized Brigade and provide additional infantry companies to guard British military installations in the Middle East. By the end of 1942 the Arab Legion had formed four such companies, each of a hundred men, and had set about expanding the Desert Mechanized Force. By that date the Arab Legion had been expanded from 1800 to 5200; it had also been divided into a police and a military branch, as it was organized from 1921–6. In Glubb's view it would have been preferable to call them the Transjordan Police and the Transjordan Army.

Men were no problem; there were more than enough. Nor was equipment, on this occasion; the British army supplied all that was required. Officers, however, were another matter. The Arab officers were either too old or too young; the bedouins lacked the essential education. The only alternative source for officers was the British army and here the limiting factor was lack of knowledge of the language and customs. As in similar circumstances where the British were expanding local forces, for example in West and East Africa, some of the officers were of high quality, some were not so good. Glubb was acutely aware of the problems the latter could cause.

[7]Manuscript report of Collet–Glubb meeting, 27–29 November 1941. Glubb's observations are to some extent borne out by the author's own experience. During an attachment to a French cavalry regiment in 1950, he became friendly with an Algerian captain who was by far the best officer in the regiment. He had served under General Leclerc during the famous march from Chad to join the British forces in Egypt and had been many times decorated. Yet he never expected to rise any higher in rank because, as he said, he was an Arab and a Muslim!

One of the former was Gawain Bell, later to become a distinguished Colonial Governor. He had first met Glubb when serving as a District Officer in Palestine. Deputed to raise a force of Camel Police in the Beersheba area, Bell modelled his force on the Desert Patrol. Greatly admiring Glubb, he had had several meetings with him. Subsequently Bell moved to the Sudan, as a member of the Sudan Civil Service. When a German push through Turkey seemed likely, Bell was released to join the Arab Legion, in which he was given the rank of *Qaimaqam* (Colonel). Already a fluent Arabic speaker, he spent a few weeks with the 1st Mechanized Regiment under Lash, before being sent by Glubb to familiarize himself with the situation in Transjordan and its people. He then moved into a small mess in Amman where among other Arab enthusiasts he found Hugh Foot. He already knew Glubb, of course, but during this period he came to know him much better. In Bell's as yet unpublished memoirs he has written as follows[8]:

'As I came to work with him in the Legion I grew increasingly to appreciate the tireless dedication of this remarkable and sensitive man. He had little patience with anyone, and British officers in particular, who sought the lighter and possibly at times the rather less reputable forms of relaxation. He found it hard to understand why anyone ever wanted leave. He never took any himself. He found it difficult to make allowances for those whose standards of enthusiasm and conduct fell even marginally below his own. But where Arabs were concerned he was ready to be less demanding. *His position in Jordan was unique and unchallenged* and quite rightly so in the atmosphere and circumstances of the time. The conception of a British deputy was something that naturally exercised him, but where could anyone with his unique qualities and experience be found? Had he been killed, or more likely assassinated, no one could have taken his place. He alone held the confidence of the Amir Abdullah, the Government and above all, of the Bedu. Glubb was the last of that small number of extraordinary Britons who, during the previous hundred years and in widely differing circumstances had made a name in the service of Arab rulers . . . He was to be

[8] Sir Gawain Bell, *Shadows on the Sand* (C. Hurst & Co., 1983), p. 144. Author's italics.

the last and the greatest of the British Pashas . . . He was the most dedicated and single-minded man I have ever known and one of the most devout.'

Another British officer who joined the Arab Legion about the same time as Bell was Michael Hankin-Turvin. As an Assistant Superintendent in the Palestine Police he was seconded to the Arab Legion in 1942, having already met Glubb the year before in the company of a party of tribal sheikhs from Beersheba. His preliminary interview was brief; a short talk followed by reading from an Arabic newspaper. He then joined a motorized squadron of 1st Mechanized Regiment in Azraq:

'The squadron was about to drive across country into Syria (the time was some six months subsequent to the Syrian campaign). This was the Pasha's method of ascertaining whether officers, otherwise suitable for secondment to the Legion, were acceptable to the troops, with whom they were thrown into such close contact. In this case there were three of us, one of whom was the traveller Wilfred Thesiger. We spent a month with the squadron . . . The Pasha made frequent visits to the regiments where he observed training and would often lunch in a squadron, kneeling with half a dozen others at a common dish . . . From time to time he would address an informal gathering of all Arab ranks, putting them in the picture as to the general progress of the war . . . He required that every soldier should know what was going on and why his unit was taking any given action, often questioning a soldier at random to ensure that this had been done.'[9]

A British officer who had joined the Arab Legion from the Palestine Police some time previously was R. J. C. Broadhurst. He was an extremely handsome man, always immaculately turned out, who became a great favourite of the Amir's. This was unusual since few British officers came in close contact with Abdullah, other than at the formal Friday audiences. Broadhurst spoke and wrote fluent Arabic and was particularly well liked by the Arabs. Glubb had great confidence in him and employed him mainly in an administrative capacity.

[9]Letter to author, 12 September 1980. Major Hankin-Turvin left the Arab Legion in 1950 to raise the Trucial Oman Levies in Sharjah (now the United Arab Emirates).

With British officers like Ronnie Broadhurst and Gawain Bell, Glubb had little cause for concern; but there were others with less experience of Arabs who could unwittingly cause offence. There were also a few whose standards considerably failed to match the Pasha's! Since the Arab Legion was still relatively small, and British officers few, Glubb was able to maintain a much closer personal watch than was possible in the post-1950 expansion. In one note to British officers he reminded them of the Arabs' sensitivity on the point of honour and dignity. He warned that Arabs are always concerned about what other people will say or think of them. Bedouins, in particular, bitterly resented the promotion of their comrades; they might resign in order to draw attention to their objections, only to apply to re-enlist a few weeks later. Bedouins had little thought for the future and often behaved like children, furiously angry at one moment, in tears the next:

'A bedouin unit needs as much care on the part of an officer as a hospital full of patients needs from a doctor . . . Every man must be studied separately, and his case discussed with Arab Officers and N.C.O.s. If possible he should be talked to alone, but in any case he should never be "roared up" before his comrades, still less before civilians or soldiers below him in seniority.' He reminded British officers of the importance of personal example. 'Every unit always reflects the qualities of its officers. If you see a certain fault to be prevalent amongst your men, the first thing to do is to examine yourself and see if you exhibit this fault . . . If you know what you want your soldiers to be like, the first thing to do is to make sure you are like that yourself . . . Silent example is the safest way of reforming other people, because it produces no resentment on the part of the reformed against the reformers.'[10]

Glubb chose quite deliberately to raise the 2nd and 3rd Mechanized Regiments at Azraq rather than nearer the city of Amman. Azraq is sixty miles east of Amman and at that time was linked by a desert track which required several hours to negotiate.[11] There was ample water and hundreds of square

[10]Extract from circular letter from Glubb to all British officers, No. A:CO/1/3.
[11]Azraq is linked today with Amman by a modern highway.

117

miles of desert which was ideal for training. For the bedouins, who composed the greater part of the Mechanized Brigade, it was 'home'; it was also far away from the contaminating effects of urban life. For British officers there was little else to do but get to know their men and train them (apart from marvellous duck shooting in the winter months). It was also far removed from the prying eyes of those who scrutinized every piastre spent in the defence budget, and who queried every item as a matter of principle. Few of them were prepared to endure the bumpy and dusty journey from Amman in order to satisfy their curiosity; the same was true of ministers and politicians, office-men all.

But Amir Abdullah came whenever he could. He was there on 3 November 1942, when Montgomery finally broke through at El Alamein. It was while he was sitting talking to the officers that the Arab Signals officer came to the tent and whispered something to Glubb, who turned to the Amir. 'Your Highness, the battle of El Alamein has been won,' he said. 'Our brigade wireless operator has been listening to the news.' Abdullah sat silent for a moment, and then he replied, 'That wireless operator, I would like him to be promoted to Corporal; let his Corporal be made a Sergeant, and I would like the Lieutenant who has just brought us this good news to be made a Captain.' 'I will see that your order is obeyed, Sir,' Glubb agreed.[12]

Both Abdullah and Glubb were desperately anxious that the Arab Legion should again take an active part in the war. As first the 2nd Mechanized Regiment and then the 3rd took shape, a Brigade headquarters was formed and Lash became the Brigade Commander. Bell took over command of the 2nd Regiment and there were great hopes that the Arab Legion would once again fight alongside the British as an allied army. But by the end of 1943, when all things possible had been done to fit the Desert Mechanized Brigade for battle, the war had moved away from the Middle East. There was nowhere for the Arab Legion to fight.

Glubb was bitterly disappointed by his failure to persuade the British authorities to employ the Arab Legion in Europe. It

[12] Sir Gawain Bell, *Shadows on the Sand*, p. 147.

was frustrating to stand on the sidelines when great events were happening; he also believed that it would be of advantage to the Arabs themselves to demonstrate their fighting qualities. Unfortunately the successes in Iraq and Syria had in a sense been counter-productive. The Desert Mechanized Regiment had done so well that the British wanted it expanded to three regiments; this meant that for the following two years every experienced soldier was employed teaching the new recruits. By the time this task had been completed the war had moved on. Moreover, whenever it seemed possible that the Arab Legion might be required for action elsewhere, political considerations overruled its employment. This happened when the 1st Regiment was moved to Iran in 1943, only to be recalled before it crossed the Iranian frontier; and again, at the very end of the war, when there was a chance of involvement in Greece.

Although reluctant to face the political difficulties of employing the Arab Legion in Europe, the British appetite for Arab Legion Guard Companies was insatiable. Since the 1st Company had been sent to guard the aerodrome at Aqir in Palestine in 1940, company after company was raised for service all over the Middle East, releasing British and Indian troops for the main fronts. By the end of the Second World War the Legion's strength had risen to 8000, 3000 of whom composed the all-bedouin Mechanized Brigade. There were about fifteen Guard Companies, amounting to 2000 men; 2000 recruits under training and 500 employed in administrative duties. Significantly, some 300 officers had been trained, many of them bedouins who had begun their service in the Desert Patrol, and others with High School education from the settled areas.

The cost of this expansion was largely borne by the British government; the technical support required was also provided by the British, which meant that bedouin officers, despite their lack of education, were perfectly competent to command their own people. This enabled Glubb to keep the bedouin regiments as homogeneous units in which the very democratic life-style of the bedouins could be maintained. He had no desire to create an 'officer class' in the Arab Legion since he considered it both unnecessary and contrary to Arab tradition:

'The attempted creation of an "officer class" is, in my opinion, an error because it does not represent any division of social classes in civil life, but is merely an imitation of European institutions. And I have found no weakening of discipline to result from abandoning these restrictions. This is because Arabs are not "class conscious".'[13]

It would therefore be true to say that when the war ended in 1945 there was not a wide measure of difference between the way of life as practised in the Desert Patrol and that followed in the three Mechanized Regiments. Glubb had succeeded in preserving the bedouins' traditions while at the same time turning them into modern soldiers. It was a remarkable achievement that had no parallel in other Forces trained by the British. The Arab Legion was indeed an Arab army, as Amir Abdullah had reminded Glubb Pasha when appointing him to be its Commander in 1939. He had faithfully fulfilled that trust throughout the war years. But the credit was not his alone; he would have been the first to acknowledge the support he received from his Arab deputy, Abdul Qadir Pasha al Jundi, Norman Lash, Ronnie Broadhurst, Gawain Bell and many other Arab and British officers.

It was as well that they had given of their best to Transjordan, providing it with a well-disciplined and highly-trained little army. For hardly had the Arab Legion detachment returned from London after participating in the Victory March on 8 June 1946 than events began to unfold across the River Jordan in Palestine which have yet to be resolved nearly forty years later.

[13] J. B. Glubb, *Relations between Arab Civilization and Foreign Cultures in the Past and Today* (Journal of the Royal Central Asian Society Vol. XXIV, Part 3, 1937). (Now the Royal Society for Asian Affairs.)

Chapter Nine

The Intractable Problem

'The root of the Palestine problem is fear, the fear of
the Jews of being forced into the sea and the fear of
the Arabs of being edged out of their own country.'

Sir Arthur Wauchope,
British High Commissioner, 1931–8

THE BRITISH PEOPLE have had good cause to regret the alacrity
with which their government accepted the Mandate for Palestine
from the League of Nations in 1922 – so many illusions shattered,
so many hopes destroyed, so many lives lost. And for what purpose, since the struggle continues still? Fear has dominated
Palestine for close on seventy years, ever since A. J. Balfour
made his celebrated announcement of British support for the
concept of a Jewish National Home on 9 November 1917.
There is no less fear today.

It is not within the scope of this book to discuss the problem
in any detail, except insofar as it has affected Transjordan, and
Jordan, and particularly Glubb Pasha. However, some knowledge of the background is essential for the understanding of
Glubb's extremely delicate personal position. Although the
servant of an Arab government, his nationality was British;
where Palestine was concerned the British were the unfortunate
men in the middle because they held the League of Nations'
Mandate to govern the country. Therefore the British were
blamed by Jews and Arabs alike for everything that went wrong
in Palestine and Glubb could not expect to be held blameless by
the Arabs he served.

Britain has frequently been taken to task for the vacillation
of its policy in Palestine, yet truth to tell no one has yet succeeded

in squaring a circle. If the Arabs were to be satisfied, the Jews (and their supporters) would blame the British, the converse holding equally true if the Jewish demands were met. The Arabs were the first to rebel from 1936-9, as has already been mentioned. A Royal Commission under Lord Peel reported in July 1937 that the cause of the rebellion was the Arabs' wish for independence and their fear of the Jewish National Home. It reached the unremarkable conclusion that the Mandate was unworkable and that Britain could not expect to reconcile her obligations to Jews and Arabs. Partition of Palestine between the two communities was the only possible solution. The Jews neither accepted nor rejected the proposal for Partition; they kept their options open. The Arabs were horrified and the rebellion gained momentum, petering out only in 1939 after great loss of life and destruction of property.

Further examination of the Partition proposal by a League of Nations mission, and by H.M.G., concluded that partition was impracticable. A conference was therefore held in London early in 1939 and a White Paper was issued in May of that year. It stated that Britain had fulfilled its obligations to the Jews and that further immigration would violate British undertakings to the Arabs and would be contrary to the spirit of article 22 of the League covenant. Jewish immigration would therefore be restricted. The Zionists were shocked, the Arabs hardly less so since the Mandate would continue for at least another ten years, thereby deferring indefinitely their hopes of independence. The Zionists insisted that the British were unduly favouring the Arabs, Anglo-Jewish relations suffering a severe blow, but the outbreak of the Second World War, in the course of which Palestine became a major British base, turned men's attention to other matters. Thus the Palestine problem was placed in cold storage until 1945.

It erupted again violently in 1946, this time the Jews taking the lead against the mandatory power. It has been a feature of the Palestine problem that it arouses the most powerful emotions, not only within the main protagonists, but equally within their supporters. Since Jewish influence is strong in the United States, it is not surprising that American support for the Jewish case was solid. The U.S.A. was by far the most powerful nation in the world in 1945 and Britain could not afford to ignore this. Moreover the consciences of decent men had been profoundly stirred by the atrocities carried out against the Jews by Hitler and his henchmen. Europe was full of displaced Jews seeking a home, whose simple desire appeared to be thwarted by the obduracy of the British. Therefore, in an effort to get the Americans to share the burden, Mr Ernest Bevin, the Foreign Secretary, persuaded them to join with the British in a commission of inquiry which was set up in November 1945.

The Anglo–American Commission reported in April 1946, recommending a continuation of the Mandate, the repeal of the restrictions on the sale of land and the immediate admission of 100,000 Jews. America's President Truman swiftly endorsed the latter recommendation but Britain stipulated that the immigrants could not be admitted without the prior disbandment of the Jewish underground forces, reckoned to be at least 65,000 strong. The Jews then set in train a programme of massive illegal immigration, at the same time embarking on an active campaign against the British garrison. The blowing up of the King David Hotel in Jerusalem (the civil and military headquarters), with a loss of ninety-one lives was but one – if the most horrific – of the numerous acts of violence carried out by the Jewish 'terrorists' or 'freedom fighters' depending upon the point of view. Palestine became once again an armed camp.

The Arab states had already made it clear, at a meeting held in Cairo in May 1946, that they would uphold the Arab character of Palestine. The country was fast falling into a state of civil war, with the Jews immensely better armed and better organized than their opponents. The men in the middle, the British, were, as ever, assailed from both sides. Few had a good word to say for the proposals made by the Anglo–American Commission and Bevin, in desperation, referred the matter to the United Nations. Their solution was to partition the country into Arab and Jewish states and for Jerusalem to be internationalized. This recommendation was endorsed by the General Assembly on 29 November 1947, the Islamic states voting against it. The Jews welcomed partition, the Arabs opposed it. Britain was unwilling to impose a solution which was not acceptable to both sides and accordingly announced her decision to give up the Mandate. The date fixed was 15 May 1948.

The people and government of Transjordan were desperately concerned over the situation in Palestine. Many had relations living there. Some, like Tawfiq Pasha abu al Huda, the Prime Minister, were Palestinians by origin. They could not stay out of the conflict, even had they wished to. Matters were further complicated by the fact that the Transjordan Frontier Force, an 'imperial' unit recruited mostly in Palestine but based in Transjordan, was widely regarded as being under the Transjordanian Government's control, although nothing could have been further from the truth. The Jews lost no opportunity in publicizing the fact that the greater part of the T.J.F.F. was deployed in Palestine seeking to keep the peace, and in blaming Transjordan, whose King (to make matters worse) happened to be the Force's honorary Colonel-in-Chief. The T.J.F.F. remained an embarrassment to the Transjordanian government until its disbandment in February 1948.

Meanwhile a change had occurred in Transjordan's relations with the United Kingdom. Early in 1946 Amir Abdullah had personally negotiated a treaty with Britain that was formally ratified on 22 March 1946. The country became fully independent, although still dependent on Britain for financial aid, and was renamed Jordan. Abdullah assumed the role of King. In February 1947 he became Supreme Commander of the Arab Legion and Glubb became Chief of the General Staff, with the rank of Lieutenant-General (*Feriq*).

The situation in Palestine was not only bedevilled by rivalries between the great powers, particularly America and Russia; there were also divisions between the Arab countries. Egypt was at loggerheads with Iraq, both aspiring to lead the Arab world. Syria believed with some reason that King Abdullah had designs on it. King Ibn Saud and King Abdullah had little love for each other. The ex-Mufti of Jerusalem, Haj Ameen al Husaini, who had been permitted by the British to return from exile in Germany, hated Abdullah almost as much as he hated the British and the Jews. On all sides the dislikes were mutual. The Secretary-General of the Arab League, Abdul Rahman Pasha Azzam, an Egyptian, was as far divorced from reality as his colleagues, wildly under-estimating the military capacity of the Jews and equally wildly over-estimating the strength of the Arabs. Perhaps only King Abdullah, wise in the ways of the world, really comprehended the difficulties ahead.[1]

Glubb's principal concern was to sound a note of caution in the futile political posturings and rodomontades of the Arab leaders and their military advisers. As an Englishman serving an Arab government he was particularly well placed to advise both Jordan and H.M.G. But he was at the same time dangerously exposed to sniping by either side; if he was not a member of the race who had caused the trouble from the very beginning by their 'infamous' Balfour Declaration, then he was sometimes thought in Whitehall circles to be 'more Arab than the Arabs'. He fully understood the delicacy of his situation, living as he did for the most part in a wholly Arab society. Hardly a day went by without his being engaged in anxious discussion with the King or Prime Minister. Palestine dominated the minds of all. 'It is one of the peculiarities of the Palestine problem,' Glubb wrote at the time, 'that it has come to outweigh all other political questions in the eyes of the Arabs . . . All friendship and co-operation will be turned to hatred – if things go wrong in Palestine.'[2] They did go wrong, grievously wrong.

Between July 1946 and January 1947 Glubb sent the Foreign Office, via Kirkbride in Amman, no less than six lengthy commentaries on the Palestine problem. Although he insisted that he was expressing a purely personal opinion, it is clear that, for the most part, his views were shared by King Abdullah and several of his ministers. 'I am aware that my subordinate rank and parochial outlook do not permit me to submit unsolicited opinions on the policy of His Majesty's Government,' he wrote; and then, having duly made his apologies, he proceeded to do just that. Throughout he adhered to the view that only Partition

---

[1] In 1953 the author asked Ibrahim Pasha Hashim, then Prime Minister of Jordan, whether there would ever be a solution to the Palestine problem. 'Of course,' he replied, 'but it will take time.' How much time? 'Well, not time as you might choose to define it. I am thinking of four or five hundred years.'!

[2] J. B. Glubb, *A Soldier with the Arabs*, pp. 58–9.

could bring about peace; but in his mind, and in King Abdullah's also, Partition meant the joining of the Arab areas to Transjordan. This was of course unacceptable to the ex-Mufti, as well as to several other Arab states.

His correspondent in the Foreign Office was Mr (later Sir) Harold Beeley who wrote to Glubb on 1 February 1947 warning him that H.M.G. had not yet decided that Partition was the answer and, even if it were, there were still many hurdles to be cleared in the United Nations and elsewhere before it could be implemented. Beeley went on to say, 'One idea which has occurred to me and which finds some support from one or two of the remarks you make in your second memorandum is that the absorption of the Arab parts of Palestine into the state of Transjordan might represent a danger rather than an advantage for King Abdullah. Is it not likely that the tail would wag the dog and that the Mufti (whether physically in Jerusalem or in Cairo) would prove to be the more powerful of the two?' In the light of subsequent events it can be said that Beeley's forebodings were not without foundation.

Glubb's principal problem was the almost total ignorance of the Arab leaders when it came to military matters. Only Abdullah appears to have appreciated the potential military strength of the Zionists; the others lived in a world of make-believe, adding up columns of figures to prove to their satisfaction that the combined strength of the Arab armies would simply swamp the Jews and hurl them back into the sea. When Azzam Pasha asked Glubb the strength of the Arab Legion and was told about 4500, he expressed surprise; he had thought there were far more. In answer to his question about the Jews, Glubb estimated they could put 65,000 trained men into the field. Azzam Pasha was again surprised; he had no idea there would be so many. But he thought it would turn out all right as he had arranged to get 700 men from Libya. Glubb remarked that 700 Libyans were not many and inquired how they were armed. 'I have sent a man to buy seven hundred rifles from Italy,' replied Azzam Pasha.[3] If it were not a matter of historical record, it would be difficult to conceive of a more irresponsible approach to the reality of war.

[3]Ibid., p. 84.

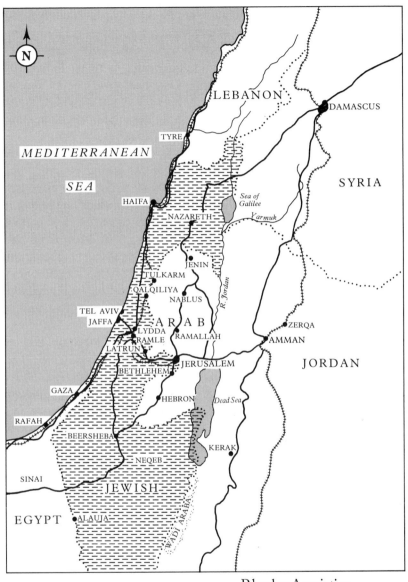

Rhodes Armistice
Demarcation Line

With the benefit of hindsight it does appear that some of Glubb's proposals were far-fetched. He attached great importance to the protection of British communications through the Suez Canal; although by that date it was clear that the British Empire's days were numbered. He recommended that Britain should acquire a large area of Sinai, south of Gaza, which would be transformed into a major overseas base. Another of his proposals was the retention of Haifa as a British enclave inside partitioned Palestine. One of his papers, written in December 1946, was fifty-seven pages in length, Beeley minuting:

'Whatever may be thought of Brigadier Glubb's proposals, his commentary on them contains a number of observations of real importance. If H.M.G. should decide in favour of partition, this paper would repay careful re-reading . . . Meanwhile, although there is much force in these arguments I do not find them so convincing as the arguments against partition. The difficulties which Brigadier Glubb so rightly fears would have to be faced, in the first instance not by an Arab government but by the British High Commissioner, supported by British forces during the period of transition. We have always realized that if we agree to something on the lines of the Arab plan we should be involved in grave troubles with the Palestinian Jewish population.'[4]

Glubb argued throughout in favour of a partitioned Arab Palestine being joined with Transjordan; in this connection he believed he was repeating 'His Master's Voice'. As far back as 11 August 1945, in a periodical report on the Arab Legion, Glubb had mentioned the possibility of a partitioned Palestine being joined with Transjordan, arguing that an independent Transjordan would be too weak and impoverished to stand on its own feet; he foresaw the problems that an over-dependence on British financial support would cause in the future. Another possibility might be the joining of Syria with Transjordan to form a Greater Syria, although this was really outside the realm of practical politics.

It is clear that Glubb was striving throughout his correspondence with Beeley to find a middle way that might suit Arab, Jewish *and* British interests in Palestine. Therefore it is not sur-

[4] FO 371/52567/E12254, minuted by Sir Harold Beeley on 20 December 1946.

prising he should have failed. He was particularly critical of the Anglo–American Commission's proposals, leading Beeley to comment, 'Events may prove Brigadier Glubb to have been an alarmist, but his forebodings are worth considering.'[5] They turned out to be correct.

It is hardly surprising that for most Palestinian Arabs the prospect of a partitioned Palestine was hard to stomach. Palestine under the British Mandate had enjoyed many advantages over her impoverished neighbour across the River Jordan. There were too those who believed that Partition must inevitably mean selling the pass to the Jews, and they were not necessarily Arab hard-liners or opponents of King Abdullah. As recently as June 1982, Abba Eban, a former Israeli Foreign Minister, said in a BBC interview about the Israeli operations in the Lebanon, 'Partition was the principle which enabled Israel to be born.' By no means every Arab who opposed Partition was a knave or a fool. Unfortunately, however, given the situation at the time, Partition did seem to be the only answer, and it might have worked had Transjordan been allowed to absorb the Arab areas. But internal Arab jealousies prevented this from happening to the eventual disadvantage of both the Arabs and the Jews.

After the British had announced their intention of giving up the Mandate, Tawfiq Pasha headed a Jordanian delegation to London in the spring of 1948. Glubb went along as military adviser. He acted as interpreter for the Prime Minister when he was received by Mr Bevin. Tawfiq explained that in view of the situation that was likely to develop after the British withdrawal, his government intended to send the Arab Legion across the Jordan to occupy that part of Palestine allocated to the Arabs. 'It seems the obvious thing to do,' said Bevin, adding a warning that the Arab Legion should not enter areas allocated to the Jews. Tawfiq and his delegation returned to Amman believing that H.M.G. had endorsed its plan to occupy the Arab part of partitioned Palestine that was contiguous with Jordan.

The army which was to carry out this task was neither large nor well-equipped. Since the end of the war the garrison companies had been run down, thereby reducing the Arab Legion's

[5]FO 371/52542/E6871/4/31, minuted by Sir Harold Beeley on 5 August 1946.

strength from around 12,000 to 6000. There were four mechanized infantry battalions, each with an organic armoured ca
squadron of ten or twelve Marmon Harrington armoured cars
these were veterans of the Western Desert, mounting a two
pounder gun and a Browning machine gun. They were thin
armoured but mechanically very reliable. Eight 25-pounde
artillery pieces had been acquired early in 1948 and were forme
into two batteries, each of four guns, but training had bee
hampered by lack of ammunition for practice. Three of the fou
infantry battalions had formed part of the Desert Mechanize
Brigade; they were chiefly bedouin in composition and com
manded by British officers; each battalion also had one or tw
British officers, regulars or on contract, in specialist appoint
ments. Company commanders were all Arabs. The artiller
batteries were commanded by British officers, assisted by tw
Warrant Officers as assistant instructors in gunnery. Ther
was virtually no second line transport, nor workshops and
engineers. The fourth infantry battalion, for which no pro
vision had been made in the annual budget, had been formed b
retaining four of the garrison companies due for disbandment
The battalion's organization was improvised, it had done little
training and there was no money to equip it. It was commanded
by an Arab officer.

The higher command organization was similarly improvised
Arab Legion Headquarters (*Qyada*) in Amman was a miniature
War Office, run on a shoe string. It controlled the police as wel
as the army, with a very small staff of Arabs and British. The
only existing field headquarters was that of the Desert Mechanized Brigade at Mafraq commanded by Lash. By a stroke of the
pen this became a Divisional Headquarters with a total staff o
twelve officers; the key appointments were held by British.

The four infantry regiments were grouped into two brigades
numbered 1st and 3rd; this was intended to deceive the Jews into
believing that the Legion was larger than was the case. A dummy
4th brigade was later located at Ramallah with the same object
Both brigades were commanded by British officers. Colonel
Desmond Goldie of the Royal Scots Fusiliers commanded 1st
Brigade; Colonel 'Teal' Ashton of the Welsh Guards com-

manded 3rd Brigade; Lt-Col. Hearst commanded the artillery. The Arab Legion was short of almost every kind of warlike stores – medicines, engineer stores, spare parts and so on – which had hitherto been supplied by the British army. The most acute shortage was ammunition. Small arms ammunition was reasonably plentiful but there was no reserve ammunition for the 25-pounders, the 6-pounder anti-tank guns and 3-inch mortars. Glubb had personally appealed to the British Commander-in-Chief in the Middle East for help over ammunition and a ship was duly loaded at Suez for Aqaba; but it had no sooner cleared Suez than it was stopped and boarded by the Egyptians. It was then taken back to Suez and its cargo confiscated. Frantic appeals to the Egyptians elicited no response. A second ship was loaded but before it could sail the United Nations decreed that neither Arabs nor Jews should be provided with arms. The ammunition was accordingly unloaded and returned to the British depots in the Suez Canal Zone. For the next sixteen months the Arab Legion had to fight a war with an ammunition supply intended by British calculations to be sufficient for one battle only.

Money was equally short. The Prime Minister, who also held the portfolio of Defence Minister, was insistent that war, should it break out, must be fought on a peacetime budget. When Glubb pleaded with him for some relaxation, Tawfiq Pasha, deeply involved emotionally with the Palestine problem, exploded with rage. Relations between the two men, only outwardly friendly, became strained for a time until King Abdullah poured oil on the troubled waters. Glubb obtained some relief when Azzam Pasha promised him the majority of the £4 million raised by the Arab League for a war chest; in fact only £250,000 was handed over, Azzam Pasha reneging on the balance. But a quarter of a million was better than nothing.

If Tawfiq Pasha, Palestinian by birth, was deeply emotionally involved in Palestine, Glubb himself was hardly less so. His mother, who was living in a hotel in Jerusalem, was resolutely refusing to leave and his son, Godfrey, had been born there. Added to which, for a man as deeply religious as Glubb, Jerusalem was indeed the Holy City. The sheer weight of his responsibilities in the face of the Arabs' wishful thinking, the obduracy of the Prime Minister, the pressures from King Abdullah, the shortages of essential equipment and ammunition, the fact that he was British and that it was the British who were abandoning the Mandate – all these combined to make Glubb feel unequal to the task. A general is always lonely in battle, even when he fights in the knowledge that his government's full authority is backing him, but in Glubb's case there was no such knowledge. He was as much frustrated as supported by his superiors, with the exception of the King and even he, occasionally, allowed his emotions to sway his judgement. Glubb felt at times that he was entirely alone. When that happened only his deep and un-questioning faith in God pulled him through.

There were personal problems too. In all his years in the Arab Legion he had never feared for his personal safety. No sentry guarded his modest residence in Amman, no armed escort protected him on his travels. However, Palestine had made Glubb a 'political' target. A less modest man would have per-ceived this sooner than Glubb who was too absorbed with his work to give the matter any attention. Had he been asked, he would probably have replied, 'Who on earth would want to assassinate me?' Nevertheless, in June 1946, a young Syrian, member of some political organization, placed a bomb under the window of the ground-floor bedroom where Rosemary Glubb was lying ill with influenza. Fortunately, she was lying with her back to the window when the bomb exploded, as otherwise she would almost certainly have been killed by flying glass. It was clear that times were changing in Jordan, as elsewhere in the world, and henceforward the Pasha was guarded day and night by hand-picked bedouin soldiers.

Rosemary Glubb says she was unaware of the explosion. 'The bulb in the bedside lamp went pop – that was about all. I got up to get another bulb, walking across the floor which was strewn with glass without hurting myself. It was only when people came rushing in that I realized what had happened. Then I was more angry because my aviary had been destroyed than I was about myself. My mother was living in Amman and insisted I moved in with her for a time. It was only then, when she started fussing over me, that I felt a little shocked. I don't remember worrying much about Jack. I had great confidence in his escort. Perhaps occasionally, when he was late returning from a visit, I felt a little anxious.'[6]

Glubb could understand, if he did not approve, the reasons given for Britain's abandonment of the Mandate in Palestine; but he believed it was Britain's duty to maintain law and order in the country until one minute to midnight. In fact, from the moment the decision was announced, the British grip loosened in the face of ever-increasing provocation. 'I could not myself avoid the feeling that the British in Palestine should have done more to keep order until the Mandate ended,' Glubb has written.[7] It is difficult to disagree with him, particularly since virtually every member of the Palestine administration was horrified by the decision to withdraw. Whatever may be said to the contrary, Palestine was signally well governed by the British, at least in material terms, and there were many dedicated men serving in the administration. They were shattered at the prospect of the chaos that would follow their departure.

The same was not true of the British people, who were sick and tired of the whole sorry business. For too many thankless years they had done their best to be even-handed, only to be rewarded by being pilloried, criticized and physically attacked by both sides. They had concluded in the end that it was not worth the death of a single British soldier to prevent Arabs from killing Jews, or vice versa. The same was true for the British Army, whose soldiers were mostly conscripts who longed to return to civilian life. They would fight well enough to defend their homeland but events like the King David Hotel bombing had sickened them of Palestine. And if today the British should be blamed for such an abrogation of their responsibilities, can we be shown any evidence that their successors have been more successful? The Palestine problem remains unsolved, an even greater threat to world peace than was the case in 1948.

Nonetheless, it is hard to imagine today the part Palestine played in world affairs on the eve of the British withdrawal. It

---

[6] Interview, 30 June 1982.
[7] J. B. Glubb, *A Soldier with the Arabs*, p. 73.

133

dominated the world's headlines in a way that was hardly equalled when the Israeli army stood at the gates of Beirut in the summer of 1982. The United States, with its powerful Jewish community, was inevitably concerned. So was Soviet Russia, albeit for entirely different reasons, and the Arab states. These emotions were roused to fever heat when the General Assembly of the United Nations voted its approval on 29 November 1947 for the Partition of Palestine between the Arabs and the Jews, the Islamic states voting unanimously against. But the Arabs were united only in their opposition to the concept of Partition. They had no concerted solution. For them rhetoric was a painless substitute for planning. Their enemies had a plan, a plan moreover that included the incorporation of Jerusalem in the new Jewish state.

The British plan, carefully prepared, was to withdraw from Palestine with as few casualties as possible by 15 May 1948, having by that date backloaded to their Suez Canal base the vast quantity of stores accumulated in Palestine from 1940 onwards. It can be said on their behalf that both they and the Jews knew their own minds, however casuistical this may sound. The Arabs, on the other hand, concerned as much with their internecine feuds as with anything else, were living in a world of make-believe. Only at the last moment did the Arab League decide to fight and then largely as a result of pressure from Egypt. They might well have preserved Arab Palestine had they been as single-minded as the Jews. Divided as they were, their cause was as good as lost before the first shot was fired; it has been this lack of cohesion that has dogged the Arabs ever since.

The Jewish forces began to apply the pressure several weeks before the Mandate was due to end. April saw the brutal massacre at Deir Yasseen that will live as long in Arab memories as Glencoe does in Scottish. Shortly thereafter the Arab working-class quarter in Haifa was attacked by the Haganah – the official Jewish army – and its inhabitants were driven out helter-skelter. Jaffa was the next major town to be attacked, with similar results. Jordan was swamped with refugees. At the same time the Jews began to infiltrate into Jerusalem, occupying the Katamon quarter of the city. The long-term strategic objective of the

Jews was to occupy the whole of Palestine west of the River Jordan, a logical aim from their point of view, but it took no account of the United Nations Partition Plan, by which the Jews laid claim to Israel. However, possession is nine-tenths of the law, and the Jewish activities were supported by many people in the west, most notably in the United States.

The British garrison, fast running down in numbers, was mainly concerned with keeping open its communications. It only intervened when the fighting looked likely to get out of hand. The Arab Legion attack on the Jewish colonies at Kafr Etzion, near Hebron, is but one example of the chaos that immediately preceded the end of the Mandate. The reason for this action was the road between Hebron and Jerusalem, along which an Arab Legion column was withdrawing with stores drawn from British depots in Egypt. These stores were vital to the Legion, and as the Kafr Etzion colonists could easily have closed the road, they were attacked by two Arab Legion companies and overwhelmed after hard fighting. The Jews tried to reinforce the colonists by parachute troops, a gallant though costly effort, but the Arab Legion won the battle. This action took place only two days before the end of the mandate.

In Jerusalem the situation was equally bizarre. The Jews were determined to take over the whole of the city before the Arab Legion could intervene. They were infiltrating troops into Jerusalem weeks before the Mandate was due to end, but so long as the British garrison remained they had to proceed cautiously. There were nevertheless numerous clashes with the Arab population. A truce, for what it was worth, had been arranged by the British High Commissioner, and only while British troops remained was there some hope of supervising it. A Truce Commission was established on 14 May 1948 to take the place of the British. It consisted of the American, French and Belgian Consuls who were expected to supervise the truce without any means of enforcing their rulings. It was an invitation to disaster.

While the various ingredients for disaster were being brought to the boil, all kinds of attempts were being made to stave off war. King Abdullah was prominent among those who believed that some kind of agreement had to be reached. To this end he had met with Golda Meir on the eve of the United Nations decision to partition Palestine. He met with her again ten days after the end of the Mandate. At great personal risk Mrs Meir visited Amman but it was to no avail. Reason had flown out of the window and the politicians had lost control of events.

Glubb, desperately anxious lest his tiny force would be thrown into battle against hopeless odds, was as keen as his master that war should be avoided if at all possible. He, too, had his contacts 'on the other side'. In Glubb's case they were Jewish businessmen connected with the Potash works on the Dead Sea; they were anxious to ensure that the enterprise would not be wrecked by war. Although Glubb had few illusions regarding the difficulties, he was willing to clutch at any straw. But he came away from his last meeting with his Jewish contacts deeply despondent, having been told by them that, 'So far as we are concerned, men with the guns are now in control.'

However, as a result of this contact, Glubb decided to make a last-minute attempt to avert a clash between the Arab Legion and the Haganah. A few days before the end of the mandate Colonel Desmond Goldie, a senior British officer serving with the Arab Legion, was summoned by Lash to his headquarters in Mafraq. Lash handed Goldie an envelope containing a message from Glubb Pasha to Shlomo Shamir, a senior officer in the Haganah. Goldie was to deliver the envelope to Shamir at Naharayim, a Jewish kibbutz west of the River Jordan. The essence of Glubb's message was that the Arab Legion was prepared to defer crossing the Jordan into Palestine for two or three days in order to provide time for the Haganah to take over the areas allocated to the Jews in the United Nations Partition Agreement, thereby avoiding any clashes between the two forces.

Desmond Goldie set off down the escarpment into the Jordan valley in his Arab Legion staff car. Shortly before he arrived at the Jisr Majami bridge he found himself in the middle of a sharp engagement. The mortars of 4th Infantry Regiment, commanded by Lt-Col. (now Field-Marshal) Habis Majali, were firing on Jewish positions west of the river. Habis was astonished to find Goldie engaged in some kind of cloak and dagger operation but was reassured when told that he was acting as a messenger for the Pasha. The firing was stopped and arrangements were made for Goldie to cross the bridge. Meanwhile, however, his driver had decided not to accompany him and Goldie proceeded on his own.

After crossing the river he found himself surrounded by an angry mob engaged in conducting their own private war with the Jews. Matters might have gone ill for him had he not been recognized by an Arab Legion soldier in the crowd. There were then cheers all round and Goldie was permitted to pass. He drove on to the kibbutz and his meeting with Shamir, who appears to have been as surprised as Habis Majali. He listened courteously to Goldie's explanation of Glubb's proposals but would not commit the Haganah. He would, however, pass on Glubb's message to his superiors. The Haganah was perfectly capable of conquering all Palestine, he told Goldie, but there would be no need for any fighting in Jerusalem provided the Arab Legion kept clear of the city. His message delivered, Goldie returned to Zerqa (and an anxious wife). Nothing however was gained by this extraordinary affair other than Mrs Meir's abortive second visit to King Abdullah.

An interesting aspect of Goldie's mission was the haphazardness of the arrangements. Glubb did not brief Goldie personally and seems to have been strangely unconcerned regarding the dangers involved. Goldie could well have been killed by angry Arabs, or by the Jews for entering their kibbutz. However well-intentioned, it is hard to understand why one of the Arab Legion's most senior officers should have been chosen for this mission; at the very least one would have expected Glubb to brief him himself. It is like something out of John Buchan.

The casual way in which the matter was handled is the more surprising because Glubb Pasha was only too well aware of how easily and quickly the situation could deteriorate. 'The catastrophic mistake made by the United Nations,' he wrote, 'had been to draw up a partition plan and order Jews and Arabs to observe it, but to send no troops to enforce it. If an army had been present, the Partition might have been carried out without an Arab–Israel war . . . The British could have remained a few weeks and then been replaced by an international force. Especially the city of Jerusalem might have been retained as an International zone.'[8]

The Arab states had no co-ordinated plan, not even an overall Commander-in-Chief. Azzam Pasha had politely hinted to Glubb that he might assume that role but Glubb had declined, equally politely. Politicians and generals from Egypt, Syria and Iraq met in Amman early in May to discuss plans. King Abdullah was appointed titular Commander-in-Chief but without staff or authority. The Egyptians declined to discuss their plans and the Iraqis were no more forthcoming. At the end of the conference Lt-Col. Charles Coaker, Glubb's principal staff officer for Operations, drove the senior Iraqi officer back to his hotel. Coaker inquired how the conference had gone. 'Splendidly,' was the reply. 'We all agreed to fight separately.'[9]

And that is what happened. On 15 May, without warning, the Egyptians entered Palestine from the south. An Iraqi armoured car regiment and infantry battalion reached the River Jordan opposite Beisan. The Syrians attacked Samakh at the southern end of the Sea of Galilee and after a brisk little action withdrew. They never appeared on the scene again. On the same day the Arab Legion crossed the River Jordan by the Allenby Bridge near Jericho. Of the Arab armies that fought in that first war against Israel, the Arab Legion alone added to its laurels – but the war which began on 15 May 1948 has never really ended.

[8]J. B. Glubb, A Report on the Fighting in Jerusalem, May 1948 (private papers), p. 6.
[9]Collins & Lapierre, O Jerusalem (Weidenfeld & Nicolson, 1972), p. 312.

Chapter Ten

Backs to the Wall

'The more difficulties are, the more the faith.'[1]

Oliver Cromwell

FEW GENERALS HAVE BEEN FACED WITH more daunting problems
than Glubb as his jubilant soldiers drove across the Allenby
Bridge into Palestine on the morning of 15 May 1948. Throughout the previous evening Abdullah and his Prime Minister had
been besieged by telephone calls from the frantic Arab inhabitants of Jerusalem, reporting the inexorable Jewish advance into
the city and imploring Abdullah to come to their aid. Deeply
troubled, Abdullah had begged Glubb Pasha to see what could
be done although he knew as well as Glubb that the tiny Arab
Legion would be swallowed up in the maze of city streets.

Glubb still clung to the hope that the Jews would not elect
to fight it out with the Arabs but would instead content themselves by occupying the areas of Palestine allocated to them in
the United Nations partition plan. 'If we move into Jerusalem,'
Glubb told himself, 'we shall use up half our army. Then we
cannot hold the rest of the country. If the Jews occupy the rest
of the country, Jerusalem itself would be out-flanked and fall.
So in the end Jerusalem also would fall.'[2] His instincts as a
soldier told him to keep well clear of the city; his political
judgement told him that this would be impossible.

Jerusalem was not only the Holy City – for Jews, Moslems

[1]From a letter to Colonel Robert Hammond dated 25 November 1648, quoted by
Thomas Carlyle in Vol. 1 of *His Letters and Speeches*, 1846.
[2]J. B. Glubb, *A Soldier with the Arabs*, p. 101.

and Christians alike – it was also the strategic heart of Palestine. The main north–south and east–west communications ran through the city. Moreover, situated as it was on the crest of the Judaean massif, Jerusalem was of vital significance tactically. But how was he to hold Jerusalem, and all of Judaea and Samaria, with less than 5000 soldiers?

The road from Jericho to Jerusalem runs through a defile. If the Arab Legion took that route it was likely to be ambushed. Glubb had therefore constructed, with the help of local labour, a rough track running up the spur behind Jericho and on beyond to Beiteen. It was up this track that Joshua led the Children of Israel after the capture of Jericho. Glubb paid for it by drawing all the money from the Arab Legion Canteen Fund – £4000 – and it was only just motorable by 15 May.

The intention was to defend Hebron District and those parts of Samaria and Judaea allocated to the Arabs; to this end Glubb deployed 1st Brigade (Goldie) to Nablus and 3rd Brigade (Ashton) to Ramallah. 1st Regiment (Lt-Col. Blackden) and 3rd Regiment (Lt-Col. Newman) formed 3rd Brigade; 2nd Regiment (Lt-Col. Slade) and 4th Regiment (Lt-Col. Habis Majali) formed 3rd Brigade. Three of the four infantry battalions were bedouin. Part of 1st Regiment was sent to Qalqiliya where it soon became engaged with the Jews. 4th Regiment moved to Latrun from where it could dominate the road to Jerusalem from Tel Aviv, as it wound its way up the Bab al Wad. 12th Garrison Company was in Hebron; 1st and 8th Garrison Companies had been sent up the Jericho–Jerusalem road on 16 May, arriving unopposed on the Mount of Olives where they dug themselves in on 17 May. There was not at that stage any intention of committing any part of the Arab Legion to Jerusalem itself.

Meanwhile the situation in Jerusalem was deteriorating hourly. It was plain to the Jews, who were operating to a carefully drawn-up plan, that if they were to seize the whole of Jerusalem it must be done fast on the heels of the British withdrawal. They had already been sapping away before the British left and were helped by the British insistence that all the Arab Legion units must have been withdrawn from Palestine prior to the end of the Mandate. This was in fact done, apart from 12th

Garrison Company which was cut off in Hebron, but it gave the Jews an immense tactical advantage. The Haganah was on the spot and pressing forward into the Old City.

The agony in Amman was intense as the Jewish pressure increased, and with it the anguished appeals for assistance from the Arabs. Glubb described King Abdullah as looking 'haggard with anxiety', and inevitably these feelings were communicated to the troops. Glubb, endeavouring with Lash to make a sensible military plan, was under constant pressure from the King to succour Jerusalem. 'His Majesty the King orders an advance towards Jerusalem from the direction of Ramallah,' read one telegram received at Lash's headquarters at 11.30 a.m. on 17 May. A longer one followed from the Minister of Defence at noon. It reinforced the King's telegram and informed Glubb that the Jews were attacking the gates of the Old City. In the opinion of the Belgian Consul, a member of the Truce Committee, counter-action by the Arab Legion against the Jewish quarter might help towards a cessation of the fighting.

Reluctantly, Glubb realized he had little other option than to commit part of the Arab Legion to the battle. After a brief visit to Amman, he was back at Ramallah early on the morning of 18 May. The news was that the Jews were reported to have broken into the Old City by the Zion Gate and were using armoured cars and mortars; the Palmach, their regular soldiers, were spearheading the assault. Glubb gave the necessary orders and soon after 8 a.m. the 1st Infantry Company moved down from the Mount of Olives and into the walled city. The Palmach, still not securely established, were driven back and soon the Arab Legion was manning the walls. But for how long? One hundred soldiers equipped only with rifles and bren guns must inevitably be overwhelmed.

As message after message arrived from King Abdullah at Lash's field headquarters near Beiteen begging, imploring, ordering the Arab Legion to intervene in Jerusalem, Glubb wrestled with the problem. Returning to Amman in the late afternoon, he says his mind was made up as his car crossed over the Allenby Bridge. As soon as he reached *Qyada* he wrote a message for immediate dispatch to Lash: 'I have decided to intervene in force in Jerusalem.' Lash was instructed to scrape together a force which would attack the Sheikh Jarrah suburb from Ramallah as early as possible on the following morning, 19 May. 8th Garrison Company was to move down from the Mount of Olives to join them.

Brigadier El-Edroos, in somewhat grudging fashion, ascribes the credit for this decision to King Abdullah whom he seems to regard as some kind of military genius. In fact King Abdullah was motivated far more by sheer emotion than by strategic considerations; it was Glubb Pasha who had to reconcile what he knew to be militarily sound with what he equally well knew to be politically expedient. Since this was a case of fortune favouring the brave, it is pointless to try to ascribe the credit for success to anyone other than the soldiers who fought so well. Glubb well knew he was taking an appalling military risk, as he had done all those years before at Al Abtiyya when faced by the Ikhwan, but in truth he had no choice; nor had King Abdullah.

Since the fighting qualities of Israel's soldiers, and the planning skill of their generals, has been made manifest to the rest of the world on many occasions since 1948, it is hard to understand why Israeli propagandists still persist in multiplying by at least a figure of five the strength of the Arab Legion force which entered Jerusalem at 3.45 a.m. on 19 May; they also grossly over-estimate the quantity of available support:

'The Legion launched the attack with four batteries of heavy guns, smaller artillery units, two infantry regiments, and large units of tanks and armoured cars. After the artillery barrage, they advanced in massed strength, tanks in the lead . . .'[3]

The true facts are that the force was very small – about two hundred men all told; they were reinforced later in the day by two companies of 1st Regiment, making a total of five hundred. The Arab Legion possessed no tanks until 1953 and no heavy artillery until much later still. The advance was led by about a dozen armoured cars, vulnerable to small arms fire, and four towed 6-pounder anti-tank guns. There were four 3-inch mortars; the so-called 'artillery barrage' was fired by four 25-pounder artillery pieces limited to a few rounds per gun owing

[3]Harry Levin, *Jerusalem Embattled* (Gollancz, 1950), p. 184.

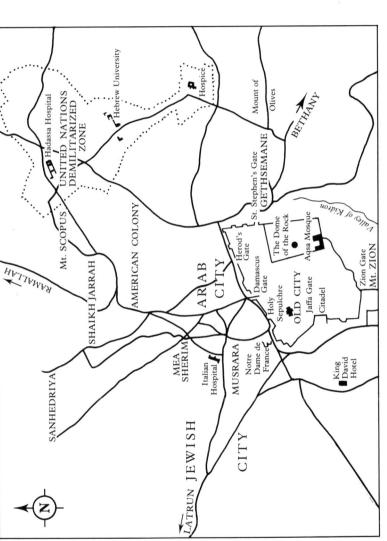

Jerusalem, 1948

N

RAMALLAH

LATRUN

SANHEDRIYA

Mt. SCOPUS

SHAIKH JARRAH

UNITED NATIONS
DEMILITARIZED
ZONE

Hadassa Hospital

Hebrew University

AMERICAN COLONY

Hospice

Mount of
Olives

BETHANY

JEWISH

CITY

MEA
SHERIM

Italian Hospital

MUSRARA

Notre
Dame de
France

ARAB
CITY

Herod's
Gate

Damascus
Gate

Holy
Sepulchre

OLD CITY

Jaffa Gate

Citadel

St. Stephen's Gate

GETHSEMANE

The Dome
of the Rock

Aqsa Mosque

Valley of Kidron

Zion Gate

Mt. ZION

King
David
Hotel

to the ammunition shortage. Militarily it was a suicidal operation but it came off. By 2 p.m. the armoured cars had reached the Damascus Gate and had linked up with 1st Garrison Company, already established on the walls of the Old City.

By the evening of 19 May it was plain to Glubb that the force already committed would be too weak to resist the inevitable Jewish counter-attack. Urgent reinforcement was needed but this would mean committing one of his precious infantry battalions to the hazards of street fighting; it must surely also mean weakening his position elsewhere. But where was the advantage in holding Samaria with Jerusalem gone? The 3rd Regiment was still in reserve near Nablus and on the afternoon of Friday 21 May, Lt-Col. Newman was ordered to move his battalion that night to Jerusalem. At 2.30 a.m. on the following morning 3rd Regiment passed through Sheikh Jarrah and soon afterwards were fighting their way into the Old City.

Most of 3rd Regiment's casualties were incurred during the fighting for the Monastery of Nôtre Dame de France which had been fortified and was strongly held by the Jews. They fought as bravely in its defence as 3rd Regiment fought for its capture, and after three days' fighting Glubb called off the attack as casualties continued to mount. 'With no reserves to replace battle casualties, with a fortnight's ammunition in stock and the districts of Nablus, Jerusalem and Hebron yet to be defended, it was wisely decided to call off any further fruitless and costly frontal attacks on heavily defended localities in the built-up area,' writes Brigadier El-Edroos. 'With a force of less than 1000 fighting men, the Arab Legion had relieved the Old City, and had occupied a thin but staunch "khaki-line" across the City – a gallant and commendable performance by any standards. More importantly, and despite the heavy casualties, the Holy Places were firmly in Arab hands.'[4]

One officer who distinguished himself during the early stages of the fighting in Jerusalem was a young Captain from Irbid, Abdullah Tell, who commanded one of the Garrison Companies. He was intelligent and well-educated and displayed a good deal of tactical sense. Later, when he met King Abdullah,

[4]S. A. El-Edroos, *The Hashemite Arab Army*, pp. 255–6.

the King was so impressed that he asked Glubb to promote him forthwith to Lieutenant-Colonel; unfortunately the King had already told Abdullah Tell that he would do this. Glubb did his best to dissuade the King, pointing out that Abdullah Tell was junior to many other Arab officers, but in the end gave in. It was as a Lieutenant-Colonel that Abdullah Tell signed the 'Cease-Fire' Agreement in Jerusalem on behalf of Jordan on 28 November 1948; the Israeli signatory was Colonel Moshe Dayan. By then success had gone to Abdullah Tell's head and he confronted Glubb with a demand for promotion to Brigadier, claiming the King had promised it to him. Glubb refused. Shortly afterwards Abdullah Tell resigned and made his way to Egypt from where he conducted many bitter attacks on Glubb Pasha.

A consequence of the Arab Legion's success in holding the Old City was the decision by the Iraqis to take over the Nablus sector. It released 1st Regiment and Headquarters 3rd Brigade, who were moved to Ramallah. This was not a moment too soon as the Israelis were to launch a series of bitter attacks against Latrun to dislodge 4th Regiment. From 25 May to 11 June the Israelis lost more than 1300 killed and wounded in their efforts, but 4th Regiment stood firm.

Glubb's troubles were increased on 30 May when H.M.G. ordered all British regular officers serving with the Arab Legion to be withdrawn east of the river Jordan; this meant both the brigade commanders, three of the four battalion commanders, all the operations staff officers and all the senior artillery officers. The command had been given in order to conform with a United Nations resolution of 29 May, but the effects were of short duration. Goldie believes it was ordered only to enable the Foreign Secretary (Mr Bevin) to make a statement to the effect that there were no British regular officers serving west of the Jordan at the time he was making the announcement in the House of Commons. Within forty-eight hours they had all infiltrated back. The instructions did not affect those officers employed on contract, although Glubb's own attention was drawn by the Foreign Office to the provisions of the 'Foreign Enlistments Act'. He paid no heed to it.

A United Nations Mediator, Count Folke Bernadotte, had arrived to mediate between the Arabs and the Jews. Glubb met him on 1 June in Amman and was immediately impressed by him. He believed him to be both brave and honest. Glubb Pasha did his utmost to co-operate where the Arab Legion was concerned; he wondered whether the same would be true of the Jews? In Glubb's opinion at that time the Jews would never be satisfied until they controlled the whole of Palestine, including the Negev. Whatever agreement they might make, it would only be a temporary expedient until they felt strong enough to advance a little farther. He still believes this to be true today.[5]

Bernadotte succeeded in arranging a truce which was to begin at 6 a.m. on 11 June. Shortly before the truce came into effect Glubb sent the 5th Garrison Company to establish a token military presence at Lydda and Ramle on the coastal plain. These two towns were to be Arab under the U.N. Partition Plan but they were surrounded by Jewish settlements and were clearly indefensible. By establishing a token presence, however, and by appointing an Arab Governor, Glubb hoped that if the truce was succeeded by a peace agreement, Lydda and Ramle would become part of the Arab area. Tawfiq Pasha disagreed with him, arguing that the Arab Legion could not possibly hold the two towns; therefore he refused to appoint a governor, although he did agree to the Garrison Company being sent to Ramle.

Glubb's lack of rapport with Tawfiq Pasha, who also held the Defence portfolio, added greatly to his difficulties. Tawfiq, who was a bureaucrat before all else, could not adapt himself to war, which cut across all his counting-house principles. Besides, he regarded the British as being responsible for the whole sorry business and yet he had to accept that his principal military adviser was British. No two men could have been more opposite in outlook and temperament and although outwardly their relations seemed good enough, beneath the surface neither man really thought well of the other. Tawfiq, office-bound and disinclined to leave it in order to see for himself, was frequently

[5]Discussion with author on 30 June 1982.

irritated by Glubb's regular absences on tours of inspection, even in peacetime. He called Glubb 'Sinbad the Landsman' because he was always travelling. On the other hand Glubb, exhausted both physically and mentally by the strain of battle, found it intolerable that Tawfiq could not see that the Arab Legion was over-stretched and under-equipped. Glubb wanted to seize the opportunity provided by the truce to reorganize and resupply, but this required more money. Tawfiq firmly refused to provide it. There would be no more fighting, he said; on that he and his Egyptian colleague, Nokrashy Pasha, were determined. Therefore there would be no more money. In any case, as he pointed out to Glubb, the Arab Legion budget had been grossly overspent, for which dereliction of duty the Chief of the General Staff would be called to account in due course. Exasperated and angry, Glubb left the Prime Minister's office determined to do as he thought best, Tawfiq or no Tawfiq.

It has to be said in Tawfiq's defence that it was not only his pinchpenny attitude that prevented Glubb from obtaining more equipment. The United Nations had imposed a ban on the provision of weapons to either side but Britain was the only country to observe this, and Britain was the obvious source of supply for the Arab Legion.

Glubb has himself observed that, 'The Arabs and Egyptians always said that the worst of the British was their strict compliance with UN resolutions, whereas the other nations ignored them. After the First Arab–Israel War Britain refused to supply arms to either side, but the Russians and Czechs poured arms into Israel.' In Glubb's opinion it was this as much as anything that drove Nasser into the arms of Russia; he just could not get the weapons he wanted from Britain or the USA.'[6]

King Abdullah's support meant a great deal to Glubb at this time. The King was a statesman, not a soldier, but he enjoyed dealing with soldiers. He saw Glubb almost daily and gave him the utmost encouragement, as did Kirkbride. Although there might not be any money with which to purchase supplies, Glubb set about reorganizing the Arab Legion. The six independent garrison companies were grouped into two more infantry

[6]Interview, 1980.

147

battalions, 5th and 6th Regiments, each commanded by an Arab. 6th Regiment was given the task of defending the Old City in Jerusalem. Glubb also succeeded in scraping together a certain quantity of engineer stores, making it possible to wire and sandbag key positions, such as Latrun. It was impossible, however, to improve the ammunition position which was desperately worrying.

The Israelis, by contrast, utilized the truce to build up and improve on their already considerable stocks. They 'disregarded their undertaking not to import war materials during the truce, and took ample advantage of that respite to rectify their almost total lack of combat aircraft, artillery and heavy armoured vehicles, and their serious limitations in automatic weapons and ammunition . . . The first bomber aircraft obtained by Israel were smuggled out of the United States and Britain. Italy was another source of supply . . .'[7]

The Israeli genius for organization, so often demonstrated in their subsequent campaigns against the Arabs, their brilliant military planning and their ruthless determination to achieve the goals they had set for themselves, was either underrated or ignored in those early days of conflict. The Arabs failed to appreciate that they were dealing with men fighting quite literally for their lives, men who moreover had survived the most vicious persecution in all Jewish history. If the Arabs were driven out of Palestine, there were still Arab states to which they could go. If the Jews were driven into the sea, they must face yet another diaspora. The knowledge of this provided them with an inner strength that the Arabs, for all their preponderance, were unable to match. But here again it has to be said, in order to be fair, that the dice were heavily loaded against the Arabs, with the two most powerful nations in the world, the United States and Soviet Russia, either overtly or covertly supporting the Jews.

Shortly after the imposition of the first truce by the Security Council on 11 June 1948, the Political Committee of the Arab League were summoned to a meeting in Cairo. Tawfiq Pasha left Amman convinced that the outcome of the meeting would

[7]George Kirk, *Survey of International Affairs, 1939–46: The Middle East 1945–50* (OUP, 1954), p. 277.

be a prolongation of the truce; both King Abdullah and Glubb had implored him to ensure that this would be so. Tawfiq returned from Cairo with the news that the Egyptian government had rejected a prolongation and that therefore the war would continue from 8 July when the truce expired. Glubb could not believe his ears. 'How are we to continue the war when we have no ammunition, and when you refuse to allow us to buy some?' he asked the Prime Minister. 'Don't fire unless you are fired on,' replied Tawfiq.

There always was a kind of *Alice in Wonderland* quality attached to service in the Arab Legion, due perhaps to the differences between the Arab and the British character, but never more so than when war broke out again between Arabs and Jews on 9 July 1948. The Jews had employed the truce to re-organize their forces and to re-equip them (with American help), and to plan their next moves. The Arabs had done nothing but talk, whistling in the dark to keep up their spirits. Since they could not agree among themselves, how could they expect to produce a coordinated strategy? For this the Egyptians were chiefly to blame; but throughout the Arab countries there was an astonishing failure to come to grips with the military realities of the situation.

Glubb has always insisted that the existence of the United Nations has introduced a new dimension into war; their policy being (with rare exceptions) to bring the shooting war to a standstill as soon as world opinion can be mobilized – in a matter of days, or at most weeks. The subsequent negotiations under United Nations' auspices are likely to be long and probably ineffectual. It is therefore essential, tactically, to seize as much territory as possible while the fighting continues, as much as a bargaining counter as for territorial possession.

The Israelis set out to do this when they launched their offensive on 9 July, pinching out Lydda and Ramle but directing their main effort against Latrun. They deployed five brigades against the Arab Legion's 2nd and 4th Regiments and were fought to a standstill. The fighting at Latrun was amongst the most bitter of the entire war; one Arab Legion 6-pounder anti-tank gun, mounted on the roof of the police station at Latrun,

149

knocked out or damaged five Israeli tanks; every one of the gun's crew was killed but each man was replaced by another as he fell. By the afternoon of 18 July the Israeli attack had been repulsed; and at 5 p.m. the second truce came into effect by Security Council resolution. At Latrun, as at Jerusalem beforehand, the Arab Legion had held their ground. Glubb Pasha had every reason to be proud of his soldiers.

Unfortunately he was again at loggerheads with the Prime Minister. The 5th Garrison Company had conducted a fine and brave fighting withdrawal from Ramle when the Jews attacked on 9 July. But they were unable to prevent the capture of Lydda and Ramle on 12 July, whereupon the forcible evacuation of the Arab population took place. Thousands of men, women and children left their homes and trekked into the mountains. It was blazingly hot, there was no water and the Jews had seized all means of transport. Hundreds fell by the wayside. When news reached Amman there was a storm of indignation. Quite unfairly, Glubb Pasha was held to be responsible. The latent antagonism between the Prime Minister and the Chief of the General Staff now came to the surface. There was an unholy row which Glubb Pasha was lucky to survive.

Despite the fact that Glubb and Tawfiq were agreed on the impossibility of defending Lydda and Ramle against strong Jewish attack, no sooner had the Israeli advance begun than rumours began to circulate in Amman that Glubb had betrayed the Arabs. Amman was full of Palestinian refugees who sought a scapegoat and Glubb Pasha would serve very well for that purpose. Mr Bevin had issued an appeal to both sides to cease fighting; shortly thereafter Lydda and Ramle fell. Glubb's detractors claimed that Bevin had instructed him to abandon the towns without fighting. At about the same time Glubb had written to the Prime Minister urging a truce, not on behalf of the Arab Legion but of the Egyptian army which was under heavy pressure.

Two hours after writing the letter he was summoned to the Palace where he was confronted by the King and the entire cabinet. Tawfiq read out his letter in a voice choking with rage while the ministers commented sarcastically on the various proposals made in it. Even the King deserted Glubb on this occasion, glowering at him and remarking that if he did not want to serve loyally, there was no cause for him to stay. Glubb was not angry, just tired and deeply depressed. He was being called a traitor in Amman; in London, in the House of Commons, a Member was inquiring why a British general was permitted to commit atrocities against the Jews. There was no point in arguing or stating his case; that had been done already but to no effect. After hearing Tawfiq out, he asked the King's permission to retire from the room.

But the war went on, with the Jews pressing hard against Beit Sira and Latrun. The Palmach redoubled its efforts to take Latrun by the time the second truce came into effect. The line held, however, and the Arab Legion remained masters of the battlefield. Immediately after the truce Glubb went to see Tawfiq again, accompanied this time by the Minister of Defence. There was no more money and the Secretary-General of the Arab League had reneged on his promise to provide £4,000,000. Tawfiq was furious when he learned that the budget was overspent. When he asked where he was supposed to get the money from, Glubb replied sarcastically, 'Why don't you stop it from my pay?' Tawfiq could stand no more discussion. Dismissing Glubb and the Minister of Defence, he drove straight to the Palace and handed in his resignation. King Abdullah tried hard to placate him and in the end it was decided that Tawfiq would stay, but that Glubb would be given a month's leave in Europe. Since everyone was worn out, it was a sensible solution. The Glubbs left for London via Cairo on 17 August.[8]

The Glubbs were changing planes in Paris on their way back to Jordan, on 17 September, when they heard the news of Bernadotte's assassination in Jerusalem earlier that day. Glubb Pasha was deeply moved. He had developed a great admiration for the United Nations Mediator, believing he was motivated

---

[8]Lash was also given leave over this period, leaving Goldie in temporary command of the Division in Ramallah. As such he had to entertain an Iraqi delegation which had come to Palestine to establish to their own satisfaction that Glubb had betrayed the Arab cause! Having been warned of this, Goldie was careful to avoid all controversial questions; since his command of Arabic was far from perfect, he was able to dodge most of them by pleading ignorance of the language.

only by a desire for peace by honourable means. The murder seemed to be so utterly pointless and would serve neither the Arab nor the Jewish cause. He had thought Bernadotte a 'splendid man', with a very sensible approach to the Arab–Jewish problem. Bernadotte's staff thought Jerusalem should be handed over to the Arabs but Bernadotte did not believe this would work; in view of this it was tragic that the Jews should have killed him.

On Glubb's return to Amman, where he was welcomed effusively by Tawfiq Pasha, he found everyone waiting for the United Nations' reaction to their mediator's murder. 'As the days passed, and nothing happened, we began slowly to realize how utterly ineffectual and impotent U.N.O. was . . . indeed there was scarcely criticism. The lesson was not lost on anyone in Palestine, whether United Nations officers, Arabs or Jews.'[9] Glubb never succeeded in achieving the same rapport with Bernadotte's successor, Ralph Bunche, and he had little time for Major-General Burns, a Canadian, who was later appointed as head of U.N.O.'s Mixed Armistice Commission.

After the first truce on 11 June, the guns had stopped firing along the front. The same was not the case after the second truce in July. In Jerusalem, particularly, the Jews continued to bombard the Arab-held part of the city with mortars, to the irritation of Glubb's elderly mother who resolutely refused to leave the American Colony hotel where she had been living for some time. It was then suggested that the best solution to the problem would be for the Arab Legion to reply in kind, selecting for their target the civilian residential area, as did the Jews, and in a remarkably short space of time the firing ceased.

Although Glubb's personal relations with the Prime Minister and the Cabinet had returned to normal, the attacks on him continued unabated. As he has commented, with unusual bitterness, 'Perhaps for generations to come, the history books

[9] J. B. Glubb, *A Soldier with the Arabs*, p. 183. Many will probably share Glubb Pasha's views on the effectiveness of the United Nations but the fact remains that U.N.O. still has a part to play in international disputes – but only up to a point. Beyond that point it becomes only a forum for propaganda, as was evident in the recent dispute over the Falkland Islands. The sad truth is that U.N.O. lacks the means to enforce the popular will.

in most Arab countries will teach that Glubb Pasha betrayed the Arabs and gave Lydda and Ramle to the Jews, in accordance with orders received from Mr Bevin in London.'[10] It was perhaps the heaviest part of Glubb's burden during his Arab service that those he served voluntarily and with sympathy for their cause chose to reward his loyalty by denigrating him. His usefulness as a scapegoat was obvious and it was therefore inadvisable to come too quickly to his support whenever he was under attack. This was exemplified by Tawfiq Pasha's attitude towards Glubb, who found his value as a whipping boy was probably no less than his value as a general. Most of those who have served the Arabs, and who have shared their aspirations, have suffered at one time or another from this curious Arab tendency to bite the hands of their friends.

It was the situation of the Egyptian army that gave the most cause for concern after Glubb Pasha's return from leave. Having advanced through Sinai to the southern borders of Palestine, the Egyptians were strung out in a line of defended localities between Gaza and Beersheba to as far east as Hebron. There was no depth to their position but they threatened the Jewish settlements in the Northern Negev. The Israelis launched an attack against them on 15 October. On the following day Glubb wrote to Goldie, then temporarily commanding in Ramallah:

'The Jews bombed Gaza and Mejdel this morning and there is a signal in from Hebron to say that the Jews have advanced between Hebron and Mejdel, and have cut the road connecting Hebron to Gaza. This is what I guess has happened. The Mufti's government in Gaza wanted to increase its prestige by starting a fight. For the past week supported by the Egyptians the Mufti's irregulars have been shooting at the Jews. The Jews have now got cross and are going to see them off. Secondly, the Jews just the chance they wanted. Now if the Jews break through to Gaza and Beersheba, the Egyptians in Hebron will be cut off. occupy both the Negev and Galilee. How are U.N.O. going to get them out? It looks as if the Gaza government have given the Jews just the chance they wanted. Now if the Jews break through to Gaza and Beersheba, the Egyptians in Hebron will be cut off.

[10]Ibid., p. 194.

153

We don't want the Jews to capture Hebron too. If we step in and occupy Hebron, we shall have no further political complications in the Hebron area! We shall appear as saviours . . .'[11]

Goldie was instructed as a first step to secure Bethlehem with two troops of armoured cars and two platoons of infantry. This would involve a risky approach march round the eastern side of Jerusalem. The force was later (22 October) increased to two companies of infantry and a squadron of armoured cars – 12 Marmon Harringtons.

On 21 October two possible courses of action for the Arab Legion to relieve the pressure on the Egyptians were debated in Amman. The first was to launch a diversionary attack in the Jerusalem/Latrun sector. This was prompted by a belief, which turned out later to be illusory, that the Iraqis might extend their front in order to release Arab Legion units for offensive action. Alternatively a force should be sent east of Jerusalem to reinforce the sub-units already moving to Bethlehem and thereby secure Hebron. In a letter sent to Goldie on that day Glubb wrote:

'Kirkbride also sent for me today and told me that he thought that for political and economic reasons, it was essential not to let the Jews take Bethlehem and Hebron. Politically we should have another Lydda and Ramle, especially as the King ordered me to send a regiment there[12] two days ago! It would again be me who had betrayed the Arab cause. Economically it would mean another 50,000 to 100,000 refugees. Would you therefore please send the armoured cars . . . It looks from the news as tho' the Jews will accept a cease fire in another two or three days, so that they can get the maximum advantage of their victory first. It is really essential to hold Bethlehem and if possible Hebron for those three days. Please arrange accordingly even if you have to send a company from 8th Regiment or anywhere else, *or weaken your front temporarily.*'[13]

In the event the Arab Legion secured both Bethlehem and Hebron. On 28 October, the reconnaissance element of seven armoured cars under Major Lockett surprised an Israeli column many times their number advancing to Hebron via Beit Jibrin.

[11]Glubb to Goldie, 16 October 1948.   [12]i.e. Hebron.
[13]Glubb to Goldie, 21 October 1948. Author's italics.

154

In a very gallant action at Tarqumiya, they forced an Israeli withdrawal, thereby ensuring that Hebron was in Jordanian hands when the cease fire came into effect. By then, however, the Egyptians had been almost eliminated by the Israelis, apart from a brigade surrounded at Falluja. The problem of how to relieve that garrison, which contained Gemal Abdul Nasser as Brigade Major, exercised the Arab League, almost to the exclusion of everything else. Glubb, who knew the League's consultations would result only in words, accepted Major Lockett's offer to walk through the Israeli lines into Falluja. This Lockett did, accompanied only by an Arab orderly. He returned to report that the Egyptians were fighting bravely although under persistent shell-fire; their morale was high.

Glubb continued to press for the Iraqis to take over Latrun in order that the Arab Legion could relieve Falluja, but the Iraqis refused. The Arab League then produced a plan whereby Jordan, Iraq and Syria would each provide a battalion. 'Who but a politician could think of such an idea?' asked Glubb. 'Three different battalions from three different armies would carry out a joint operation in mountainous country at night – apparently without even a single commander.'[14] Exasperated by such folly, Glubb sent Lockett back to the Egyptian commander in Falluja with another plan. The Egyptians would withdraw east on an agreed night, abandoning their stores and much of their transport and equipment; the Arab Legion would advance to meet them, engaging the Israeli blocking force from the rear. Lockett returned safely but the Egyptians had rejected the plan. They continued to hold out until the Israeli–Egyptian armistice was agreed on 24 February 1949; then they marched out with the honours of war. Theirs had been a valiant effort.

In the midst of the anxiety about the Egyptians, Glubb was informed that Mr Bevin had told a questioner in the House of Commons that Glubb would not be liable to five years' imprisonment for enlisting in a foreign army without the King's permission! Bevin's statement coincided with an outbreak of rioting in Amman in protest against developments in Palestine, during which Glubb Pasha had been publicly denounced as a

[14] J. B. Glubb, *A Soldier with the Arabs*, p. 215.

traitor to the Arab cause. Fortunately he was too busy to waste any time worrying about such nonsense. Regardless of the financial consequences, he was expanding the Arab Legion as fast as men could be trained. In less than twelve months the Legion had been doubled in strength; having started the war with four battalions, these had been increased to eight by the end of 1948, with two more in the process of being formed. Considering the multitude of pressures to which they were subjected, this expansion represented a considerable organizational feat on the part of Glubb and his very small Anglo–Arab staff.

Meanwhile, on 1 December 1948, the formal incorporation of the Arab portion of Palestine into the Hashemite Kingdom of Jordan was agreed by the principal Palestinian leaders assembled in Jericho. On 13 December the Jordanian Parliament altered the constitution accordingly; henceforward the two halves of Jordan would be known as 'West Bank' and 'East Bank'. Although this was an inevitable consequence of Partition, it aroused a storm of protest in the other Arab countries. The Egyptian-sponsored Government of All Palestine which had been established in Gaza withdrew to Cairo, from where it rejected Abdullah as ruler of Palestine. The ex-Mufti was of course a prime mover in this action which demonstrated, yet again, the inability of the Arabs to cease their internal feuds in order to concentrate on the wider issues.

There was certainly no evidence of a desire to continue the fighting. The Arab League which at Egypt's urging had rushed so heedlessly into war laid down their arms without a thought for each other. Egypt agreed to an armistice with Israel in February 1949, Lebanon following suit soon afterwards. Syria had long played no active part. In February 1949 the Jordan government accepted an invitation from Dr Bunche, United Nations chief negotiator, to send a delegation to Rhodes to discuss an armistice with Israel. On 11 March 1949 the terms of such an armistice were agreed by the Jordanian and Israeli delegations.

While these discussions were taking place in Rhodes the Iraqis announced their intention to withdraw their troops from Palestine without entering into negotiations with Israel. There were some 19,000 Iraqi soldiers deployed in the area of Nablus,

Tul Karm and Jenin. The Israelis then said they would occupy the Iraqi sector when the Iraqis withdrew in order to 'keep order'. Furthermore they informed Dr Bunche on 13 March that Israel would regard any attempt by Jordan to take over the Iraqi sector as a breach of the armistice agreement and that hostilities would ensue.

There was consternation in Amman. Attempts to persuade the British and Americans to use their influence with Israel met with no response. With great reluctance the Jordan government accepted a compromise negotiated by Dr Bunche whereby a further 400 kilometres along the Iraqi front would be ceded to Israel. An armistice was then formally signed in Rhodes on 3 April 1949. The Jordanian delegation were greeted on their return with vituperation and vilification in the press. King Abdullah and Glubb were pilloried as traitors. It was a sorry reward for all that the Arab Legion had accomplished in Jerusalem, Latrun and Hebron. As Count Bernadotte had commented at one stage: 'There are plenty of people fighting in Palestine, but only one army – and that is the Arab Legion.'[15]

Abdullah was unmoved by the clamour. He knew that Jordan was unable to fight Israel on its own. He had no faith in either the Egyptians or Syrians. Iraq was torn by internal feuding and could not be relied upon. His long-standing quarrel with Ibn Saud continued unresolved. Therefore it made sense to come to terms with Israel. In any case Abdullah had Mr Bevin's agreement to the union of Arab Palestine with his kingdom east of the Jordan. As Supreme Commander of the Arab Legion he gave his Chief of the General Staff unstinted support and encouragement. Without it Glubb could not have long continued his efforts to expand the Arab Legion in order to deal with its vastly increased responsibilities.

It is now time to consider Glubb's performance as a military commander in the field. Although he was universally admired by his subordinates, there were those who thought he was out-of-date tactically and inclined to interfere too much and too often with his subordinate commanders, even down to the level of platoons on occasions. But Colonel Desmond Goldie has

[15]Ibid., p. 215.

157

N

MEDITERRANEAN

SEA

LEBANON

DAMASCUS

TYRE

ARAB

SYRIA

Sea of
Galilee

HAIFA

NAZARETH

Yarmuk

Mejama
Bridge

JEWISH

Shaikh
Husain
Bridge

JENIN

TULKARM

QALQILIYA

NABLUS

R. Jordan

TEL AVIV
JAFFA

QIBYA

ARAB

ZERQA

LYDDA
RAMLE

RAMALLAH

Allenby
Bridge

AMMAN

LATRUN

JERUSALEM

JORDAN

ARAB

BETHLEHEM

GAZA

FALLUJA

KAFR
ETZION

TARQUMIYA

HEBRON

Dead Sea

RAFAH

BEERSHEBA

KERAK

NEQEB

SINAI

JEWISH

EGYPT

ALAUJA

WADI ARABA

U.N. Partition Plan

made it plain that many of Glubb's actions were due to political considerations rather than military. Goldie says that Glubb often found it necessary to point out to his British officers, 'I've no doubt you are technically correct from a military point of view in what you suggest, but you must realize that this is not a proper war in the accepted sense. This is a *political* war, where small armies are directed against some comparatively unimportant position in order to exploit a political objective.'[16]

It has to be remembered that Glubb's formal military education ceased in 1920 while he was still a Lieutenant. During the years when his British army contemporaries were attending the Staff College, or the Imperial Defence College, Glubb was pacifying the desert tribes and militarizing the Arab Legion. That he was conscious of these limitations is clear from a passage in his memoirs:

'I was only a bogus general and had never received any staff training. My active command in the Second World War had only been in command of one regiment against the Iraqi *coup d'état* or the Vichy French. At the end of the war I commanded 12,000 men, but only in the role of guarding, garrisoning or patrolling the Middle East. Moreover we had been supplied and our vehicles maintained by the British army. Now we had suddenly and without money to improvise all our own base and administrative services.'[17]

This was not false modesty. Several of his former officers have remarked how shy the Pasha seemed to be when in the company of senior British generals. 'It was almost,' said one, 'as if he felt they were in some way superior to him.'[18] It is doubtful, however, whether they would have achieved as much as Glubb did with so little. He fought his battles on slender budgets and with insufficient supplies. He had none of the technological advantages of the modern general for controlling the battle. There were no light aircraft or helicopters to carry him rapidly to Lash's headquarters in Ramallah; instead a tedious four hours'

[16]Major H. D. B. Goldie, 'The Arab Legion', *Journal of the Royal Scots Fusiliers*, (1949), p. 33.
[17]This has been taken from the draft version of Glubb's memoirs but has not been included in the published version, *The Changing Scenes of Life*.
[18]Statement to author.

journey there and back by staff car. Radio communication was non-existent; wireless messages took time to encode, send and decode and the telephone was insecure, as well as unreliable.

Besides, the control of operations was only part of his work. He was deeply involved in the political issues, ranging from problems with his own government to negotiations with the United Nations Mediator. He had to organize and expand the Arab Legion, obtain supplies and preserve public security in Jordan itself. It would have been easier to have borne these heavy responsibilities had he felt he had his government's full confidence, but this was sadly lacking. He was subjected to pressures from all sides. On top of this, although he knew Lash well and liked him, he recognized that his military experience was negligible; his chief operations staff officer, Charles Coaker, was a young Gunner major and his senior Arab officers, Abdel Qadir Pasha and Ahmed Sudqi Bey, were both essentially policemen and hopelessly out of date as soldiers. Perhaps only Broadhurst was close enough to be a friend, but he too was a policeman by training and involved principally in administration. When everything is taken into consideration, it is a miracle that Glubb Pasha survived.

On one point everyone, British and Arabs, are agreed. He was *very* brave. He even seemed to grow physically in stature when the bullets were flying. There is an account of Glubb and Lash engaged in conference outside Sheikh Jarrah as the mortar bombs exploded around them. Lash is reported to have commented that he earned his pay that day but Glubb seemingly thought nothing of it. He could become so absorbed in what he was doing or thinking that he was oblivious to anything else. The last word perhaps should be left to one of his earliest recruits in the Desert Patrol who acted as his escort during a visit to 3rd Regiment during the bitter fighting for Nôtre Dame in Jerusalem. 'The Pasha did not know fear,' he said. 'I was very afraid that day but I was ashamed to show it. He put his trust in Allah and I tried to do the same – but it was very difficult!'[19]

[19] Statement to author by a *Nageeb* (Staff-Sergeant) in the 2nd Armoured Car Regiment in 1954. The *Nageeb* was later decorated for gallantry. He was a member of the Dhafir tribe from Iraq who joined Glubb's Desert Patrol in 1932. 'I was only a lad at the time,' he said, 'I can't remember how old – possibly only fifteen.'

Chapter Eleven

The Legion Expands

'In Jordan the Legion is the main factor in the smooth transition from nomadic to settled life.'

The Times, 12 February 1950

WHEN THE ARMISTICE between Jordan and Israel was signed at Rhodes on 3 April 1949, the Arab Legion consisted of nine infantry battalions. There were virtually no supporting arms and services, such as artillery, engineers, signals, transport, etc. Although it was true that the Arab Legion alone of the Arab armies had come out of the war with credit, having saved the Old City of Jerusalem for the Arabs and having out-fought the Jews at Latrun, no one knew better than Glubb at what cost. Almost all its ammunition had been expended, as had most of its supplies. The officers and soldiers had been fought to a standstill. Had the Jews continued the battle, they must inevitably have prevailed through sheer weight of numbers and superiority in *matériel*. In their criticism of Glubb Pasha, the Jordanian politicians chose to ignore this fact, but King Abdullah was wiser. He knew how close-run the battle had been.

It would not have mattered so much had the Arab Legion been free to return to its peacetime garrisons on the East Bank. Instead it found itself responsible for defending the border with Israel known as the Demarcation Line, that extended for more than 200 miles from Jenin in the north to Hebron in the south. Within that frontier lay scores of villages and towns, incorporated into Jordan on 24 April 1950, referred to usually as the West Bank, whose inhabitants hated and feared the Jews above any other race on earth. In far too many instances lines drawn on a map in Rhodes separated villages from their markets and villagers from their fields. 'Day after day,' said one of these villagers, 'I climbed a hillock outside this village and watched the Jews tilling the fields which had been ours for hundreds of years.' It did not make for peace.

Glubb Pasha's task would have broken many men. He had at one and the same time to produce a balanced army, expand it in size, procure for it arms and ammunition, deploy it to defend Jordan's recently acquired territory, find and train sufficient officers to lead it, and most difficult of all devise a way to defend the West Bank without scattering the Arab Legion in penny packets throughout the area.

Glubb remembered the Territorial Army in Britain and it occurred to him that something of the same kind on the West Bank might serve to defend the villages until the Arab Legion could come to the rescue. The force he had in mind would be named the National Guard (*Haras al Watany*) and be trained by the regular army. Every village would be armed and equipped up to section or platoon strength, trained and led by Arab Legion N.C.O.s, and grouped into battalions commanded by Arab Legion officers. There would be an Arab Legion wireless operator with every sub-unit. Their task would be to defend their hearths and homes against Israeli tip-and-run raids across the Demarcation Line until the regular army could intervene. There was, too, a secondary reason for forming this National Guard, '. . . to bring Palestinians into a larger share of the defence of their country.'[1]

Clearly this was the most sensible and economical way to carry out a task which otherwise would have required an expansion in the strength of the Arab Legion beyond the capacity of Jordan to sustain financially. It made sense to the unprejudiced. Unfortunately it was not seen as such by politicians from either bank of the River Jordan. Those on the East Bank doubted the wisdom of arming villagers, lest they used the arms to rebel against the government, or for criminal reasons, or to raid the Jewish settlements. Politicians on the West Bank opposed the

[1] P. J. Vatikiotis, *Politics and the Military in Jordan* (Cassell, 1967), p. 80.

scheme because many of them were not reconciled to their in-corporation into Jordan; they were afraid lest the integration of the villagers into Jordan's defence might weaken their influence politically.

Glubb went to infinite lengths to seek out and win over to his side those who opposed the concept of a National Guard. Nevertheless, long after the National Guard had been success-fully established, some of the other Arab countries tried their utmost to persuade the Jordanian government to separate the National Guard from the Arab Legion. The reason for this was entirely political. They argued that since Palestine was a prob-lem common to all Arabs, anything that helped to confirm the incorporation of the West Bank with Jordan should be resisted. It was even suggested that the National Guard should be com-manded by an officer from one of the other Arab armies. But the Jordanian government stood firm and the National Guard became a true success story; by 1956 it was 30,000 strong.

Money was always short in the Arab Legion. The subsidy provided by the British tax-payer in 1948-9 when the Legion was at war amounted to no more than £2.5 million. The war cost £6 million. The Arab League's contribution was £250,000, the Jordan government's £300,000. The balance was provided by Britain, in effect financing the first of the Arab Legion's wars with Israel. It was always believed in Jordan that the subsidy was paid directly to Glubb Pasha but he has always insisted that this was untrue. One Jordanian politician criticized Glubb in 1955 for the fact that funds provided by H.M.G. for the up-keep of the Arab Legion were not paid into the Treasury and as a consequence, 'the Minister of Defence had no say in expendi-ture on the Legion'.[2] Glubb denies this, saying that his financial powers were limited to no more than £200. He could not 'write-off' a damaged tent or lost greatcoat without reference to the Finance and Defence ministries, every proposed item of expenditure being scrutinized by the bureaucrats in London and Amman. There is certainly no reason to doubt Glubb's word. Indeed, the subsidy would not have been so freely forth-

[2]Unpublished diaries of Colonel J. B. Slade-Baker, Vol. V, 1 April 1955 (St Antony's College, Oxford).

coming were it not for the fact that the British Treasury had confidence in Glubb's house-keeping.

No sooner had H.M.G. shrugged off its responsibilities in Palestine than it took alarm at the fast deteriorating situation in the Middle East. This coincided with the rapid run-down of British forces which made it increasingly difficult to meet Britain's commitments in the region. As a first step the British intervened and halted the Israeli offensive against the Egyptian early in 1949, invoking for the purpose the Anglo-Egyptian Treaty which was already a dead letter and certainly now requested by Egypt. However it prevented an Israeli conquest of Sinai. Next, the British Commander-in-Chief in the Middle East (General Sir John Crocker) was instructed to report on the state of the Arab Legion, and whether it could, or would, take over some of the operational commitments previously carried out by British forces.

Crocker found that both King Abdullah and Glubb were anxious to expand the Arab Legion, but only if additional money could be provided by H.M.G. Crocker advised accordingly stipulating that the British element in the Legion should be considerably increased. This would ensure better organization and training, as well as make certain that the money provided for military purposes was not diverted into other channels. He recommended the formation of an Infantry Division, with all the necessary supporting arms. He particularly advised that a senior British officer should be appointed to command the 1st Arab Legion Division. Although General Crocker was impressed by Glubb Pasha, he did not feel the same about Lash, who lacked any kind of formal military training. When Crocker left the Middle East Command soon afterwards, his recommendations were endorsed by his successor, General Sir Brian Robertson, who had been a contemporary of Glubb's at the 'Shop', and who like Glubb had begun his military service in the Royal Engineers. He and Glubb struck up an immediate rapport.

The reorganization was to include the formation of three Infantry Brigades, each commanded by Brigadiers on loan from the British army. Five of the ten Infantry Battalions were to have British Commanding Officers, as would the three Artillery egiments and the Armoured Car Regiment. An Engineer Regiment would be formed, again under British command. The senior staff officers in the Arab Legion headquarters and headquarters of the Division were to be British, and Glubb would be provided with a senior British officer of Colonel's rank to act as his chief of staff. A Tank Regiment and a second Armoured Car Regiment would be raised and a start made in the formation of an Arab Legion Air Force under a Wing-Commander on loan from the R.A.F.

King Abdullah and Glubb did not agree to these recommendations without serious misgivings. It was clear that the influx of British officers would change the pattern in the Arab Legion. It had been easy until then to absorb a handful of British officers into an Arab army; their presence was hardly noticed. It would not be so easy when there were seventy or more of them, accompanied by their families. However, given the threat from Israel, the King and Glubb had little choice but to agree with the British terms. The Arab Legion could not hope to deal with its increased commitments on the West Bank unless it increased in strength and obtained modern equipment and supplies. Money had not only to be found for pay and equipment; barracks, workshops and stores had to be built, trucks, land-rovers and aircraft purchased, and vastly increased reserves of ammunition provided. Inevitably the subsidy had to be increased but there was never enough money to go round. It used to be a joke in the Arab Legion that if you needed a tooth extracted it was a mistake to wait until the end of the financial year when the hospital might well have run out of anaesthetics. Nevertheless it was amazing how much was achieved with so little. Glubb may have had to fight his financiers every inch of the way but he was an expert in making bricks without straw.

In an attempt to emphasize the fact that British officers owed the King of Jordan the same loyalty as his Arab officers, every officer was provided with the King's Commission, identical with that provided for Arab officers. This was in Arabic, signed by the King, and was intended to be hung prominently in the office of the officer concerned.

There was no difficulty in finding the soldiers as the Legion

started to expand. From 1950 onwards the army was Jordan'
principal industry. Finding the officers was a different story
When Peake formed the Arab Legion in 1921–2 he had found hi
officers from among the Arabs who had served in the Imperia
Ottoman Army, most of them aged between twenty and thirty
They were in their forties when war broke out in 1939, and th
majority of them were employed chiefly in police duties. Non
had been given higher military training. There was of cours
some expansion between 1939 and 1945, officers being pro
moted from the ranks or admitted as cadets, but most of those ir
the former category were handicapped by lack of education
When expansion really took off in 1950 there was a need fo
about 1000 officers, many of them for the technical arms like th
artillery and engineers. A knowledge of English was essential i
these officers were to benefit from training courses in Britain
there being no such facilities in Jordan at that time. This mean
that Glubb was forced to recruit more sophisticated young mer
than hitherto. The solid middle-aged bedouin who had joinec
the Desert Patrol as a *jundi* and had risen to lieutenant or captair
by sheer staying power could not be expected to compete witl
slide rules and logarithms at the School of Artillery in England
It followed that a very different type of Jordanian officer cam
onto the scene. They were high school educated, bilingual ir
English and Arabic, and some of them had met and marriec
British women when on courses in Britain. Not surprisingly
they were much more politically aware than the 'old sweats' o
the Desert Patrol. Many of them were posted to the technica
corps where the higher standards of education were needed
This was noted of course by the younger and more intelligen
bedouin officers who had no intention of being left behind in th
race; they too began to study English and adopt the ways of th
settled Arabs. Some of them married out of their tribes. The
entire character of the Jordanian officer corps changed during
the decade following the Second World War. It became more
sophisticated, in many ways more professional and much less
bedouin in background. Whether Glubb Pasha liked it or not,
the Arab officers in the Arab Legion could no longer be expected
to stay out of politics.

Glubb's aversion to politics may have originated in his experiences in 1927 when as Administrative Inspector of the Diwaniya Division in Iraq he found himself in conflict with his Arab superior. This left him, he wrote, 'with an intense aversion to party politics which so often tempt those who indulge in them to place the interests of their party before those of their country.'[3]

He had an almost pathological distaste for politics, and by extension for politicians. 'I would like to emphasize that I had nothing to do with politics,' he has written. 'I avoided any such subjects because I realized that I would in any case be blamed for them . . . The easiest thing is always to blame the British. Consequently I never opened my mouth about politics. I was most careful to be purely the army commander and to serve under the Minister of Defence, the Prime Minister and of course the King. Fortunately the politicians were completely ignorant of military affairs and took no interest in them whatsoever, so I had a completely free hand. You may remember also that the police were under the *qyada* and so I was Director of Public Security as well. The politicians were 100% office men and scarcely ever toured the districts and knew very little about the tribes or the country people.'[4]

Although there is no doubt of Glubb's sincerity in making that observation, it is somewhat naïve. It was impossible to hold a post such as his in an Arab country without becoming involved in some fashion in politics. However hard Glubb tried to avoid political issues, no educated Jordanian could be expected to believe him. He was after all dealing with government ministers almost every day and could expect to be blamed as much as they for real or fancied grievances.

Neither his Arab nor his British officers would have found it easy to believe that Glubb did not in fact possess the most delicately tuned political antennae. On the contrary they were full of admiration for his skill in steering a course through the political labyrinth. 'It is quite impossible to compare the life I led [in the Arab Legion] with that of the British army because politics played such a large part in one's actions and thoughts,' wrote

J. B. Glubb, *Arabian Adventures*, p. 171.   [4]Letter to author, 13 February 1980.

Colonel Desmond Goldie,[5] and if this were true of an ordinary
battalion commander, how much more so must it have been the
case with the army commander. Dr Albert Hourani, who greatly
admired Glubb, believed he understood politics much more
acutely than he chose to admit, even to himself, since otherwise
he could not have remained in his post for as long as he did.
Hourani considers Glubb to have been a very remarkable man
but believes he was temperamentally unable or unwilling to
understand the urban population and the intelligentsia. Indeed
so far as the latter were concerned, his lack of sympathy may
well have become dislike. Although Glubb was far too intelligent
to dismiss city-dwellers out of hand, he was much happier in the
society of bedouins and villagers.[6]

Hourani's view is to some extent supported by Brigadier
El-Edroos who said in his history of the Hashemite Arab Army

'The eventual pacification and the successful recruitment of
the Bedouin of Transjordan into the ranks of the Legion was
due solely to the personal efforts, leadership and diplomatic skill
of Major (later General) J. B. Glubb. The dash, offensive spirit
and élan displayed by the all-Bedouin Desert Mechanized
Force in the subsequent campaigns in Iraq and Syria in 1941
was a tribute to Glubb Pasha's prowess as a leader and commander of Bedouin troops. His later attempts to distinguish
between Bedouin and non-Bedouin (*Hadari*) personnel were
however, less than successful. In the opinion of Arab officers
they were quite unjustifiable . . . and suspect. One can fully
appreciate and sympathise with Glubb's genuine and sincere
loyalty towards the Bedouin, who, like the tribal Pathan, has
many manly and admirable qualities – including a delightful
sense of humour. But the cold, hard fact remains, that the
Turkish Army recruited Arabs from all over the empire and
employed them in all theatres of war with considerable success.'

This is, of course, perfectly true, apart from the fact that the
Turks did not recruit bedouins because they considered them to
be untrainable. Glubb was the first man to find an answer to

[5] Major H. D. B. Goldie, 'The Arab Legion', *Journal of the Royal Scots Fusiliers*
(1950), p. 31.   [6] Interview with Dr Hourani, 24 November 1980.
[7] S. A. El-Edroos, *The Hashemite Arab Army 1908–79*, pp. 213–14.

his problem and richly deserves the credit for it. Moreover, as
we have already seen, there were sound political reasons for
urning the bedouin regiments into some kind of praetorian
guard. Nevertheless both Hourani's and El-Edroos's observa-
ions have been to some extent confirmed by Glubb himself
when he wrote:

'The attitude of ministers and officials was inherited from
he Turkish official class. In the last years of the Ottoman
mpire, it was dominated by the desire to imitate Europe. Thus
officials and ministers in Jordan almost took a pride in not
understanding bedu language or the customs of the tribes (of
whom eighty per cent of the population consisted).'[8] Glubb
pecifically excluded King Abdullah from this criticism, point-
ng out that his early years in the Hejaz gave him an instinctive
ympathy for the tribes. Moreover, as a member of the Ottoman
Parliament before the First World War, Abdullah had acquired
much more comprehensive grasp of world affairs than any of
is ministers, such as Tawfiq Pasha abu al Huda.

Tawfiq Pasha was Jordan's longest-serving Prime Minister
nd Glubb worked closely with him for more than ten years.
Tawfiq was a super effendi if I can put it that way (these exist
even in England),' he wrote. 'He never went anywhere except
rom his house to his office and vice versa . . . He thought I
hould never leave my office as he never left his . . . Tawfiq
Pasha was a professional politician. He was normally effusively
riendly to me but I knew that behind my back he told everyone
hat I was to blame for most of the country's problems.'[9]

The interplay between the bedouin and non-bedouin element
n the Arab Legion was apparent to most of the British officers.
Those serving in bedouin units considered their soldiers to be
he most reliable, but those serving in *hadari* regiments were
qually convinced of their soldiers' martial qualities. There was
not at that time much disposition on the part of educated *hadari*
fficers to claim bedouin descent but it would be wrong to con-
lude from this that there was some kind of division between the
wo elements as there had been in the past. By 1950 the bedouins
were gradually becoming assimilated, losing in the process the

[8]Letter, 13 February 1980.   [9]Ibid.

characteristics they had brought with them from the deser

If, as Glubb Pasha has claimed, the years between 1939 an
1951 were indeed Jordan's 'Golden Age', it was most tragicall
brought to an end on Friday, 20 July 1951, when King Abdulla
was assassinated as he entered the Great Mosque in Jerusaler
for the noonday prayer. The King had a very special affectio
for Jerusalem and insisted on praying there regularly, althoug
he was warned on many occasions of the risks he ran among th
great crowds. Kirkbride pleaded with him not to visit Jerusaler
so often, to which Abdullah replied, 'My dear man, until m
times comes no one can harm me, and when it does come, n
one can guard me.'[10] Soon after the King's murder, Kirkbrid
applied for a transfer and was moved to Libya. The triumvirat
who had co-operated so successfully for so long had been broke
up. Glubb was left to battle on alone.

His relationship with the late King had been one of complet
trust and devoted loyalty. Abdullah was much the older man
with a greater understanding of world affairs than Glubb's. H
could be exacting, imperious and short-tempered at times, bu
invariably there would be a twinkle in the end. His ambition
extended far beyond the confines of his tiny kingdom, and alon
among the Arab leaders of that time Abdullah realized that th
Arabs would sooner or later have to reach an agreement with th
Jews, but as equals, not as suppliants. This, coupled with hi
long-standing feud with the ex-Mufti of Jerusalem, mad
Abdullah a marked man in the eyes of Arab extremists.

The King's death caused consternation in Amman. Th
government panicked and called out the troops. But in the even
nothing happened. It was established that the murder had bee
instigated by relatives of the ex-Mufti. Abdullah Tell, who wa
living in Cairo and working for Haj Ameen, was reputed to b
an accomplice. He denied this but was tried *in absentia*, foun
guilty on the evidence and sentenced to death. Five other con
spirators were found guilty and executed. According to Ann
Dearden, 'the evidence appeared conclusive and the passage o
years has cast no doubt on the trial'.[11] Abdullah Tell was late

[10]Sir Alec Kirkbride, *A Crackle of Thorns*, p. 165.
[11]Ann Dearden, *Jordan* (Robert Hale, 1958), pp. 93–5.

ardoned by King Husain and permitted to return to Jordan.

King Abdullah had been accompanied to Jerusalem by his eldest grandson, Husain bin Talal, to whom he was devoted. Husain was aged sixteen at the time of the assassination. A bullet aimed at the King hit the young prince but ricochetted off a metal bar on his tunic; that bar almost certainly saved his life. His calmness impressed everyone. His behaviour at his grandfather's funeral similarly impressed Lt-Col. P. F. Walsh, a senior staff officer at *Qyada* who had been responsible for many of the arrangements:

'By the graveside there were crowds of mourners, relatives, dignitaries, bedouins, palace attendants, the lot, all highly emotional and upset. The Amir Naif was visibly affected, in tears supported by an assistant by each arm. The one figure who remained calm and dignified throughout the proceedings was the young Husain who was, as you know, his grandfather's favourite. It struck me then that he was the ideal person to succeed ultimately the old Abdullah.'[12]

King Abdullah had two sons by different wives, Talal and Naif, both of whom stood in some awe of their strong-minded father. The eldest, Talal, was a man of great charm with a most attractive personality and a firm sense of duty, but unfortunately he suffered from ill-health which grew worse with the years. At the time of his father's murder Talal was undergoing treatment in Switzerland. Motivated by his sense of duty he at once returned to Jordan and ascended the throne. The stresses of high office, however, proved too much for him and he abdicated, in favour of his son, Husain, after only nine months. He then went to live in Turkey where he died in 1972. His abdication was the occasion for much sorrow in Jordan where he was deservedly popular, not least with Glubb Pasha, who was very fond of him.

Talal had married Zein, also a member of the Hashemite family. Her father, Shereef Jameel bin Nasser, had fought with distinction under Amir Feisal during the Arab Revolt. Queen Zein was a very beautiful and intelligent woman. Her brother, Shereef Nasser bin Jameel, was commissioned into the Iraq

[12]Letter to author, 7 March 1980.

army and later joined the Arab Legion in which he rose to become Commander-in-Chief in 1969–70, a particularly troublesome time in Jordan. He died some years after his retirement from the army.

Husain bin Talal was born in Amman on 14 November 1935. He was sent to school in Egypt, to Alexandria's Victoria College. That was followed by Harrow in his early teens, by which time it had been decided that he would attend an abbreviated course at Sandhurst after Harrow. He was at Sandhurst when called upon to succeed his father and was formally crowned King in November 1953, at the age of eighteen. Glubb had known him since he was a small boy and was very fond of him but there was a gap between the two men's ages which proved impossible to bridge. It should have been clear – perhaps it was to some – that the relationship Glubb had enjoyed with Abdullah, and which he might have enjoyed with Talal, could never be established with Husain.

It was inevitable that while the young King was trying to adjust to the unfamiliar world of government, into which he had been so unexpectedly thrown while still a schoolboy, Glubb's influence in the country became ever more marked. Ministers might come and go but 'The Pasha' seemed irremovable, a rock in the shifting political seas. He was credited with an authority he did not possess and blamed whenever things went wrong – as they frequently did in Jordan during those troublesome years. In the Arab Legion he was regarded as all-powerful, by Jordanians and British alike. Only Glubb knew the limitations of his powers and he did not choose to publish the facts abroad.

Despite political crises and the ever-worsening situation along the border with Israel, Glubb drove on with single-minded devotion to improve Jordan's defences. He had not the slightest doubt that the Israelis would seize the first opportunity to occupy all Jerusalem and advance their boundaries to the line of the River Jordan. Anything he could do to thwart such a plan must be done. His visits to the Foreign and War Offices in London were regarded with some apprehension by the officials concerned. The Pasha could be persuasive and was prepared to take on various operational tasks from the British army in the

Middle Eastern theatre, always provided that he was given the money to do this. There were certain attractions in such offers, British soldiers costing a great deal more than their Arab Legion equivalents, but there were political implications that sometimes made the deal less attractive in Whitehall than in Amman.

Glubb's working day began at 5 a.m. when he and his wife enjoyed a cup of tea. Seldom spending a full day in the office, he would usually visit a unit, attend a training exercise or visit the West Bank. There were official functions to attend, ministers to be briefed and the King to be waited upon. In Kirkbride's time the two men met regularly for an exchange of views; with his successors Glubb met less frequently. Often there would be long trips by land-rover into the desert, or bumpy flights by Arab Legion aircraft to Aqaba or Jerusalem. When he got back to the office there would be problems to be considered, papers to be signed and letters to be dictated. And always there would be a crowd of petitioners waiting patiently for a moment of *Abu Hunaik*'s time – to explain about the lost camel, or to ask for something to be done about cousin Feisal, or just to borrow a few dinars with which to buy food or medicines. They were long, long days, particularly wearing when the hot winds blew in summer.

Fridays are the Moslem Sabbath but the Pasha seldom missed church on Sundays. Whatever the pressures he would be there, reading the lesson at Matins or Evensong, occasionally taking the service in the tiny church out at Zerqa. His devoutness was well known and added to the respect in which he was held in a predominantly Moslem community. One American visitor to Amman found it difficult to understand why this should be so, forgetting that Arabs were among the earliest Christians. There were many Christian Arabs serving in the Arab Legion. However it was a bedouin camel-herd who, when discussing Glubb with the writer, described him as, 'A true servant of God'.

It was the situation along the border with Israel that took up most of Glubb's attention during the years of the Legion's expansion. Villagers who slipped across at night to pick a few melons growing in their former fields could hardly be blamed for doing this, but the Israelis never hesitated to fire on them.

There was also a flourishing smuggling trade. Israel was short of meat; Jordan was short of fish. Mutton for mullet was therefore a fair trade, and there were other goods as well. But much the most serious were the *fedayeen* raids organized by Egypt and other Arab states. These invariably resulted in severe reprisals by the Israel Defence Force, usually long after the actual culprits had returned to Cairo or Damascus. The government of Jordan discouraged such raids; not because it had any more cause than the other Arab governments to like Israel but because it would be Jordanian citizens who would suffer the consequences of Israel's retaliation.

The Arab Legion suffered from a distinct disadvantage when it came to dealing with Israeli border raids. The natural communications in Palestine had run along the coastal plain and up into the foothills. There were only rough tracks leading down from the mountainous Judaean massif towards the coastal plain and more often than not the Israelis had ample time to get clear away before the Arab Legion could arrive on the scene. Moreover the rugged terrain was particularly suitable for ambushes, especially at night. There were incidents almost every night and always the Pasha had to be informed. Sooner or later the officer in charge of a sector would hear his telephone ring, often at 4 a.m. or thereabouts. 'Is that you, so-and-so?' the reedy voice would inquire. 'Yes, sir.' 'Then can you tell me what is happening at such-and-such a village? We have picked up reports of an Israeli raid.' The explanation would follow, after which there was always a pause, as if for reflection at the other end. 'Thank you, sir,' the Pasha would say, 'I am sorry for troubling you.' One Arab officer was so impressed after the Pasha had telephoned at some unearthly hour for six or seven nights running that he concluded that Glubb could sleep on his feet, like a horse. It led to much discussion round the coffee-hearth.

As more and more British officers and their families arrived in Jordan, the Arab Legion changed beyond all recognition. A smart headquarters was built for the 1st Division at Khaw, near Zerqa, and a School of Artillery was established. The Training Centre at Abdile, outside Amman, was greatly extended, and plans for a Staff College were under active discussion. The tiny

Arab Legion Air Force was beginning to expand and there was talk of a new *qyada*. It was all 'go' in the Arab Legion between 1950 and 1954; new units raised, new barracks built. Throughout this period Glubb still endeavoured to keep his finger on the Legion's pulse, vetting all appointments and keeping an eye on those officers whose personal habits or political opinions had brought them uncomfortably to his notice.

Memories of those days recall to mind the Confidential Report system in use in the Arab Legion. These had to be compiled on every officer and soldier and comprised a five or six page booklet which listed every known military virtue and failing. On every page were columns marked Excellent, Good, Fair, Bad and Nil. The reporting officer was required to put an X against such abstruse questions as 'Give the extent of this man's belief in God,' or, even more difficult to answer, the extent of a man's interest in sex. In the case of the latter it was hard to know in which column the X should best be written, an 'Excellent' signifying either too great an indulgence or monastic abstinence. One never knew.

Such overseeing of every aspect of the soldier's life was of course perfectly possible in the Desert Patrol, and even later in the Desert Mechanized Brigade, but it became an impossible task once the Legion was 20,000 strong, even for a man like Glubb Pasha who positively enjoyed detail. At the height of the crisis of King Talal's abdication, he still found time to write to General Cooke about Dress Regulations. The Arab Legion was not a particularly dressy army but Glubb kept an eagle-eye on turn-out. One of the more tedious requirements was the wearing of collars and ties however hot the day. Rolled-up sleeves were equally frowned upon. Shorts were taboo and even today women tourists in Jordan are warned against wearing them.

King Abdullah was a stickler for protocol and woe betide the European woman who entered the royal presence short-sleeved and short-skirted. Europeans often forget that Arab etiquette requires the removal of shoes rather than headgear on entering a room. The British habit of walking about stripped to the waist, as the R.A.F. airmen did at the Amman air base, shocked many Jordanians to the core.

175

Glubb was probably one of the few genuine Arabists who did not consider it necessary to adopt Arab dress. Unlike T. E Lawrence, who attended the Peace Conference in Paris wearing Arab robes, or Harold Ingrams in the Hadhramaut who wore the *Futa* of South Arabia, Glubb's uniform was patterned on that of the British army. He wore, of course, the red and white checkered headcloth of the Arab Legion, known as *shamagh*; o. the red and blue forage cap, called *sidara*; but otherwise he wore a khaki tunic and trousers, always with a black Sam Browne bel and sword frog. He wore khaki serge in winter and khaki drill ir summer. He was not very impressive in uniform until one noticed his five rows of medal ribbons and realized that he had no need to draw attention to himself by the cut of his tunic. Of duty he always wore English clothes.

The border between Jordan and Israel was described by Glubb as the 'Frontier of Hate'. It was an apt description and each year it was worse than the last. He was fiercely criticized for the Arab Legion's apparent unwillingness to launch heavy raids into Israel, this supposed passivity being regarded as a tacit admission of Israeli superiority. But the problem was much more complicated than it might appear on the surface Glubb's sheet anchor was the Anglo–Jordanian Treaty by which Britain was pledged to come to Jordan's assistance if attacked However H.M.G. was chiefly concerned with damping down the fires along the border and therefore anything which might lead to a major battle was to be discouraged. The subsidy might be at risk if Jordan was labelled as the aggressor. For this reason the Arab Legion had to wait until it was attacked before it took offensive action.

The second reason for the Jordan government's policy was the vulnerability of the country to Israeli attack. Jordan's vital strategic centres on the West Bank lay within a few hours' march of Israel. The Arab Legion was not only out-numbered when compared with the Israel Defence Force; it was virtually naked when it came to air support. Control of the air was vital on the West Bank where the main communications passed through so many defiles. Israel had air superiority until such time as the Arab Legion Air Force could be properly equipped and trained.

t was essential therefore that Israel should not be provided
with any kind of excuse to launch a major incursion across the
Demarcation Line. It followed that any retaliatory raids carried
out by the Arab Legion had to be most carefully planned and
controlled. There were such raids but they never received the
publicity accorded to the Israelis and the *fedayeen*.

On the night of Wednesday, 14 October 1953, a border raid
took place that was to have far-reaching consequences. The
village of Qibya, a mile or more inside Jordan and about fifteen
miles from Ramalla, was the target for a particularly vicious
reprisal attack by the Israel Defence Force. The unit designated
for this raid was Special Unit 101, raised and commanded by
Major Ariel Sharon. At 9.30 p.m. the village was surrounded
and attacked, allegedly in revenge for a *fedayeen* raid on the
village of Tirat Yehuda on the previous night. Three Arab in-
filtrators were reported to have thrown a grenade through a
window, killing a woman and two children. This may have provided the pretext but the attack on Qibya was so carefully
planned and so ruthlessly executed that not even the Israel
Defence Force could have organized it in less than twenty-four
hours.

The National Guard in Qibya put up a stout fight but they
had run out of ammunition by midnight. The headquarters of
the Arab Legion 3rd Brigade at Ramallah was informed at 10.30
p.m., and the Brigadier ordered a rifle section of ten men from
the neighbouring village of Budrus to investigate. They became
involved with the Israeli covering troops and never reached
Qibya. Meanwhile the shelling and mortaring of Qibya and two
adjacent villages added to the confusion. Soon after midnight
the Israelis broke into Qibya, firing indiscriminately from the
hip as they charged through the dust and darkness. They then
proceeded to blow up the stone houses with explosives, burying
more than seventy women and children under the rubble. The
relief force from the Arab Legion arrived on the scene at dawn
to find only a few dazed survivors wandering around the
shattered village. It was a massacre on the scale of Deir Yasseen.
Nothing in Jordan would be quite the same again.

Chapter Twelve

The Slide Begins

'I do not see how the Pasha can long survive this'
[i.e. Qibya]

Entry in author's diary, 18 October 1953

THE QIBYA MASSACRE marked the watershed in Anglo–Jordanian
relations. Had the Israelis set out deliberately to wreck those
relations, they could hardly have planned it better. There was a
howl of rage and horror on both banks of the Jordan. The scape-
goats were the British officers of the Arab Legion, headed by
Glubb Pasha. The British commander on the West Bank,
Brigadier 'Teal' Ashton, was summarily dismissed; as was his
Arab subordinate, Lt-Col. Kamel Abdel Kader, whose 10th
Regiment included Qibya within its defensive sector. The 1st
Arab Legion Division was hastily deployed in the Jordan valley,
more as a demonstration than for any useful purpose, where it
languished in discomfort for several weeks. This smacked of
closing the stable door after the horse had bolted and as such was
commented on by certain Arab officers.[1]

Glubb Pasha took advantage of the concentration of so many
of his officers to address them at Shuneh, beside the Dead Sea,
on Sunday, 18 October 1953. This was in many ways a *tour de
force*. Speaking in alternate Arabic and English sentences without once losing the thread of his discourse, Glubb held the
attention of his audience for more than one hour. He described
the events at Qibya without attempting to put any gloss on them,
explaining the consequences for the Arab Legion. 3rd Brigade
was to be brought back to Zerqa from the West Bank; 1st and

[1]Comments made to the author by one of his bedouin officers.

nd Brigades were to replace it, the former based on Ramallah, the latter on Nablus. Ashton's dismissal was mentioned only in passing. This annoyed some British officers who felt that Ashton had been made the scapegoat for the whole sorry business although the commanding officer of 10th Regiment had shown little initiative. This British reaction shows only too clearly how blind they were to the political realities. At the end of Glubb's address the assembly dispersed in solemn mood, one senior Arab officer commenting that the way ahead was strewn with land mines.

Rioting broke out two days later in most of the principal towns on both the East and West Banks. Amman was the most seriously affected. There the 9th Infantry and 2nd Armoured Car regiments were moved into the town from Zerqa to support the civil police. There was a certain amount of stone-throwing and much abuse but no requirement for the soldiers to open fire. The most ominous feature of the riots was their anti-British tone, much of the abuse being directed against Glubb. 'Death to Glubb Pasha!' was a common cry.

Brigadier Ashton was also singled out for censure by the mobs, particularly on the West Bank. He was virtually unknown to most of the other British officers, as he had always lived a bachelor's existence at Ramallah close to his headquarters. Speaking excellent Arabic and favouring an Arab life-style, Ashton enjoyed an excellent rapport with his officers and soldiers, although some of the former thought he unduly favoured the bedouins. His interests were painting and shooting. On one occasion a visiting British general was received in Ashton's bedroom; he was sick at the time. The general found him lying on the floor wrapped in a blanket and surrounded by the remains of his breakfast. 'He looked like a gypsy,' said the general. Ashton could, indeed, be unconventional but no one could doubt his devotion to the Arabs and their cause in Palestine. It was sadly ironic that he should be the scapegoat for Qibya.

Some British officers felt he had received a raw deal and it was not until many years later that Glubb Pasha provided a convincing explanation for Ashton's dismissal:

179

'From the point of view of the politicians the way out of being blamed for Qibya was to make out that the British were responsible. They immediately decided to sack Teal (the Arab commander was also sacked). I had three alternatives. (1) To obey the orders of the government. (2) To resign myself. A great many people would have welcomed this. They were afraid to sack me lest the British cut off the subsidy, but if I had resigned H.M.G. could not blame them. (3) I could have refused to obey the orders of the government. They might then have justifiably asked H.M.G. to remove me. In any case the propaganda always stated that I obviously was not serving the Jordan government but H.M.G. who were doubtless giving me secret orders. If I had refused to obey, I should have put myself and H.M.G. apparently in the wrong. I had always been most scrupulous to behave towards the Jordan government exactly as I should have behaved towards H.M.G. if I had been serving them. As far as I can see I had no alternative but to carry out their orders [i.e. the Jordan government's].'

In an earlier but revealing paragraph in the same letter Glubb wrote, 'You ask why I had to sack Teal Ashton after Qibya. I find this an alarming question because it shows that you and probably no one can have any idea of my position. I remember Lash once complaining to me that he never knew what I was doing because I never told him or anyone else. So the fault is obviously mine.'[2]

Glubb is correct. He seldom communicated with his British officers, apart from a very few. Some of them felt he would have been happier without them which is undoubtedly true. Lt-Col. Walsh recalled an occasion when he attended a Queen's Birthday Reception in the British Embassy in Amman. It was very hot and crowded. 'I remember the Pasha saying to me near a window, "It was so much nicer when there were only four British officers in Amman!"'[3] Glubb himself wrote, 'Before 1948 I had only one or two British officers for many years. I found it easier that way and was perfectly happy.'[4] Few British officers met Glubb Pasha other than on official occasions, or at

[2]Letter to author, 14 February 1966.   [3]Letter to author, 7 March 1980.
[4]Letter to author, 14 November 1974.

180

he beginning and the end of their service in the Arab Legion. It is probable that those employed on contract by the Jordan government felt closer to him than the regular officers. Glubb Pasha preferred to leave it to General Cooke to deal with the atter.

If Ashton's dismissal left a sour taste in some British mouths, it did go part of the way towards allaying Arab criticism. The fact that there followed a slow but subtle change in Anglo–Jordanian relationships escaped the notice of most British officers. This was due partly to the commendable ability of the Arabs as a race to separate personal amities from wider political animosities, although there had not been much off-duty social intercourse between the British and Jordanian officers, as much as anything because Jordanian women did not, in those days, attend mixed parties. With few exceptions Jordanian social occasions were all-male, making them more formal than they would otherwise be. Although social relations were easy and friendly, few of the British succeeded in establishing close personal relations with their Jordanian colleagues. The language barrier was partly responsible for this. English was not used so freely in Jordan twenty-five years ago. The number of British officers who could conduct a conversation in depth in Arabic was small indeed and the same was true for Jordanian officers in the English language. This was even more the case when the women met each other at formal tea parties where kitchen Arabic on the one side and broken English on the other inhibited anything more than an exchange of civilities and trivialities. There was also an education barrier. Few Jordanian officers had enjoyed an equivalent education to the British; those who had mixed much more freely than the others. There was of course one element in Jordanian society which was well educated but it was made up of Palestinians who had come to Jordan as refugees. They were however regarded with a fair amount of suspicion as a possibly disruptive element. Only a few of them were taken into the Legion, and then on sufferance.

It also should be added that the marked difference in rates of pay created some kind of a barrier. This had not mattered when there were only a few British officers, but there were sixty or more of them serving in the Arab Legion by 1953. They received the same pay as they would have drawn in the British Army, supplemented by a generous secondment allowance. They were also provided with adequate accommodation. In order to stretch the subsidy to the utmost, Glubb tried to keep down the pay of the Jordanian officers, which in itself caused a difference in life-style. Moreover there was an acute shortage of accommodation for Jordanian officers. Glubb has since said that he received few complaints on this score but resentment did undoubtedly exist, perhaps not among the bedouin officers but certainly among the more sophisticated *hadari* ones.

All this is hindsight. None of it was easily apparent at the time. In Zerqa camp, the Legion's base, British officers and their families lived the typical garrison life of the army overseas - entertaining among themselves, playing games, shooting at Azraq, visiting Jerash and Petra, and spending their annual leaves in Cyprus where they were flown in Arab Legion aircraft. Jordanians were so charming and the life so pleasant that any possible resentment of the British presence that they encountered was almost entirely ignored; indeed it was taken for granted that the Jordanians enjoyed having the British in Jordan just as much as the British enjoyed being there. Unless they were informed to the contrary, there was no reason to suppose otherwise. It was certainly difficult to detect any change in the atmosphere.

Since Glubb Pasha relied almost entirely on General Cooke to deal with the British officers, the relationship between the two men is of particular significance. As Commander of the Legion's only Division, Cooke was in more ways than one Glubb's right-hand man. The Pasha has subsequently praised Cooke both in writing and in speech but it would be difficult to deduce from their correspondence that the two men were very close.

Major-General Sidney Arthur Cooke, always known as 'Sam', was something of an enigma. A tall and very handsome man, always immaculately dressed, he was a bachelor with a passion for gardening. Born in 1903, his father an officer before him, he was commissioned in 1924 from Sandhurst into the

Lincolnshire Regiment. He was a regimental officer *par excellence*, meticulous in his work, punctilious in his duties. He took part in Wingate's first Chindit operation in Burma in 1943 and received the O.B.E. for his services. In 1949 he was serving in the Canal Zone in Egypt when the British rushed a small force to Aqaba to forestall its capture by the Jews. Cooke commanded that force as a Brigadier. He was therefore known to Glubb when his name was proposed as Lash's relief by the Commander-in-Chief in the Middle East in 1950. Glubb accepted him and Cooke arrived in Jordan as a Brigadier, his promotion to Major-General being gazetted in September 1951. He was six years younger than Glubb and looked younger still.

Cooke's forte was organization and administration. Much of the credit for establishing the organization of the Arab Legion on sound modern lines must go to Cooke Pasha, as is freely admitted in the Jordanian Armed Forces today. But although he had survived with credit one of the most gruelling operations in the history of the British army, Cooke did not evince much interest in training or operational planning. He left this to Glubb and his senior staff officer at *Qyada*, and to the brigade and regimental commanders. How much of this was due to personal inclination, and how much to a wish to avoid any conflict with Glubb, is hard to say.

Cooke must often have wished that the same arrangements applied between the Pasha and himself. Glubb bombarded him with letters on almost every conceivable subject from the training of buglers to the preparation of a Staff College syllabus. The demi-official correspondence between the two men, conducted invariably in the most formal fashion without the use of first names, is revealing for two reasons. Firstly, for its volume: there were sometimes three or four letters in the same day. And secondly, as an example of Glubb's concern for detail. Nothing was beneath his notice, from adverse comments on the drill and turn-out of a regimental Quarter-Guard to the selection of an officer to attend a Signals Course in England. Glubb was still trying to command the Arab Legion, now more than 20,000 strong, in the same fashion as he had commanded the 300 men of the Desert Patrol.

One of Cooke's more difficult problems was Glubb's habit of suddenly posting an officer or soldier without any previous warning. This would result in protests from the man's commanding officer who might have had other plans for the individual so abruptly removed from his command. The Pasha's reason for the action may have been based on security but this was seldom explained to the indignant commanding officer. It then became Cooke's task to pour oil on the troubled waters, sometimes without knowing the full story. These arbitrary moves were something of an occupational hazard for unit commanders in the Arab Legion. One example of them involved Lt-Col. Kenneth Heisch very early in his service in Jordan:

'I had been told to find a Wakil (Warrant Officer) for the Training School. The Records Officer came up with a splendid recommendation – all the right qualifications – excellent man – now in Kerak – but immediately transferable. Many thanks – transfer him. A few days later came the familiar voice on the phone. "Oh, Heisch, come down and see me, will you." The Pasha then explained sorrowfully that it had taken him three months of careful diplomacy to remove a Wakil as far from Amman as possible, and now I had recalled him. Why? After due apologies I admitted that I had thought at the time that the Records Officer had been a bit over-effusive in his recommendation and should have been alerted. At this he smiled in a tired sort of way and told me to ask him first in future.'[5]

Then there was the case of Ali Sherif, interpreter. Ali, of Algerian descent, was a refugee from Jaffa where his family had once been prosperous. Now he lived in a Zerqa slum, his family huddled together in two rooms in a mud hut. Why should Ali have any love for the British? They had hanged his uncle in Haifa Jail during the rebellion in Palestine in 1937 and had since deprived Ali of his patrimony. Ali was well-bred, intelligent and educated; officer material, one would have thought. But he was only a warrant officer in the Legion and, as a Palestinian, suspect. Nevertheless his commanding officer thought well of him and sent his name forward for officer training.

A year passed without acknowledgement. Attempts to

[5]Letter to author, 17 January 1981.

184

obtain information were stonewalled. The commanding officer was about to leave Jordan, his tour with the Legion completed. A Jordanian friend gave a farewell dinner in his honour. There he was told that Ali had been arrested that afternoon. All inquiries drew a blank. Cooke Pasha was approached but without result; perhaps he did not try very hard. Eventually Coghill, Glubb's security adviser, was consulted. 'Ask no questions and you'll be told no lies,' was his immediate reaction, but the C.O. persisted. Coghill agreed to see him and disclosed the fact that Ali was a member of an extreme Islamic fundamentalist sect. Each member had a death-list. Prominent on Ali's were the names of his commanding officer and his commanding officer's wife.

Apparently he had been under surveillance for some time but nothing had been said to his commanding officer. Yet, as interpreter, Ali had seen virtually every document received at regimental headquarters. He was a regular visitor to his C.O.'s house where he had taught both him and his wife Arabic. They, too, had visited Ali's house. If it was true as alleged, surely it was unwise to employ him in such a sensitive appointment? Coghill shrugged his shoulders, 'You are probably right, but this is the Arab Legion.'

There was little General Cooke could do to prevent these arbitrary postings. Most British officers thought he was too weak to intervene but this was probably unfair. There was usually so much politics involved that Cooke simply had to accept the fact. He chose instead to immerse himself in administration and the study of Arabic. He even translated the British Army's manual, *Games and Sports in the Army*, into Arabic – a daunting task. If by this he had intended to teach Jordanians cricket, or to discourage the bedouins from cheating when taking part in a tug-of-war, he was to be disappointed. When two bedouin teams were pulling against each other it was necessary to surround the arena with barbed wire to discourage spectators from joining in.

Most of the Arab officers liked and admired Cooke Pasha. He was in their eyes much more 'the very image of a modern major-general' than Glubb Pasha, whom they regarded more as a father-figure. Some of the British officers, on the other hand, considered 'Sam' Cooke to be too much of a staff officer, out of his element when in the field, and they would have liked him to stand up more to Glubb Pasha. His own staff officers were very fond of him and did their best to shield him from Glubb's epistolary onslaught. One of them was to remark later that in his view Glubb was 'very jealous of surrendering anything of his power and influence to anybody . . .'[6] Certainly in this respect Cooke and Glubb fitted in well together; a more aggressive personality would inevitably have clashed with Glubb, who was determined to run the Arab Legion on the lines he believed right. After all he had had years of experience in dealing with the Arabs. One of Cooke's most valuable characteristics was his imperturbability, as was mentioned in his obituary. 'There was a dependability about Sam Cooke which was worth a great deal when the tensions were high.'[7] He died on 26 March 1977.

Cooke never made public his opinion of Glubb Pasha, but in private he always spoke of him with great affection. There can be no doubt that he greatly admired Glubb. Glubb, too, was fond of Cooke. They had come through a great deal together and it almost seemed in retirement that they were closer in spirit than when serving together in Jordan. Cooke became 'Sam' to Glubb, thereby having conferred on him almost the highest accolade in the Pasha's gift; although in Cooke's case Glubb always remained 'the Pasha'. In a curious way this exactly reflected the relationship that existed between the two men.[8]

Undismayed by the storm of protest following Qibya, and apparently unrepentant, the Israelis became increasingly aggressive along the Demarcation Line. They made no attempt to conceal their policy for dealing with cross-border raids. Retaliation was to be swift and stern. The United Nations Mixed Armistice Commission, set up expressly at Rhodes to deal with

---

[6]Unpublished diaries of Colonel J. B. Slade-Baker, Vol VII, 24 January 1956.
[7]*The Times*, 26 March 1977.
[8]Glubb Pasha found it difficult to adopt the modern fashion of addressing people by their first names. He often refers disparagingly to this practice in his correspondence. He had known the author for thirty years, but waited until he was in his sixties before writing to him as 'Dear James'!

border incidents, was boycotted by Israel. Moreover Israel refused to continue with the Local Commanders Agreement, which had been intended to decentralize the handling of local disputes by authorizing local commanders of both sides to meet and discuss the situation. From early in 1954 onwards relations between Israel and Jordan grew worse and worse. There was a nasty flare-up in Jerusalem from 1–4 July which could easily have escalated into something much worse had it not been very skilfully handled by the local Jordanian commander, Lt-Col. Peter Young and his 9th Infantry Regiment. There was, too, always the possibility that the Israelis would drive down the Jordan valley from the Sea of Galilee and cut Jordan in half. This led to the deployment of a small Jordanian force to act as a deterrent during the hottest months of the year when the 'going' was particularly suitable for the employment of armour, the Arab Legion possessing no tanks at that time.

Meanwhile, as a result of Qibya, the Arab Legion devoted much greater attention to the training of the National Guard. More experienced officers and N.C.O.s were seconded to the National Guard, each appointment being vetted by Glubb Pasha. He spent more and more time on the West Bank visiting National Guard posts and watching their training. There is a well-known Arabic proverb which reminds us that under the eye of the master the horse will grow fat. The knowledge that the Pasha was so interested in the National Guard, his brainchild in the first place, ensured that brigade and regimental commanders included the National Guard in their training exercises and made certain that their subordinates did the same. The result was a minor triumph on the night of 1 September 1954 when a major raid carried out by the Israelis on the village of Beit Liqya was successfully repulsed by the village's National Guard led by an Arab Legion N.C.O. It was unfortunate that the Arab Legion sub-unit, hastening to the scene of action, was ambushed by the Israelis, but it did however force them to withdraw. Israel was later condemned by the Mixed Armistice Commission for a flagrant breach of the Armistice Agreement.

The Arab Legion's ability to deal with these border incidents was greatly hampered by the lack of adequate intelligence.

Glubb has been criticized for his failure to establish an adequate intelligence organization and there is certainly some substance in this. Even his staunchest admirers believe more could have been done. There was virtually no intelligence during the first Arab–Israeli war and not much improvement thereafter. Compared with the Israelis it was hopelessly amateurish. One British officer, to be numbered among Glubb's most devoted supporters, considered that Glubb preferred to pick up information through gossip, as he had always done during those years in the desert, either from his Arab friends, or from selected individuals. There appeared to be little or no attempt to collate and evaluate the information, or if there was it was not apparent to unit commanders farther down the line. This contrasted markedly with the Israel Defence Force's Intelligence which was as good as any in the world.

The turmoil along the border during 1954 was reflected within Jordan itself. The problem and politics of Palestine dominated all discussion among educated Jordanians, and this included officers in the Arab Legion. Perhaps the bedouin officers were less affected but even they could not avoid becoming involved. On his inauguration the King had appointed a new Prime Minister, Fawzi al Mulqi. Fawzi had been a student at Liverpool University, where he had acquired very liberal views. He had been Ambassador in London when Husain was at Sandhurst and the two had become friendly. Fawzi was a strong believer in democratic institutions based on the British model, a view not shared by Glubb Pasha, who considered that political institutions which suited one country were not necessarily suited to another. Glubb in fact favoured King Abdullah's methods of government as being better suited to the people of Jordan.

Fawzi's progressive reforms went some way towards proving Glubb to be right. The Communist Party, although small in size, benefited from Fawzi's lifting of restrictions on the press. The newspapers were full of seditious propaganda, some of it directed against the throne. This frightened the conservative elements in the country and annoyed the King. Fawzi threatened to resign and the King took him at his word. The old war-horse,

Tawfiq Pasha, was called out of retirement to form a government. He was of course up to every kind of political trick and at once advised the King to dissolve parliament and call an election. Tawfiq then set about ensuring that only his candidates were elected on 16 October 1954.

He sent for Glubb and asked him to ensure that the army voted for his candidates. 'I protested against such a suggestion,' Glubb has written.[9] Eventually it was agreed that soldiers voting would be shown a list of candidates, the government's being quite clearly marked. This led to much criticism, even in bedouin units; in the 2nd Armoured Car Regiment, for example, a deputation of officers met with their commanding officer to make a solemn protest. It is doubtful whether Tawfiq's list had much effect on the voting; most of the bedouin soldiers were uninterested in politics in those days. Tawfiq might well have got his majority without resorting to such gerrymandering.

Nonetheless charges of rigging the election came as a godsend to his opponents and did Glubb's reputation an immense amount of harm. Anyone who knew Glubb would have known that skulduggery of this kind was anathema to him but inevitably he was tarred with Tawfiq's brush. 'The real ruler of the country is Glubb Pasha; people feel he is the real King and do not like it . . .'[10] was the comment of one educated Jordanian. There was serious rioting in Amman where for the first time Arab Legion soldiers and policemen had to open fire to disperse the mobs.

'During the thirty years from 1921 to 1951,' wrote Glubb, 'the stability had been due to the personality of King Abdullah; for three years after his death this tradition survived. From October, 1954, onwards, Jordan was to become just one more unstable, passionate, blood-stained Arab country.'[11]

The deteriorating political situation was not immediately apparent to Glubb's British officers. It was inconceivable that the Pasha would ever be dismissed. There was hardly ever any discussion about his possible successor. But General Cooke

[9] J. B. Glubb, *A Soldier with the Arabs*, p. 351.
[10] Unpublished diaries of Colonel J. B. Slade-Baker, Vol. VII, 10 December 1954.
[11] J. B. Glubb, *A Soldier with the Arabs*, pp. 365–77.

was due to retire in 1956 and there was much speculation about *his* successor. Glubb has since said that he intended to leave the selection to the War Office. Although the British officers could be charged with naïveté for failing to consider what was happening politically, it has to be said that British officers on the whole keep away from politics; their job was to command and train their soldiers and this they did with exemplary zeal.

It was however apparent to some officers that the Pasha was under attack, their enlightenment being due to the fact that their Arab officers had told them so. At the dress rehearsal for the annual Arab Legion Day Parade on 13 April 1955, an occasion when only Jordanian officers took an active part, Glubb Pasha reviewed the parade as was his custom, on a handsome Arab horse, cantering down the ranks to be greeted with loud and sustained cheers. One British officer gazing on this spectacle was moved to comment, 'Isn't it remarkable that the Pasha should evoke such loyalty!' He was not much impressed when his companion commented that all was not gold that glittered, and that many of those shouting *for* the Pasha might soon be shouting *against* him.

Matters were brought to a head by the ill-starred efforts of H.M.G. to persuade Jordan to join the Baghdad Pact. The Pact was essentially an attempt to thwart supposed Soviet ambitions in the Middle East. It had begun with a Treaty of mutual co-operation between Turkey and Iraq in February 1955. Britain joined the Pact in March, to be followed later by Pakistan and Iran. In view of her Treaty with Britain, Jordan's adherence would have seemed to be a natural development. When the President of Turkey, Mr Jellal Bayar, paid an official visit to Jordan in November 1955, the Baghdad Pact was among the subjects discussed. King Husain, with the threat from Israel in mind, wanted to expand the Arab Legion to form three Infantry and one Armoured Divisions. When he whispered this to his C.G.S. at the only official meeting attended by Glubb, the Pasha replied that it would be splendid, but where was the money to come from? The Turks were unforthcoming on this score but advised Jordan to approach Britain, with whom they were already allied by Treaty.

H.M.G. reacted promptly to Jordan's approaches. It offered ten Vampire airplanes as an outright gift. There was also an offer of a substantial amount of military equipment. Furthermore, were Jordan to join the Baghdad Pact, Britain would be willing to renegotiate the Anglo–Jordanian Treaty. As proof of its bonafides Britain was prepared to send as its plenipotentiary the Chief of the Imperial General Staff (General Sir Gerald Templer) who duly arrived in Amman on 6 December 1954 and remained until 14 December. Early in the discussions it was agreed that Britain would equip and maintain a considerable reinforcement to the Arab Legion, amounting in all to one Infantry and one Armoured Division. This pleased King Husain and his ministers but caused a tremendous outcry against the Pact in Jordan. Husain advised Templer to go home until the hue and cry had died down, and in the meantime appointed a new Prime Minister.

But things did not settle down. Gemal Abdul Nasser, President of Egypt, was opposed to the Baghdad Pact, chiefly because of Iraqi involvement and inspiration; he hated Nuri es Said, Iraq's Prime Minister. He also feared that the Pact might deflect the Arabs from their main aim; the overthrow of Israel. Nasser's extremely effective propaganda machine went into action and the money required to finance subversive activities was made freely available. Egypt's hostility to Israel, and the fact that Nasser had set himself up to be the leader of the Arabs in opposition to Israel, coupled with the extensive propaganda activities, swayed the judgement of many Jordanians. On 16 December 1955 rioting broke out on the streets of Amman and within hours had spread to every large town on both banks of the Jordan. It was reported that Nasser's agents distributed £6000 in the streets of Amman in one night to encourage rioters. According to Glubb the Egyptian Military Attaché was out in the city warning policemen not to disperse the rioters. 'If you lose your jobs,' he was alleged to have told them, 'the Egyptian government will pay you pensions enough to support your families.'[13] He was ordered out of the country some time later.

The rioting spread like a prairie fire, engulfing the main

[13] J. B. Glubb, *A Soldier with the Arabs*, p. 398.

towns and refugee camps. The Arab Legion was stretched almost to breaking point in its efforts to deal with the situation, sometimes for as much as ten or twelve hours a day for days on end. There was a sinister undertone to the riots quite new in Jordan. For the first time in its history the Arab Legion lost a British officer, killed while dispersing a mob outside Zerqa cantonment; he was Lt-Col. Pat Lloyd, commanding officer of the 4th Light Anti-Aircraft Artillery Regiment. The situation at one stage became so grave, and the Arab Legion was so exhausted, that King Husain seriously considered asking Iraq to help with troops.[14]

Throughout this trying period, which lasted until the end of January 1956, Glubb Pasha was constantly on call. He was also constantly under attack. Since he was considered by so many Jordanians to be all-powerful it was natural that he should be blamed for everything. Opposition politicians had been agitating for his departure for some time, 'not because they had anything against him personally (on the contrary they knew he had done a tremendous lot for Jordan), but because they felt that so long as he was there no Government would ever be free.'[15] Glubb was also fiercely criticized for employing British officers in the Arab Legion to quell the rioting. This was said to have created the worst possible impression among the people.

When law and order was once more restored, two things were certain. Firstly, Jordan's adherence to the Baghdad Pact was a dead letter. Secondly, Glubb Pasha's personal position had been seriously eroded – much more than was apparent to his British officers, perhaps more than was apparent to Glubb himself.

[14]Sir Anthony Eden, *Full Circle* (Cassell, 1960), p. 345.
[15]Unpublished diaries of Colonel J. B. Slade-Baker, Vol. V, 1 April 1955.

Chapter Thirteen

The Dismissal

'I should like you to be very clear that Glubb Pasha
gave to this country great and distinguished service.'

King Husain to the author, 10 January 1982

KING HUSAIN AND GLUBB PASHA are both born soldiers. They
love soldiering and all that goes with it. They are both very
brave men. To this day King Husain looks back on his time at
Sandhurst as almost the only period when he was free from care,
learning about the profession he loves. He differed very little
from the young Sapper subaltern who set out for France in
1915, his courage high and determined to do his duty. Glubb
has always claimed that he was first and foremost a soldier, and
the same might well be said of Husain bin Talal. Yet for all their
devotion to the military profession, they were often in conflict
between 1953 and 1956.

The King was being subjected to pressures that weighed all
the more heavily because of his youth and inexperience.
Nationalism was sweeping across the world and Jordan could
not be expected to escape the infection. The French and British
empires were fast falling apart. New leaders were emerging, like
Nasser, whose popularity was owed to their success in ridding
their countries of foreign domination. It was not easy to accept
that Jordan should be an exception. Most Jordanian officers
were nationalists, as most British officers would have been in
their place. The situation was further complicated in Jordan
by the threat from Israel and the presence in the country of
thousands of refugees whose homes and livelihoods had been

wrested from them. Britain was the country primarily responsible in Arab eyes for this state of affairs. It is surely not surprising that the British should be hated as a nation although many individuals were held as exceptions. The King was just as much affected by these sentiments as his officers. He shared their resentment that such a state of affairs should have ever come to pass.

He also felt deeply that he and his people were not masters of their own destiny. Jordan's dependence on British financial support saw to that. The expenditure of every pound provided in the subsidy was carefully scrutinized in London. The Arab Legion could not increase its establishment without first making out a case for doing so that satisfied the British Treasury and War Office. Whereas every other Arab country controlled its armed forces, in Jordan the British held all the key posts. They commanded the army, the artillery and the armoured corps. All the infantry brigades were commanded by them and half the infantry battalions. They commanded the air force, small though it was, and held all the senior technical appointments.

Glubb Pasha had, in fact, carefully prepared a plan for the replacement of British officers by Jordanian officers but it was based more upon British considerations than Jordanian. It was an honest plan and well-intentioned but it omitted to give sufficient weight to the political and psychological factors. Had the Pasha not been the man that he was, deeply respected by almost all Jordanians, the Anglo–Jordanian partnership must have been dissolved much sooner.

His every action since the Armistice with Israel in 1949 had been dictated by his conviction that sooner or later Israel would reopen hostilities at a time and place of her choosing. He knew the Israeli generals had not welcomed the Armistice, believing that the whole of Jerusalem was within their grasp; it was also common knowledge that in their eyes Israel's only defensible frontier must lie along the Jordan. Glubb knew far better than any Jordanian politician the strength and skills of the Israel Defence Force; without a massive injection of weapons, men and aircraft, the Arab Legion would be rapidly overwhelmed by sheer weight of numbers. He made plain his fears in a letter written eighteen years after his departure from Jordan:

'. . . after 1948 we were under constant threat of attack by an Israel ten times as strong as Jordan. The Jordanians did not realize this, and the politicians liked to say that we could have defeated Israel in 1948 if we had wanted to, but I refrained from doing so on orders from H.M.G. . . . I was acutely conscious that Israel might renew the war, that we could not possibly resist, and that our defeat would be attributed to British treachery. As a result my chief reliance was on retaining the Anglo–Jordanian Treaty, which I hoped would deter Israel from attacking us. Neither H.M.G. nor the Jordan Government talked much about the treaty, but it was my chief hope. I reckoned the Arab Legion might hold the Israeli army for three days, during which I hoped H.M.G. would do something.

'It was this constant fear of attack by Israel which dominated all my thinking. To put up enough resistance to enable Britain to intervene was our only hope, and to enable us to do that, maximum military efficiency was my object. Supposing we had cut down on British officers, that efficiency would have fallen and the Israelis could have walked over us in thirty-six hours, as they did in 1967. But as long as there were any British officers there, the politicians would have blamed them for the débacle. So the alternatives were 1. either to maintain maximum efficiency and hold on to Britain, or 2. for *all* British officers to go, so that we could not be blamed when the débacle came. The Jordan Government, by sacking all the British officers, chose the second course . . .' [i.e. in 1956].[1]

The reasoning is sound, the concern genuine. Glubb Pasha's love for Jordan and its people was at least as deep as his love for Britain. Nor was he questioning the ability of Jordanian officers to command battalions and brigades, provided they had the training and experience to do so. Some of the senior Jordanian officers were very good; some were not so good. The same is true in all armies. The trouble in Jordan was that there were so few experienced officers. By 1953 the Arab Legion had expanded in five years from 6000 to nearly 20,000. More than 1000 new

[1]Letter to author, 14 November 1974.

officers had had to be trained; many of them lacked education and relatively few of them possessed a sufficient knowledge of English to benefit from training courses in Britain. It is also important to remember that this expansion was taking place with the threat from Israel overhanging Jordan like a thunder cloud.

The majority of Jordanian officers were young and inexperienced. Jordan is a young country with 30% of its population under the age of thirty. Like young men everywhere they were full of ardour and high ideals. Glubb's view on the likely outcome of a war with Israel could not be expected to carry conviction with those who believed one Jordanian soldier to be equal to at least four Israelis. They were also convinced that at the first sign of Israeli aggression every other Arab country would rush to Jordan's aid. Nor do young officers in any army invariably agree that their senior officers know best; not infrequently they consider them to be out-of-date and lacking fire.

With hindsight it seems clear that Glubb seriously miscalculated the political effects of not hastening Jordanian officers to senior command appointments within the Arab Legion. Similar mistakes were made elsewhere during Britain's withdrawal from empire; in almost every instance the British moved too cautiously in training local officers to take over from them. The yardstick for promotion was efficiency and this was too often measured by comparison with the British officer's slow and stately progress up the promotion ladder in peacetime – so many years and so many training courses from subaltern to captain; so many more from captain to major, etc. Those who planned these programmes were high-minded men but they overlooked the fact that even in the British army junior officers were rapidly promoted in war. War demanded emergency measures, as did the gales of nationalism sweeping round the world.[2]

Glubb was on the horns of a dilemma. He was of course too

---

[2]The author's experience while serving in the Arab Legion convinced him that Arab officers had been promoted too slowly. Consequently, when he became Commander of the Federal Regular Army in Aden in 1961, he initiated a crash programme for Arabization, although he realized that this must affect the Force's efficiency for a time. By 1963 the force had its first Arab commanding officer and the British element had been reduced by nearly fifty per cent. Of course in Aden Israel was not a problem, but the Yemen always represented a potential threat.

shrewd not to see that there might be political dangers, but he feared an Israeli attack even more. If the Arab Legion were to withstand such an attack it would require its complement of British officers until such time as their Arab subordinates possessed sufficient experience to take over from them; in Glubb's view this was to be measured in years rather than months. A less honest man might have attempted to fudge the issue but Glubb preferred to rely on reasoned argument. The King and his friends and advisers heard him out politely, but when emotion prevails, reason takes a back seat. They could not accept Glubb's conclusions. To some extent they were prisoners of their own, and Nasser's, propaganda, which was demonstrated all too clearly during the war with Israel in 1967.

The tragedy was that Glubb was truly devoted to the young King whom he had known all his life. His relations with King Abdullah had been as close as it is possible for them to be between monarch and servant. He had been very fond of the unhappy King Talal whom he has described as 'a perfect gentleman'. He wanted to achieve the same relationship with King Husain but the task was an impossible one. The difference in ages and outlook created an insoluble problem. From 1953 onwards the King and Glubb were frequently at loggerheads despite every attempt by both sides to reach agreement. Glubb was fifty-eight and the King barely twenty, but Husain never permitted his impatience to affect his courtesy; he must be one of the best-mannered men in the world. Glubb has attributed their differences partly to that age gap, and partly to the influence on King Husain of a small group of young officers constantly gathered around him. The strength of Glubb's fondness is clear from a passage in *A Soldier with the Arabs* in which he describes the King's negotiations with General Templer over the Baghdad Pact:

'I felt a deep affection for the young King, so courageous, so entirely deprived of disinterested advisers and plunged in such a vortex of intrigue, falsehood and power politics. It occurred to me that, if he could survive until he reached forty-five years old, he might well become another King Abdullah. For King Husain's grandfather had also been headstrong and impetuous

in his youth; it was only when his hot-headedness became
cooled with age that he became a great ruler.'[3]

Hope for the future, however, could not alleviate the situation at the time. The King was understandably unsure of himself and shy when dealing with his grandfather's trusted adviser
and friend. He had all the Hashemite charm but he also had a
will of his own. It could not have been easy for him to discuss
strategy and military organization with a general who had won
his spurs in the First World War. It was virtually impossible for
there to be a meeting of minds, particularly since the King
believed that Glubb's influence extended far beyond the Arab
Legion (as indeed it did). Glubb complained that the King blew
hot and cold, and that he never knew what precisely he had
in mind. A diary entry in May 1954 reveals something of the
conflict:

'I was told today by a senior staff officer at *Qyada* that the
King is angry with the Pasha and that they have frequent arguments.'[4] The senior staff officer was Kenneth Heisch who as
Assistant Adjutant-General was in a position to know the facts;
he was also intimately involved in the plans for Arabization.

Glubb Pasha's account of the events that followed suggests
that the conspiracy for his dismissal was restricted to a handful
of young officers under the leadership of Lt-Col. Ali abu Nuwar.
Ali owed his rapid promotion to his friendship with the King
whom he had come to know while serving as Jordanian Military
Attaché in Paris. Husain had visited Paris on his leaves from
Sandhurst and Ali had been his guide. Glubb knew that Ali,
intelligent, well educated and sophisticated, was ambitious and
deeply involved politically. That was why Glubb had posted
him to Paris to keep him out of harm's way. But on Husain's
return from Sandhurst he had insisted on appointing Ali as
one of his A.D.C.s and ordered his promotion out of his normal
turn. Glubb had protested but deemed it politic to comply.

The names of Ali abu Nuwar and his confederates first
came to notice after the circulation of a subversive pamphlet
early in 1956. This had been prepared and circulated under
Egyptian arrangements but purported to emanate from the

[3] J. B. Glubb, *A Soldier with the Arabs*, p. 396.   [4] Author's diary.

Jordanian 'Young Officers Movement'. Nasser had his own reasons for wishing to get rid of the British in Jordan and Egyptian funds were made freely available for that purpose. The Egyptian Military Attaché in Amman, an agreeable character, was the paymaster for the pamphlet. Glubb gave the names of Ali abu Nuwar and several other officers to the King with the warning that they were actively disloyal, but the King disputed this, and stated that they might be misguided but were at heart true Arab patriots.

The 'Young Officers Movement' had been in existence for several years, possibly as far back as King Abdullah's time. Lt-Col. Peter Young, the C.O. of 9th Infantry Regiment, has said he knew of it in 1954.[5] His was a bedouin unit and he appears to have assumed that the Movement was confined to the better-educated officers of the Artillery and Engineers. But there were in fact bedouin officers involved in the Movement, at least one of them among the guiding spirits. The name of another was reported to General Cooke in 1954 but no action was taken.[6] It now appears that the 'Young Officers Movement' was much more widespread than was thought at the time.

Contrary to the opinion widely held by Jordanians and British alike, Glubb did not have informers in every unit. He did not believe there was any need for them. He kept open house in Amman where officers and soldiers could drop in whenever they chose, regardless of rank, to exchange gossip or submit a petition. This was the tradition of the desert and the Pasha was acting in the same way as every bedouin sheikh. Not surprisingly, bedouin officers and soldiers predominated at these coffee and tea drinking sessions. The late Sir Patrick Coghill was the Pasha's security adviser but he does not appear to have been very close to him.[7] It was sometimes said that Glubb's closest confidant was Coghill's deputy, Colonel Abdur Rahman

[5]Peter Young, *Bedouin Command* (Kimber, 1956), p. 174. It was also known as the Free Officers Association.
[6]It was not until the author was researching for this book in Glubb's papers that he learned the officer in question had been under suspicion since 1950. From the Shammar tribe in Nejd, he was one of his best officers, invariably selected whenever a special task was required. No one had seen fit to warn the author about him. He spoke quite freely about politics. Unusually for a bedouin officer he was unmarried.
[7]From letter to author, November 1980, written shortly before Coghill's death.

es Sahan, who was an Iraqi from Zubair, a market town on the edge of the desert. He had joined the Desert Patrol in the early days. His cousin, Khalid, was the first Jordanian to command a bedouin unit – the 2nd Infantry Regiment – which he did in a fine swashbuckling style.

Glubb certainly knew a great deal more than he chose to reveal but even so his Intelligence does not seem to have been very efficient. Spies were employed across the Demarcation Line in Israel but they were not much use. Certainly very little information was disseminated regarding the 'Young Officers Movement', most of whose members felt that it was time for Glubb to go, as well as for the replacement by Jordanians of British officers in an executive capacity. Whether the British were good, bad or indifferent, they constituted an affront to the dignity of their Jordanian comrades in the eyes of other Arabs. It was as simple as that.

In a review of Peter Young's book, *Bedouin Command*, published in 1956, the *Daily Telegraph*'s military correspondent, General H. G. Martin, criticized the failure of British Intelligence to foretell Glubb's dismissal:

'It was not until 1954 that Colonel Young himself first heard of the Young Officers Movement, and then only by chance. It was by chance also that in January last [1956] he happened to see a highly-subversive pamphlet entitled "Pamphlet No. 36 issued by the Arab Legion Liberal Officers Rally". Pamphlets Nos. 1 to 35 appear to have passed unnoticed by our Intelligence. Finally, all of the Legion's sixty-four British officers, from General Glubb downwards, appear to have been taken unawares by the events of March 1 [1956]. An Intelligence system that could not keep those on the spot better informed may well have given Whitehall a highly-misleading picture.'[8]

There is some substance in this criticism. Several journalists visiting Amman commented on the slide in the Pasha's popularity and presumably their views were noted. But it has to be remembered that Glubb was still enormously respected by the vast majority of Jordanians, even by those who, like the King, felt he ought to retire. Moreover, Arabs make good conspirators,

[8]*Daily Telegraph*, 1956.

as the Turks discovered when they ruled the Arab world. There was also a slight improvement in the political situation immediately after the riots had been suppressed. This was due to the fact that the raids carried out by the Arab Legion on the refugee camps in the Jordan valley had led to the seizure of documents which disclosed that it was not only Glubb Pasha and the British officers who were under attack; the throne itself might be in danger.

The riots were suppressed with a heavy hand but they kept on breaking out afresh, particularly on the West Bank. The 3rd Artillery Regiment, a *hadari* unit, was particularly effective in dealing with rioters in the refugee camps near Jericho. It was commanded by Lt-Col. Jack Tyrrell, a very robust officer. Late in January a special Task Force was formed, Special Force 3, to deal specifically with the rioting in the refugee camps in the Jordan valley and Hebron. Its commander was Colonel Sadiq Shara, a very competent officer, whose troops were the 1st Armoured Car and 9th Infantry Regiments. Both their commanding officers, Lt-Cols Rea Leakey and Peter Young, had very distinguished war records. These were bedouin units that stood no nonsense from the rioters. During the course of these operations, which lasted for nearly two weeks, Sadiq disclosed to Leakey and Young that his sympathies lay with those officers who wanted Glubb to go. He made it plain that in his opinion Jordanian officers were fully competent to take over from the British as brigade and battalion commanders. He also thought Arabization was coming about too slowly. Leakey was sufficiently impressed to report the matter to Jim Hutton, Glubb's chief of staff, on his return to Zerqa, but nothing came of it.

Sadiq's military competence and connections with the 'Free Officers' ensured his rapid promotion to Major-General after the British had left. In 1958, during the short-lived union of Jordan with Iraq, Sadiq was Chief of the Joint Staffs in Baghdad. When Qasim and Aref led the brutal revolution there on 14 July 1958, Sadiq was arrested and sentenced to death. He was lucky to be released some days later. In 1959, when Sadiq was Deputy Chief of Staff in Amman, a Jordanian brigadier, also named Qasim, attempted a military coup which failed. At the time

Sadiq was accompanying King Husain on an official visit to Washington. As the King well knew, Sadiq was implicated in the plot. He was arrested and tried and sentenced to death on his return to Jordan. He spent several uncomfortable months in the death cell until released and pardoned by the King, who re-employed him after a decent interval. In 1977 Sadiq was Jordan's Foreign Minister.[9]

It is hard to explain why, in view of the rapidly deteriorating situation, British officers by and large seem to have been oblivious to the threat to the Pasha's position. Lord Trevelyan records that a British journalist visiting him in Cairo after covering the riots in Jordan told him that Glubb would not last another three months.[10] Much the same view was reached by the British Military Attaché in Baghdad who visited Jordan on his way to Beirut and was so disturbed that he wrote a lengthy report. It seems to have made little impact on the War Office. Glubb's own attitude was very much one of 'business as usual' although he was greatly concerned by the violence. When the axe did fall, everyone was taken by surprise. One event that certainly contributed to Glubb's downfall was the briefing he had given the King some weeks previously.

With the intention of interesting the King in operational planning, Glubb had suggested he should be given a top secret briefing on war plans. Since security was all-important, Glubb had proposed that the audience be restricted to the King, Prime Minister and Ministers of Finance and Defence. He was there-fore considerably nonplussed when the King appeared with his A.D.C.s and several court officials. However he continued with the briefing. Afterwards the King jumped to his feet, pulled a piece of paper from his pocket and angrily denounced the plans he had just heard. 'I do not agree with any of the plans we have heard,' he said. 'I will never surrender one hand's-breadth of my country. The army will defend the demarcation line. Then we shall attack. I will sanction no withdrawal.' There was loud applause from his audience, after which the King went on to

[9] Sadiq was a friend of the author's. They spent several very hot and uncomfortable months in the Jordan valley in 1954 guarding against an Israeli armoured attack, Sadiq commanding 8th Infantry, and the author 2nd Armoured Car, regiments.
[10] Humphrey Trevelyan, *The Middle East in Revolution* (Macmillan, 1970), p. 65.

omplain about the system for promotions, the building of a
ew headquarters and several other matters. 'Finally,' he said,
we are grateful to the Chief of the General Staff for all the work
he has done, but I think now it is time for him to enjoy a rest.'[11]

Glubb withdrew with the ministers, all of them dumb-
ounded. A few days later Glubb had an audience with the King
and offered to explain the various points he had raised. The
King smilingly brushed it all aside, saying they were of small
mportance. It is clear, however, that the King had intended his
emarks to be taken quite literally since, after Glubb's dismissal,
he told Slade-Baker:

'We hoped that General Glubb would retire honourably and
n a manner which would not hurt his feelings, especially after
all his good work. Nothing happened.'[12]

Possibly something would have happened had the King
ressed the point, but instead, according to Glubb, he was twice
eassured by the King when he offered to resign. By then the
King was deeply involved in the Baghdad Pact negotiations,
which were closely followed by the riots, and the opportunity
or Glubb Pasha to fade quietly out had passed. It is a sign of
King Husain's magnanimity that after Jordan's defeat in 1967,
when the army did take the offensive under extremely adverse
onditions, he asked Glubb to call on him in London and admitted that Glubb's plan had been the right one. But by then
King Husain was ten years older and wiser.

Since Glubb Pasha would have resigned without demur had
he matter been pressed, there must have been a reason why he
did not do so. Perhaps it was the Prime Minister's assurance that
hese were just the changing moods of any young man, or the
oyalty he felt for Jordan, that led him to hang on. He denies that
H.M.G. ever put any pressure on him to stay. On the contrary
he was told on several occasions that, although H.M.G. hoped
he would stay on, not a finger would be lifted to support him if
he Jordanians did get rid of him. Sir Geoffrey Furlonge, British
Ambassador from 1952–4, believes Glubb would have been wise
o leave earlier. He thought he had lost his touch with the Arab

[11]J. B. Glubb, *A Soldier with the Arabs*, p. 366.
[12]Unpublished diaries of Colonel J. B. Slade-Baker, Vol. VII, 6 March 1956.

officers; he says he advised the Foreign Office to this effect bu
a suitable successor presented a problem. Dr Albert Houran
agrees with Furlonge. He thought Glubb should have left afte
the war with Israel in 1949; from then on the Pasha's influenc
perceptibly declined. King Husain has said that he warned th
Foreign Office on several occasions that he was losing patienc
with his C.G.S. And yet, when the moment of truth arrived, th
Foreign Office seems to have been taken by surprise!

King Husain has given several reasons for his decision to dis
miss Glubb Pasha.[13] Firstly, he thought Glubb was too old an
out-of-touch with military developments. Secondly, he did nc
agree with the plans for the defence of the West Bank. Thirdly
he was very dissatisfied with the stocks of artillery ammunitio
and exasperated by Glubb's inability to extract more supplie
and equipment from the British; since this must have meant a
increase in the subsidy, Glubb can hardly be held to blame
Fourthly, the programme for the replacement of British officer
by Jordanians was taking far too long. Fifthly, the King resente
the fact that Glubb kept promotions in the army and police i
his own hands. He was particularly annoyed when Glubb re
instated the officer dismissed after Qibya without authority fron
anyone.

It is also clear that the King thought Glubb Pasha had al
together too much influence in the country. Indeed, Glub
Pasha himself believed that the most immediate cause for hi
dismissal was an article published in *Picture Post*, claimin
Glubb to be the 'uncrowned king of Jordan', though Kin
Husain has denied this. He was willing to concede that Glubb
did his best to stay out of politics but his prestige was such that h
was dragged in willy-nilly. The final showdown appears to hav
been caused by the Prime Minister's reluctance to accede to th
King's demand that the police should be removed from Glubb'
control; and by the presentation to the King by Glubb of a lis
of officers for dismissal on political grounds. 'Their only fault
as far as I could see,' says the King, 'was that they were national
ists and ambitious.'[14]

What the young King did not know – how could he? – wa

[13]King Husain, *Uneasy lies the Head* (Heinemann, 1978), pp. 107–25.   [14]Ibid

hat the ambitions of some of his advisers and confidants
hreatened the very throne. There were many Palestinians in
ordan who were followers of the ex-Mufti, arch-enemy of the
Iashemites. There was also Egypt in the wings, ready and
villing to subvert anyone prepared to further Nasser's ambitions
or his country. Syria, too, had no love for Jordan or its royal
amily.

Once the King had made up his mind, he acted with all the
ingle-mindedness and ruthlessness of youth. If the deed were
o be done, it were best done swiftly. He could see no advantage
o be gained from delaying what was certain to be hurtful. In any
ase he was anxious to avoid any trouble in the Arab Legion. As
t turned out, the hurt was the more because it was so unexpected.
The story is best told perhaps by Glubb:

'On the morning of 1 March, I spoke to the officers of the
1st Armoured Car Regiment. I left Zerqa at 11.30 a.m. to return
o my office. As we drove through Amman and passed the
'rime Minister's office, I noticed the King's car and escort out-
ide the building.

' "There must be a meeting of the Council of Ministers," I
aid casually to an officer with me. "I see our lord's car outside
he Prime Minister's office."

'I went to my office and started to work on the papers on my
able. Officers came in and out. Then the telephone rang. The
Minister of Defence was speaking.

' "Could you come down to the Prime Minister's office for
minute?" he said.

' "Certainly," I answered. "Do you want me now?"

' "Yes," he said, "please come now."

'I got into my car and drove to the white stone building of
he Prime Minister's office. I was shown into his private room.
There was no one there.

' "His Excellency is in conference with the Council of
Ministers," said the orderly.

'A few minutes later the door opened and Sameer Pasha,
he Prime Minister, entered, followed by Felah Pasha Medadha,
stout jovial party and rather a friend of mine. Sameer Pasha
eemed nervous.

' "It is very sad for me to have to say this to you," he began. "His Majesty came here this morning and he said that he thinks that it is time you had a rest."

'I realized, of course, the meaning of this tactful approach.

' "Has anything happened?" I enquired. "What is the reason?"

' "I don't know anything about it," said the Prime Minister, obviously relieved that I seemed to be taking it calmly. "The King asked me to summon the Cabinet this morning. When the ministers arrived, he walked into the room and said you were to be dismissed. 'These are my orders. I want them executed at once,' he said. I hope you are not upset," Sameer Pasha added.

' "You need not worry about me," I said. "I will not intrigue or make trouble. I have lived most of my life in Jordan. I shall never create difficulties for her or the King."

' "I daresay it's only a temporary phase," said Sameer Pasha. "Perhaps in a few days we'll be welcoming you back. I've been Prime Minister several times, then I've been dismissed, and now I'm back again."

' "That may apply to politicians," I said, smiling, "but I don't think it can apply to me."

' "Perhaps you think I should resign sooner than agree," continued the Prime Minister. "I had thought of that, but if I did so, the King could easily find another Prime Minister who would be willing to carry out his orders. So it would not help you if I did so."

'It occurred to me that some people resign in protest at what they consider unjust, even though obviously someone else will succeed them.

' "I would not suggest what course your Excellency should follow," I replied.

'I felt no particular emotion. When something suddenly happens to change one's life, one cannot realize it at once. There was a box of cigarettes on the table. I took one and lit it.

' "To whom do you want me to hand over, and when do you want me to go?" I asked.

' "Can you leave in two hours?" enquired the Prime Minister.

206

'"No, Sir!" I said with emphasis. "I cannot! I have lived here for twenty-six years. Almost all my worldly possessions are here, to say nothing of my wife and children."

'"You could go and leave your family behind," he hazarded.

'"I'm afraid I can't do that either," I said.

'Eventually we agreed that I would leave at seven o'clock the next morning. We rose and moved to the door. The two Ministers shook hands with me; I had worked with them both, on and off, for twenty years or more.

'I went back to my office. I collected a few personal things. The heap of files on my table had grown taller while I was out.

'"You can lock up," I said to my orderly. "I shan't be coming back."

'When I got home, my wife was in the drawing room. As I came in, she jumped up smiling.

'"Hullo!" she said. "How nice! You're back earlier than usual. Were things slack today at the office?"

'"My dear," I said, "the King has dismissed me. We leave Jordan at seven o'clock tomorrow morning – and we shall never come back."'[15]

There was only a handful of people at the airport next morning to bid them farewell. Many were in tears. The British Ambassador, Mr Charles Duke, was there, together with the Minister of Defence and the King's Chamberlain. The latter handed the Pasha a signed portrait of the King across which he had written in his own hand:

'With our acknowledgement of the good services and untiring exertions and with our best wishes for His Excellency General Glubb Pasha. 1/3/56. Husain Talal.'[16]

The aircraft took off a few minutes later. With scarcely more ceremony than that which had greeted him on his arrival in the country twenty-six years before, the man whom a former Prime Minister of Jordan had described as a 'founder member of this kingdom' disappeared into the skies. Behind him he left a host of friends – but he has never returned.

On more than one occasion since then Glubb Pasha has laid much of the blame for his dismissal at President Nasser's door.

[15] J. B. Glubb, *A Soldier with the Arabs*, pp. 422–4.   [16] Ibid., p. 428.

He believed Nasser wanted to get rid of him in order to clear the way for Jordan to become an Egyptian satellite, but this seems unlikely. Nasser was essentially a pragmatist. He took advantage of situations rather than created them for his own purpose. In any case the King hotly denied that he had been subjected to Egyptian pressure. 'It is absolutely untrue,' he said. 'No pressure has been brought to bear by any country. On the contrary I do not want to accept financial assistance from Egypt or from any country as a replacement of the British subsidy. We are perfectly satisfied with our old relations with Great Britain and we want them to continue and improve.'[17]

Very soon after Glubb's departure Sir Alec Kirkbride arrived in Jordan in a purely personal capacity. He was to open an archaeological museum in Jerusalem. Sir Anthony Nutting has this to say of the visit:

'Kirkbride duly went, and on his arrival in Amman was overwhelmed with greetings. In the town he met a demonstration with banners and slogans, proclaiming *Death to the Imperialists* and *Down with British Interference*. He had not gone more than a few yards when he was recognized and a crowd surrounded him, calling him their long-lost friend and bidding him welcome back to Jordan . . . At the Royal Palace it was the same. The palace staff ran to shake his hand as he climbed the palace steps to the entrance. And inside, the King, quite beside himself with joy and relief at seeing Kirkbride, poured out his heart to this lifelong friend of his family. As he talked his pent-up indignation against Glubb came tumbling out. He could not, he said, have tolerated the General for another day; he had been patronized for too long and he was sick and tired of it. He could never be master in his own house so long as Glubb commanded the Army; and once he had made up his mind to get rid of him what was the sense in delaying? For Glubb to have stayed under an extended period of notice would have been to invite trouble in the Army.'[18]

This was reported by Kirkbride to Eden on his return to London. Nutting was present at the interview. Although Eden

[17]Unpublished diaries of Colonel J. B. Slade-Baker, Vol. VII, 6 March 1956.
[18]Anthony Nutting, *No End of a Lesson* (Constable, 1967), p. 31.

was loath to accept that Husain had acted on his own initiative, he had to face the facts. Nevertheless he continued to maintain that somehow or other Nasser did have a hand in it.

But all the evidence goes to show that the King acted of his own accord. He may have consulted with some of his intimate friends but the final decision was surely his. Twenty-six years later his Commander-in-Chief, at that time one of his A.D.C.s, confirmed this. 'His Majesty was still very young and it required great courage,' said General Zeid bin Shakir, adding, 'He did not sleep at all the night before he dismissed Glubb Pasha.'[19]

[19] Interview, 4 January 1982.

Chapter Fourteen

A State of Shock

'It was like losing a father.'

Comment made by
an elderly bedouin friend, January 1982

GLUBB PASHA HAD LEFT BEHIND HIM a country torn by conflicting
emotions. The Palestinian refugees took to the streets in their
thousands, singing and dancing to celebrate his dismissal; they
needed a scapegoat to account for their misfortunes and the
Pasha would do as well as anyone. The majority of Jordanians
were more surprised than anything else; it marked the end of an
era, rather as people felt on the death of Queen Victoria. Some
of the bedouin officers in the Arab Legion rattled their sabres
recognizing that in the Pasha's departure they had lost a powerful patron. But Glubb had made it clear to General Cooke that
he wanted no blood spilt on his behalf; everyone was to carry on
as normal. It was not the least of the many services he rendered
Jordan.

In a statement by King Husain which was read to the
National Assembly by its president, Ibrahim Pasha, the King
said it was his wish that 'General Cooke should retain his command and that the British officers should participate in training
the Army and continue on his staff as advisers.' However there
was to be no question of British officers continuing to hold
executive appointments; plans had already been carefully drawn
up for their supersession. Brigadier Raadi Ennab, Glubb's
deputy in charge of administration, was promoted to Major-
General and appointed Chief of the General Staff. He had begun
his service in the Turkish army, joining the Arab Legion in

921; ever since then he had been employed in police duties or dministration. He lasted only three months before Ali abu Nuwar took over from him. Ali had risen from Major to Major-General in less than four years. This was not calculated to endear him to the many able officers he had passed over in the course of his meteoric rise. Some British officers were relieved of their commands within days, others within weeks. Lists had been prepared for their replacement. Those who had been prominent in suppressing the riots were the first to go. Although the atmosphere remained tense for some time, there were few cases of deliberate rudeness and several British officers were 'dined-out' by their regiments. Those who were retained were formed into a Training Mission under a British commander. However their stay was brief. In October, after the Anglo–French landings at Port Said, they were packed off home.

Glubb's dismissal came as a shock to many governments. He had been in Jordan for so long as to seem a fixture and his influence was generally regarded as being for the good. The reaction in Britain was much more violent, even hysterical in some quarters, leading Glubb, on his return, to write a letter to the *Daily Telegraph* to put the matter into proper perspective. He made it clear that the Jordan government was fully within its rights to dismiss him; he was after all its servant. Not that most people in Britain knew anything about Glubb; many confused him with T. E. Lawrence and one elderly country squire thought he commanded the Foreign Legion. But the British government and particularly the Prime Minister were very irate. Eden was almost as angry with Glubb as he was with King Husain. 'Why did the fellow allow it to happen?' he is reported as saying when the news arrived from Amman.[1] He personally cabled the King in an attempt to persuade him to rescind his decision and instructed the Ambassador in Amman to use all his influence with Husain for Glubb's recall. To no avail. The ambassador, Charles Duke, who was friendly with the King, made no more impression on him than Eden.

There is no doubt that King Husain was surprised by the

Told to the author by the late Brigadier I. F. M. Spence who was with Eden when the news arrived from Amman.

vehement British reaction. He emphasized over and over again to Colonel Slade-Baker, who had a long interview with him six days after Glubb had left, that the Pasha's dismissal was not intended to be, and should not be interpreted as being, in any sense an anti-British move. It had been an entirely personal matter confined to one man. The reason given by Husain for the sudden dismissal of Glubb was the King's fear of a division in the army had the Pasha been permitted to remain, even for a few days.[2]

On the night of Glubb's dismissal the British Foreign Secretary, Selwyn Lloyd, was dining with President Nasser in the Tahera Palace in Cairo. During the meal a message arrived for the British Ambassador, Humphrey Trevelyan, informing him of Glubb's dismissal. Later in the evening Nasser was also handed a message but no mention was made of events in Jordan. Nasser afterwards insisted that he did not know of Glubb's dismissal until after the dinner party. This is probably true although both Eden and Lloyd were convinced that Nasser had fixed the entire business. Glubb himself has inclined towards the same view but all the evidence suggests that it was incorrect. King Husain took orders from no one. The decision was his alone.

There were sixty-four British officers serving in the Arab Legion; without exception they were taken by surprise. Lt-Col. Peter Young has provided an excellent description of how he first heard the news:

'On this evening [1 March] for the first time in months I went to the cinema . . . I am sorry to say that I disobeyed orders and left my bodyguard at home. I also forgot to mention where I was going. The film was *Desirée*. We had barely sat through a wrongful arrest and a *coup d'état* or two, when someone loomed up and said that Qaid Young was wanted below. There I found the Brigadier's driver Lutfi who took me to his house . . . As we drove up Arthur Green opened the door. "Come in. Something's happening. Glubb is out." My comment is unprintable. I accepted a whisky and soda and heard that Brigadiers Galletly and Hutton, Sir Patrick Coghill, Lt-Cols Gray and Griffiths had also been relieved of their commands. There was a direc-

[2]Unpublished diaries of Colonel J. B. Slade-Baker, Vol. VII, 6 March 1956.

ne to the H.Q. of 1 Brigade which for some reason had not been
ut. Brigadier Galletly had himself phoned through this infor-
nation. It was impossible to get through to the General [Cooke].[3]

' "We're still in. Can't understand it, can you?"

' "I suppose they're not afraid of us" . . . A few minutes
assed before the telephone rang again. The Brigadier walked
ack into the hall, and I followed him. "It's Ali Hiyari," he said.
There was a bit of talk, then he beamed at me: "You're out," he
aid. It was like being given l.b.w. in a cricket match. "And what
bout me?" asked the Brigadier. There was a little more talk. As
e put down the receiver, he said: "I am to remain in command
or the time being. I wonder how long that will be . . . It's His
Majesty's orders. There's nothing we can do about it." I went
ome and rang up the Regiment . . . I tried to ring up General
Cooke to satisfy myself that the orders were genuine. I was sur-
rised to get through, but it was Brigadier Hutton who answered.
"Yes, the orders are perfectly genuine. These are His Majesty's
rders. All these changes of personnel are to go through. It only
emains for you to give whoever is taking over from you as good
handover as possible, and then come over here [i.e. to Zerqa]
vith your family . . ." "[4]

Although the British officers, and most of the Jordanian,
vere stunned by the news, many of the latter believed it was
ime the Pasha went. He was too old, they said. Ali Hiyari had
emarked at a private dinner party a year previously that he did
not think British officers would be required in the Arab Legion
or much longer.[5] The British resented the manner of Glubb
Pasha's dismissal as much as anything. It seemed a harsh way to
reat a man who had devoted so much of his life to Jordan and

Galletly commanded 1 Brigade (Ramallah), Green 2 Brigade (Nablus). Hutton was
Glubb's chief of staff, Coghill Security adviser. Griffiths commanded 1st, and Gray
rd, Infantry regiments, both bedouin units. Young commanded 9th Infantry
egiment, also bedouin.
Peter Young, *Bedouin Command*, pp. 175–7.
Ali Hiyari was an able officer who succeeded General Cooke in command of the 1st
Division. On 13 April 1957 he was appointed C.G.S. in place of Ali abu Nuwar who
had gone into exile. Five days later he inexplicably deserted to the Syrians while
investigating a reported concentration of Syrian troops on the Jordan border. After
ome time the King allowed him to return and has since employed him in a number
of important posts. Ali gave the author dinner shortly before he left Jordan and told
im that he was leaving at the right time. He said the British were on the way out.

213

whose personal probity was a byword throughout the land. It was the more resented in Britain because Jordan owed it creation to Britain and had been supported by the British tax-payer for nearly forty years. King Husain's action seemed to be completely out of character.

The King has said he feared a division in the army and he was almost certainly correct. The praetorian guard of bedouins which King Abdullah, Kirkbride and Glubb had set out to fashion towards the end of the Second World War was still very much in existence in 1956. Glubb Pasha meant a great deal to them, particularly to the older bedouin officers and N.C.O.s whose lack of education placed them at a disadvantage in the competition for promotion. King Husain was well aware of this as were his advisers, both bedouins and *hadari*. If Glubb was to go, he must be out of the country within hours. They were mostly young men who had grown up in Glubb Pasha's shadow. None of them seems to have anticipated that he would go quietly his over-riding consideration that Jordan should be spared any turmoil on his behalf. Since the British Prime Minister appears to have shared their views, they should not be condemned out of hand.

In the event the only reason why a counter-coup did not take place was because Glubb had expressly forbidden any such action. His orders were loyally obeyed by the British command-ing officers in bedouin regiments. One of them was taken to one side by his officers when the news was received from Amman. They were convinced that the King had acted under duress. They begged to be led to Amman to restore the Pasha. He refused, saying it would be disloyal to the King and contrary to Glubb's orders.

The experiences of another commanding officer are worth recounting in more detail. It should be understood that in the confusion reigning in the immediate aftermath of Glubb Pasha's dismissal it was believed in many quarters that he was the victim of a plot engineered by Ali abu Nuwar and some of his supporters. The King, it was thought, was virtually the prisoner of these men. Many bedouin officers believed that in reinstating the Pasha they would also be helping King Husain.

The British officer in question was attending a party in the Arab Legion officers' club when he was suddenly summoned by some of his officers and driven on a circuitous route to his camp. On the way he was told of Glubb's dismissal. When he arrived at the camp he found his regiment drawn up and ready to be led into Amman, 'to restore the situation'. Protesting that he required more information, the commanding officer suggested they should consult General Cooke whose house was nearby. They told him that the road had been closed by an armed picket and that they would certainly be fired upon, but the C.O. insisted. Accompanied by several of his officers he walked down the road and past the picket without being halted. They found the G.O.C.'s residence ablaze with light. Cooke Pasha was briefing a gathering of British officers on the day's events.

When he inquired the reason for the deputation, he was horrified to learn that the regiment was about to set out for Amman, fighting its way through if needs be. 'He almost went down on his knees to implore me to prevent it,' said the C.O. 'He told me that Glubb Pasha had expressly forbidden anything of the kind. I was to return to the regiment, stand it down and hand over command to whoever had been appointed to take over from me. After explaining the situation to my officers we returned to the camp where my relief was already waiting for me. He saluted smartly and apologized for any inconvenience he might be causing me. It was all very civilized. We spent a short time in the office, after which I was driven to my house where my wife was waiting for me anxiously. She had simply no idea of what had been happening. When we left Jordan some time later my entire regiment turned out to escort me to the airport. It was quite a send-off!'[6]

Meanwhile the man who was at the centre of the storm flew home to England after a short stay in Cyprus. He was entirely unaware of the reception awaiting him and his family at London Airport. Glubb was essentially a modest man, his modesty bordering at times almost on naïveté. Appreciating that Jordan was a small and poor country, in no way to be compared in wealth and influence with Egypt, Iraq and Syria, he did not con-

[6]Told to the author in January 1982 by the officer concerned.

sider himself to be an important figure in the Middle East. The contributions made by King Abdullah and Kirkbride were, in Glubb's view, immensely more important. As a soldier he had done his duty to the best of his ability, and with good results, but no more than that. He had no false pride. He and his wife were simple in their tastes and life-style, sustained, in the moments of crisis which afflict every family occasionally, by their profound religious faith. Glubb did not even query the right of King Husain to dismiss him although undoubtedly he would have preferred that it had been done less precipitately. His chief immediate worry was financial. What would they do for money - and where would they live?

The dense crowd of reporters, photographers and camera men assembled at Heathrow on their arrival overwhelmed Glubb and his family. The children were tired and fractious after the long flight from Nicosia. The Pasha and Rosemary Glubb were under strain, physically and emotionally. It would not have been surprising in the circumstances if they had given vent to their feelings but neither uttered a word of criticism. Nothing in Glubb Pasha's distinguished career became him more than his behaviour that night and during the weeks that followed.

A few friends were there to greet them, among them Brigadier and Mrs Robert Elliot. 'His wonderful control, and with that I include Rosemary, astonished us all,' said Elliot. 'There was no word of regret, no bitterness, no thought of self-pity nor despair, but solely the thought that nothing connected with his going should ever disturb or weaken the ties between Great Britain and Jordan.' The Elliots had gone to Heathrow 'vaguely hoping that he would see us, with other friends, in the crowd and feel happier'. It was fortunate they were there. Together with the police they succeeded in smuggling the Glubbs out of the airport lounge by a back entrance and set off for Camberley with the press in hot pursuit. Unable to shake them off they stopped at an inn, where Glubb held an impromptu press conference until even his questioners had had enough. 'In times of utter physical prostration, journalists sometimes seem to be without pity,' Glubb commented later.

The family was temporarily split up in Camberley, the

children staying with the Elliotts, the Glubbs with Mrs Elliot's mother. 'Nothing could have exceeded the kindness of the Elliots,' wrote Glubb. 'As long as we live we can never repay the debt we owe them.' It had indeed been a bizarre homecoming for a man who disliked the limelight, and for his wife who felt the same. 'It may seem brutal to say so,' Elliot has written, 'but it was actually the best thing that ever happened to him. I am sure he would not be alive today otherwise. He might even have retired "in the normal course of events" and like lesser men before him have just disappeared from sight.'[7]

The Prime Minister telephoned the day after his arrival to say that the Queen had made him K.C.B. He was to have a long audience with her a few days later. The government had for once acted both promptly and with imagination. It behaved less generously when Glubb approached the Foreign Secretary for financial help; he was told that H.M.G. accepted no financial responsibility for him. The Ambassador in Amman was instructed to approach the Jordan government but was told that it, too, was under no obligation to assist.

Glubb has admitted that he was an imbecile all his life where money was concerned. It sounds incredible but he never had any form of contract with the Jordan government; nor did his salary compare with that paid to a British army general. The Glubbs lived very unostentatiously and did not entertain a great deal, the entertainment allowance sufficing to provide his constant stream of Arab visitors with tea and coffee. He had supported from his own pocket the schooling of numerous orphans and other young children and had paid for the hospital treatment of dozens of soldiers and their relatives. There were two children at boarding school in England whose fees had to be paid and somewhere found for the family to live. He had arrived with only a few pounds in his pocket and there were virtually no savings. Improvident is probably a better word than imbecile in Glubb Pasha's case, but both for him and for his wife there had been many more important things to worry about than money.

[7] Letter to author, 15 August 1980. The late Brigadier Robert Elliot commanded the Arab Legion Artillery from 1952–4. He died in 1982.

Fortunately there was a small, almost derisory, pension due to him. Glubb had approached the British Resident in Transjordan in 1933 with the request that some kind of pension should be arranged for him. The Colonial Office were not responsive at first but on 28 April 1934 the Chief Secretary to the Palestine government had informed Peake Pasha that Glubb had been appointed an Assistant District Commissioner (Grade G) in Palestine. The post was pensionable. When the Mandate ended Glubb had only completed fourteen years of pensionable service and his pension was only a few hundred pounds, but it was all he had. For years he assumed that his pension was that of an Inspector in the Palestine Police and it was only when researching for this book that the original letter was found.

Help did come, from an unexpected quarter. After his impromptu press conference on the way from Heathrow to Camberley, Glubb was approached by a *Daily Mail* reporter with the offer of £6000 for a series of six articles. Glubb was overwhelmed – no one had offered him such a large sum of money in his entire life. He immediately closed with the offer, probably unwisely because there would be other offers later. Robert Elliot wrote the introductory article for the series, giving it the title, *This man Glubb*. Not long afterwards there came an offer from Hodder & Stoughton, the firm that published *The Story of the Arab Legion* in 1948; it went into several editions. Hodder offered a generous advance for a second book, in Glubb's view, with the intention of helping him out rather than in any expectation of a best-seller. In fact *A Soldier with the Arabs*, which was published in 1957, sold well, Glubb being 'news' at the time.

For a man who had spent so much of his life dealing with importunate tribesmen and tortuous politicians, Glubb was curiously simple-minded when it came to dealing with his personal affairs. The house he bought in Mayfield is an example of this. It was a large and rambling building which had stood empty for three years. The garden was equally large and difficult to maintain. However, it was going cheap, and for this reason Glubb bought it, only to discover that it cost a fortune to run. He and his wife have remained there ever since, but not without some difficulty.

Glubb had been a compulsive writer for much of his life. He would cover reams of paper in his large flowing handwriting. It came easily to him. Lord Caradon who, as Hugh Foot, was Assistant British Resident in Amman in 1939, provides us with an interesting comparison between Kirkbride and Glubb. 'While Kirkbride was cynical, Glubb was enthusiastic. Kirkbride never said or wrote anything unless absolutely necessary; Glubb wrote enormous memoranda in English and a stream of orders and notes and messages in Arabic.'[8] Glubb did not abandon this practice in later years; his monthly reports on the Arab Legion had almost a Blackwoods flavour about them. He had read widely, chiefly history and philosophy, and he had a retentive memory. In his makeup there was much of the academic although he lacked the disciplined mind that comes from years of formal study. His writing therefore tended to be discursive at times, and occasionally rather dry.

Between 1956 and 1982 Glubb wrote twenty books in all, the last of them, his memoirs, in less than a year when he was aged eighty-four. He wrote with the same single-mindedness that had guided him throughout his years as a soldier, striving always to be fair. Inevitably the appeal of his books was to a limited readership and it is not the intention here to subject them to critical review. Four of his books were devoted to the history of the Arabs, involving years of research. His publisher advised against the project, doubting its popular appeal, but Glubb went ahead regardless. His publisher was right, but Glubb had the satisfaction of writing an academic work. His two best books are probably his account of the struggle against the Ikhwan in the 1920s, *War in the Desert*, and his diaries of the First World War published by Cassell in 1977 under the title *Into Battle*.

If a man is not a hero to his valet, the same probably holds true for his secretary. But Glubb Pasha was an exception. At the time of his dismissal his secretary was Mollie White, who showed both courage and initiative in securing Glubb's personal files from the safe in his office. She did this after Glubb Pasha had left *Qyada* for good, collecting the files in a bundle and walking out boldly through the security guards milling around in the

8 Sir Hugh Foot, *A Start in Freedom* (Hodder & Stoughton, 1966), p. 66.

outer office. Had she been stopped, there would undoubtedly have been trouble. She continued to work for him after his return to England, under somewhat different conditions.

'When we were back in England,' she has said, 'the public relations men who were working with him in connection with his lectures and tours did not know what had hit them! Not only were they always trying to track him down for appointments, but of course he always got his own way about everything. I think I am right in saying that one lot gave up the unequal struggle after a short while. Back in Jordan he was just as difficult to pin down . . . He never worried about what others thought, saying in effect, "If I worried about everyone who talked about me, I should never have any sleep!" Always calm and serene, at a time when the press were trying hard to provoke him into saying something nasty about King Husain, the Pasha played it very cool and simply changed the subject with a sweet smile . . . He hated being organized. After we left Jordan I worked for about a year for him, and I certainly did work. The Pasha was in great demand for lectures, tours etc., and getting him to appointments was a job in itself. On one occasion he went off to catch a Green Line coach at a stop just down the road. A little while after leaving he returned, saying, "Oh, Miss White, the coach didn't stop for me." It was a "Request" stop and he had failed to put out his arm!'[9]

The Jordan government had been meticulously correct in the handling of the Pasha's household effects. They had mounted a strong guard on the house and the contents were carefully listed. It was certainly not looted, as was wrongly reported in certain newspapers. Everything marked for return to England was packed and eventually arrived home safely. Articles and furniture no longer required were auctioned, sometimes with strange results. A valuable dining table went for a song but a cheap baby's basket-cot fetched a great deal more. The money came in useful but it amounted to very little.

The Pasha was not the only one to find himself in financial straits. There were about a dozen British officers with contracts with the Jordan government at the time of Glubb's dismissal.

[9]Interview, 1981.

They were dismissed in their turn. One or two of them were critical that Glubb did not make more fuss on their behalf with H.M.G. However Lt-Col. Kenneth Heisch, himself on contract, who was responsible for personnel matters, considers this criticism to have been ill-founded:

'As regards aid to local contract officers,' he has written, 'there was little if anything he could do. As employees of the Jordan government we were not the responsibility of H.M.G. and any risk we took of eventual unemployment was recognized and accepted by us. There was in fact a superannuation fund agreed by the Jordan government, based on rank and duration of service, which assured us of a lump sum when we left. I don't recall the actual amounts but my impression at the time was that this was a generous bonus. My sole connection with H.M.G. was approval to wear my *Istaqlal* (Grade 3)[10] with the stipulation that this privilege did not include any order of knighthood which has always puzzled me! It really surprises me that any ex-local contract officer should feel the British government owed them anything.'[11]

[10]The Order of the *Istaqlal* (Independence) was one of the Jordanian decorations.
[11]Letter to author, 28 January 1981.

Chapter Fifteen

---◆---

Epilogue

'He was the best little great good man that ever girded
a sword on his side; he took all things in good part,
and interpreted every action in the best sense.'

Rabelais

IN HIS ACCOUNT of his service in the Western Aden Protectorate
Lord Belhaven has written, 'I have yet to learn of the man who
has gained from the stake he laid down in Arabia.'[1] Despite the
manner of his departure from Jordan, Glubb Pasha would not
agree with him. Although the last few years in Jordan had been
difficult and disappointing, the years before them had been
golden ones, full of excitement, achievement and promise. The
Pasha's face would light up whenever he talked of them. He
may have been inclined to over-gild the lily on occasions, such
as when he asserted that he had never known a bedouin tribesman to tell a lie;[2] Charles Doughty would certainly have
dissented, as would probably those British officers who commanded bedouin regiments in the Arab Legion. Nevertheless
those golden years provided a sense of fulfilment that nothing
in the future could diminish.

Glubb's loyalty to those comrades of the early days is evident
in every book he has written about them. 'With his unfashionable
penchant for the Bedouin, as against the urban Arab,' wrote
James Morris, 'and his staunch desert values, he represents a
style of Arabism that has faded; a straight-eyed, open-air, un-
cluttered loyalty, now replaced by the theoretical profundities

[1] A. Hamilton (Master of Belhaven), *The Uneven Road* (John Murray, 1955).
[2] Comment by Glubb to author, June 1982.

of scholars and politicians.'[3] Morris, who considers Glubb to have been one of the best of the 'Anglo–Arab patriarchs,' also says of him, 'he was not one of the patronizing kind, nor one of the gunboat conservatives, not stuffy or complacent, neither aloof nor ingratiating. He moved sensibly with the times, and when at last the Arabs threw him out, feeling the need of him no longer, he accepted their ejection without rancour or recrimination.'[4]

There is the example of Glubb's iron self-control on the night of his dismissal. Although he must have felt sad, and perhaps even bitter, Rosemary Glubb cannot recall any words of complaint or recrimination. 'We were so busy deciding what to take with us and packing it up that time passed in a flash, and there wasn't a moment to brood.'[5] His secretary who worked for him during the first year in England was amazed by the way he settled down. 'I don't believe anyone could have adjusted to the circumstances in the way he did – so philosophically,' she has said.[6]

There may well have been a certain feeling of relief. Walking a tightrope is after all a demanding operation, both physically and mentally, and the Pasha had been doing this for nearly ten years. 'I remember him telling me quite clearly, probably in 1950,' wrote the late Lt-Col. P. F. Walshe, 'that he had no wish to remain longer than necessary and that he would like to go and hand over to an *Arab* officer within three or four years at most.'[7] Colonel Bob Melville, the Arab Legion's liaison officer in London for many years, believes Glubb told him in 1952 or 1953 that he would like to retire but that the Foreign Office had asked him to stay on for a little longer (but Glubb could not recall any such request being made to him). He has however written revealingly about his enforced retirement that, 'it was a peaceful relief to be no longer a public figure. One of the chief drawbacks of being in the public eye is that the fact undermines one's character by causing one to think of one's self – a preoccupation destructive of the spirit of service.'[8]

[3]Review by James Morris of *War in the Desert* (J. B. Glubb) in *Books and Bookmen.*
[4]Ibid.   [5]Interview with Lady Glubb, 1982.   [6]Interview with Miss White, 1981.
[7]Letter to author, 7 March 1980 (author's italics).
[8]J. B. Glubb, *The Changing Scenes of Life* (Quartet, 1983), p. 192.

For a man who had invariably risen at 5 a.m. and seldom retired to bed before midnight, it must indeed have been a pleasure to have more time to spend with his family. It must have been an even greater one for Jack and Rosemary Glubb to put behind them the constant, if unspoken, fear of the assassin's knife or bullet, the vilification in the newspapers and the vituperation on the radio. It must have been a joy, too, to have some privacy after nearly twenty years of living in public, surrounded by soldiers of the escort, petitioners, hangers-on, and the constant coming and going of staff officers, orderlies, sheikhs and politicians with axes to grind.

And yet no man can be expected to regard with equanimity the collapse of a life's work. That Glubb Pasha was deeply concerned about the future of Jordan and of its brave but impulsive young King is clear from a letter he wrote to Desmond Goldie on 11 March 1956:

'It was rather a sad ending in Jordan – I imagine that H.M.G. may have a chance of holding on to the political connection and the airfields, but I am afraid that the Arab Legion will go downhill very fast now. It is sad to think of, because it really was a great little army for a few years.'

However Glubb was proved wrong. Britain no longer has any airfields in Jordan, nor any wish for them. She possesses very little political influence although there is still a residual affection for the 'auld alliance'; despite misunderstandings on occasions, Britain is still the 'second home' of most educated Jordanians. The Arab Legion on the other hand, now known as the Jordanian Armed Forces, having recovered from the traumas of the 1960s and 1970s, is probably as well trained and led as it ever was; it is certainly far better equipped. The credit for this is due entirely to King Husain, who has set and insisted upon standards far exceeding those of other Arab armies. He has been helped of course by some able collaborators, without whose loyal support he might well have failed, but the drive, enthusiasm and personal example have come from the King. No one has been more delighted than Glubb Pasha that this should have been the case.

He did, however, consider Jordan's abrogation of the Anglo–Jordanian Treaty both unfortunate and unwise; without the

Treaty, Jordan was wide open to attack by Israel, as indeed happened, with disastrous results for Jordan, in 1967. Glubb's criticism of the King's action in unilaterally abrogating the Treaty in March 1957 has since been proved correct but it is hard to see how the King could have acted differently at the time; he was under great pressure to act, not only from the other Arab states, but also from his own officers and ministers. Politics is the art of the possible and as King Husain himself has said, 'It is not always possible to take the course one's heart would like when one's head says otherwise.'[9] And it was probably true that the British were glad to get off the Jordanian hook on which they had been impaled for so long. It was now the Americans' turn to be the world's whipping-boy.

Despite many invitations, Glubb has never returned to Jordan. Nor has he kept open house in Sussex, as he did in Amman, for any Jordanian who happened to be passing. He has eschewed the latter, knowing the splendid hospitality of the Arabs, simply because he could not afford it. As for the former, he gave his reasons in a letter in January 1982:

'It is very heartwarming to know they still remember me in Jordan. All the same, I think I prefer to remember it as it was. I am sure it is a mistake to go back. It is always best to keep one's memories. However I am delighted that the country is still doing so well. It was unique in the Middle East. There used always to be *coups d'état* and troubles in Syria and Iraq but Jordan was always as stable as a rock. Long may it continue so. They were a charming people.'[10]

The Pasha is now a part of Jordan's history (although Peake Pasha is all but forgotten). For those below thirty Glubb too is no more than a name – a legend perhaps? But for the middle-aged and the elderly he means a lot more. 'How is the Pasha?' they ask, usually adding, 'May God remember him for good.' Some are surprised to learn he is still alive; all speak of him with great affection. Sir Gawain Bell recounts a story that is in many ways indicative of the regard in which he is held, even by those who were no more than children at the time of his dismissal.

Bell was travelling from Damascus to Amman in a taxi in

[9]Audience with King Husain, 10 January 1982.   [10]Letter to author.

1963. 'I had a seat beside the driver,' he writes, 'and in the back were two Syrians. One was a man of twenty-five or so, an Arab Legionnaire returning from leave. The other was a little younger; a schoolmaster from near Deraa in the Hauran. As we approached the Jordan frontier the talk between the two turned to the Arab Legion, now the Jordan Armed Forces. The schoolmaster brought up the dismissal of Glubb Pasha in 1956. "What a fortune that man must have made," he said. "Commander of the Jordan Army for the best part of twenty years. Think of it; the stores, the arms, the ammunition – everything. He must have taken a very nice rake-off throughout all that time." "My dear fellow," the Legionnaire replied, "you've got it all wrong. I personally never saw Glubb, but a lot of us in the army knew him and talk of him, and I can tell you from what they've told me that so far from making a piastre out of the army, Glubb constantly helped men in need from his own pay, and that he used to send to hospitals in the Lebanon, at his own expense, fellows suffering from tuberculosis." "Are you sure?" queried the schoolmaster. "I'm convinced," answered the Legionnaire. "I'll take your word for it," said his companion, after a long pause, "although it sounds very extraordinary. I never thought he was that sort of a man." I remained silent throughout this conversation [says Bell], but as we drove to the Frontier Post I felt happy in the thought that justice had been done, in however small a way.'[11]

It was Glubb Pasha's bad luck that the great Arab boom was still twenty years away in the future when he left Jordan; otherwise his knowledge of the Arabs might well have brought him lucrative employment. It is nevertheless strange that H.M.G. could find nothing for him. They may have thought it might be embarrassing at a time when Britain's relations with the Arabs were so delicate; or perhaps the Prime Minister, Harold Macmillan, who was busy mending fences with the U.S.A. and within his own Party, agreed with his predecessor that Glubb could have done more to avert his dismissal. Glubb himself never pretended he had any claims on the British government. 'I think you are wrong when you say I was a key figure in the Middle

[11]Sir Gawain Bell, *Shadows on the Sand*, p. 145.

East for twenty-five years,' he wrote. 'If I had been in Iraq or Egypt, this might have been so. But Jordan was too small to cut much ice, whether one did a good job or not.' [12]

There was no repining. He had to get on with finding a job. When Foyles suggested that he might turn his hand to lecturing, Glubb at once agreed. For the next five years he travelled all over England, Scotland and Wales lecturing to universities, schools and societies. Rosemary Glubb often accompanied him. The work was not very remunerative but it did provide the opportunity to see something of a country he had hardly known since 1919; and lecturing, together with his writing, did bring in enough money to keep the wolf from the door. Then Foyles Lecture Agency proposed a lecture tour in the U.S.A. where the financial rewards were much greater.

All the arrangements were made for him. He was therefore surprised on arrival in New York to be handed a prepared statement to be read out to the press conference arranged for him at the airport. The statement expressed admiration for the brave people of Israel etc., etc. Glubb refused to read it. He had no strong feelings for or against the Jews but he insisted that if a statement had to be made, he preferred to draft it himself. He was then warned that unless he read out the statement as prepared for him, he would probably be blackballed at most of the rich clubs where Jewish influence was strong. He nevertheless refused to comply and as a result the financial reward of the tour was less than it would otherwise have been; however, it was most successful and Glubb was asked to return.

Thereafter an annual lecture tour in America became a regular feature of his life. He early realized that he was as capable as any agent to arrange his programme, plane tickets and hotel bookings. This saved him money and he was able to bring to it the meticulous attention to detail that had characterized his years as a soldier. He also, fortunately, retained his health, energy and enthusiasm until well into his seventies. One of his closest American friends, Colonel James Pooley Davis, who had at one time been American Military Attaché in Jordan, had this to say about him:

[12]Letter to author, 18 October 1974.

'The Pasha made several trips to the States to lecture under the auspices of foreign affairs groups, universities and civic clubs. He made one trip a year and travelled from coast to coast, usually by air. His trips must have been strenuous because when he had a speaking engagement there usually was a session with reporters first, at the airport or wherever he was staying. One year he came to Seattle to address the Foreign Affairs Council on the Middle East situation. The next night he spoke to a packed auditorium at the University of Washington on Arab Life and Customs. His next stop on that trip was "just down the road" at Oregon State University . . . where he conducted a seminar for students studying the Middle East that afternoon and gave another lecture in the evening. Following that we drove to Palo Alto for a lecture at Stanford University.

'On one of his trips he gave a lecture at Lewis and Clark University in Portland, Oregon. The students were so impressed that they later raised a subscription to bring him to the university to lecture for one term. During that time he had the opportunity of seeing some of the great variety of the north-west, and showed intense interest. He seemed quite at home, whether lunching above a fishing wharf on a Pacific Coast Indian reservation, boating on a long mountain lake surrounded by rocky steeps reminiscent of Jordan, or riding down a prehistoric river bed cut through lava, to see a huge hydro-electric dam.'[13]

Lecturing, writing and travelling took up so much of his time that inevitably Jordan faded into the background. He had not so much beaten his sword into a ploughshare as turned it into a typewriter. It was a life he thoroughly enjoyed, apart from the discomforts of air travel and airports. He had found, in every sense of the word, a new vocation and one that provided a better financial reward than a Lieutenant-General's pay in the Arab Legion. But as the 1970s followed the 1960s, the wear and tear of an active life began to exact its toll. In 1971 he spent part of the fall semester at Troy State University in Alabama and while there had several fainting fits. He was then aged seventy-four. Soon afterwards he collapsed in Birmingham, Alabama, where he was due to speak, and was taken to hospital. On medical

[13]Letter to author, 20 April 1982.

advice the rest of his tour was cancelled and the Pasha returned home to undergo treatment. He has never set out on his travels again, although he never ceased to write books and a succession of articles.

Glubb's attraction for young American students lay in his modesty, simplicity and approachability. He was the least pompous of men. Americans see their admirals and generals cast in a heroic mould but Glubb Pasha was not that kind of man. Short in height, not particularly distinguished in appearance, neatly but never elaborately dressed, always courteous and never condescending, Glubb Pasha was no Macarthur wading ashore in the Philippines or a Patton striking poses with pearl-handled pistols. He would have considered such behaviour extremely bad form. He much more resembled the kind of professor the students met on the campus, a trifle distrait in appearance perhaps; kindly if a little absentminded; learned beyond dispute; and if a man of war, then one more likely to succour a damsel in distress than lay waste a city. There was always about the Pasha a distinct air of authority – but never a hint of arrogance.

If it were necessary to find one word to describe Glubb Pasha, that word must surely be 'balanced'. He was indeed a supremely well-balanced man, and this despite his Cornish–Irish emotionalism, quick temper and impatience with those who failed to match his own high standards. Some part of this balance was perhaps due to a happy childhood and his close relationship with his father and mother; a larger part was due to his profound Christian faith. Early in his career he convinced himself that leadership was in essence love for one's fellow men, and he made this conviction his guiding star throughout his life. He came to believe that it was only the spirit of love which could really move men and women; only love could prevent war, which he regarded with loathing and horror. He even sincerely believed that it was realistic to love one's enemies. 'If only the Israelis had loved the Arabs and tried to do them good,' he has written, 'they would by now have held as powerful a position in Western Asia as they do in the United States. But successive Israeli governments have continued to suppress the people of Palestine, to rule them by martial law, to evict them and seize their lands and to deny them any part in government.'[14]

This has been described as naïve by worldly-wise statesmen and diplomats who prefer to regard the world through less rose-coloured spectacles. But the world, with its now terrifying ability to destroy itself, must one day make up its mind whether Glubb Pasha is right, or whether the holocaust is inevitable. For his part, Glubb has no doubts, and it has yet to be shown that he is wrong.

Even modest men are entitled to a proper pride in their achievements but it is probably true that Glubb Pasha attached little importance to their outward manifestations. He was the first recipient of the Lawrence Gold Medal presented by the Royal Central Asian Society for 'work of outstanding distinction in the Near and Middle East'. He was similarly honoured by the Royal Scottish Geographical Society. In 1942 he was presented by Amir Abdullah with a Shereefian gold dagger, an award made to only one other Englishman, T. E. Lawrence. There were presentation swords from King Feisal I, King Ibn Saud and King Abdullah. There were Honours from Jordan and Britain. The Pasha was proud to receive them but he preferred to regard them as rewards to the men he had led than as personal distinctions. He was a humble man.

Although by nature a warm-hearted man, the Pasha could appear rather cold in public; certainly with his British sub-ordinates. He was more relaxed in Arab society. He also had the somewhat disconcerting habit, to a junior British officer, of addressing one as 'Sir'. Knowing the importance attached by Arabs to dignity, he always kept a proper distance, but he was a charming host in his own home. He did not much care for the use of Christian names and he appeared to take the most flippant remark seriously, as if unable to credit that anyone could make a joke about a serious subject. General Cooke once remarked of him, 'The Pasha is always "on parade".' His long years in Arabia had insulated him from the changes in British society brought about by the Second World War, and he did not much

---

[14]Glubb Pasha's memoirs. In 1974 he published a book, *The Way of Love: Lessons from a Long Life* (Hodder & Stoughton), explaining his philosophy.

care for them when they came to his notice. He was an Edwardian in manner, because he preferred it that way.

The *Daily Telegraph* described him as 'quiet and studious' in its report of the presentation of the Shereefian gold dagger on 11 November 1942. He was not quiet by nature and when at home with his family enjoyed playing games and singing songs with his children. But he had lived for many years among the garrulous and quarrelsome bedouins whose lives were necessarily lived in public; the only way he could achieve an inner privacy was by appearing always to be quiet, attentive and patient. His Arab companions of those days always refer to his patience. His enthusiasm surfaced at times, more often in Arab than in British company, but he never allowed it to run away with him; his emotions were always under control. He was certainly studious by inclination, playing no games and caring little for social life. He did however enjoy chatting in the evenings with friends, Arabs and British, sipping tea or coffee with the former, and sherry or whisky with the latter (but one glass was enough). A heavy cigarette smoker at one time, he gave it up completely. On the few occasions he visited the British officers' mess in Zerqa he never attempted to be convivial – just polite, interesting in discussion and always friendly.

His work was his life and he did not find it easy to delegate; his load therefore grew heavier as the Legion expanded. He could be a hard taskmaster, making little concession for those whose dedication did not match his own. He was far more inclined to make concessions for his Arab than his British officers, few of whom were really close to him. One of them has commented:

'You never knew what was going on with Glubb. His mind had begun to work like an Arab's. He was all subtleties. He had the kind of mind that could understand the illogic of the Arabs and anticipate it. He knew they would act from their emotions, and he knew what those emotions were. He dealt as an Arab with the King's palace, as a Bedouin with the tribes, as a British officer with London. No one except Glubb knew everything that was going on.'[15]

[15]Collins & Lapierre, *O Jerusalem* (Weidenfeld & Nicolson, 1972), p. 197.

This, if true, was part of his strength. He took few into his confidence and this made him indispensable. He ran the Arab Legion as he had run the Desert Patrol, relying on his own judgement and knowledge of the Arab mentality. No British officer could hope to match his knowledge of the Arabs; no Arab officer could be expected to know how to deal with the War Office in London. In Amman he was judged by the results which, until Qibya, seemed fair enough. In London, too, his handling of a succession of difficult situations was hard to fault. Thus he combined in his own person two quite different lines of approach. The British Government was hoping for some kind of accommodation between the Arabs and Israel that would lead to peace in the Middle East. The Jordan government in its inner heart wanted to see the Palestinian Arabs back in their own land. In no way could these divergent aims be reconciled and it was Glubb's misfortune to be the man in the middle. In the end he was certain to lose.

He elected to concentrate on the military aspect of the problem, but he might have been better advised to consider the political aspect. Had he been a less honest and less dedicated man, he would probably have decided to give up an unwinnable contest and hand over to an Arab successor. But in his judgement this would have meant abandoning Jordan and would have conflicted with everything he had been brought up to believe in – duty, loyalty and service. He therefore chose to ride out the storm which finally engulfed him.

Two of his British staff officers have emphasized that the Pasha was 'predominantly an operational soldier'. He felt an affinity for those holding command or staff appointments 'at the sharp end', particularly for those with outstanding war records. 'Those in administrative, supply and financial staff appointments were regarded with some impatience, generally benign, but in the expectation of error, disturbing his fine balance of Arab equilibrium.'

The Pasha was never arrogant but like many people who have faith in their own judgement he could at times be peremptory and demanding. He was also chary of praise where his British subordinates were concerned. His own sense of duty was so high that he expected the same from lesser mortals. He was more lavish of praise with his Arab subordinates. Some of his British subordinates wondered occasionally whether he was fully aware of their toil although it is true that without exception they respected and admired him. 'He could be awfully demanding at times,' one of them has said, 'but at least one knew he was working twice as hard as oneself, as well as being subjected to much greater pressures. He was a great man.'

It required about two years to gain the Pasha's confidence. He did not care for mistakes but he disliked nervousness more. He was no bully but liked to be faced fairly and squarely. 'Once one was accepted by the Pasha one was accepted completely,' Kenneth Heisch has written. 'It was very satisfying to take him a letter for signature and see him sign it with barely a glance. His own burden of work was enormous and many a time the phone would ring at 11 p.m. or later with some requirement for the morning. He assumed his staff would cope with whatever action was required and very, very seldom made any acknowledgement. One came to appreciate that silence was in itself an accolade. It is hardly necessary to add that to work for this remarkable man was a rare privilege.'[16]

Glubb particularly disliked being organized by his staff and he could be forgetful on occasions, departing in his car just before he had an appointment in his office. There would then be frantic telephoning to recall him. At heart he was a very kindly man with a strong distaste for scenes of any kind, mainly because he was by nature quick-tempered. He inherited from his mother an iron will, as well as her devout Christian faith. Without these he could scarcely have survived the pressures from 1947 onwards.[17]

Glubb Pasha will probably be longest remembered for his sympathy with, and knowledge of, the bedouin tribesmen of Arabia. Within the Arab Legion he was remarkably successful in bringing together the bedouins and those recruited from the settled communities. However, in his determination that the

[16]Letter, 17 January 1981.
[17]Lady Glubb (senior) made her home in Jerusalem and refused to leave it during the fighting in 1948. After her son's dismissal she reluctantly returned to England, living to the age of ninety-seven. She was a great personality.

Arab Legion should not become politicized, as had happened in the Syrian and Iraqi armies, he might be accused of allowing his heart to rule his head, since it was inevitable that the simple values of the desert would sooner or later become eroded by contact with the urban population.

As an Englishman commanding an Arab army Glubb Pasha found it impossible at times to steer a straight course. As he tacked in accordance with changes in the wind, some people found it difficult to understand his actions. Some even thought him devious, 'more Arab than the Arabs', but they never knew the full story. He could be wilful at times, even mischievous, in his determination to have his own way. He was a strange paradox, on the one hand simple and open, on the other subtle and complex. Although usually he was patient, sometimes he could be impulsive. It is possible that he fought an inner battle between his desire for a life of action against a wish for a life of learning and of study. This could explain how he adjusted so easily to the great change in his life from the age of sixty onwards.

He was a much more complicated man than ever appeared on the surface. He believed in the values he had been taught by his mother and father when Britain still ruled an empire, but he was never an imperialist. He had only contempt for those who claimed a superiority on the grounds of race or colour. He believed we had as much to learn from the Arabs as they had from us. It saddened him greatly in his old age to see his countrymen abandon so recklessly so much that he had been brought up to cherish. It may have made him appear reactionary at times but this was far from being the case. His study of history had convinced him that few empires survive for more than two centuries. He was therefore reconciled to the passing of the British Empire but believed the British had still a lot to give to the world by way of example. He regretted that we appeared to have lost the will to do so.

His philosophy stemmed from his faith, which was based on the power of love. For him, as for the simplest bedouin camelherd, God was ever-present, all-seeing and all-beneficent. The bedouins knew that he was a devout man and respected him the more for it. His soldiers were never mere names or numbers;

234

they were always individuals. St John Armitage tells a story of the Pasha visiting the fort in Wadi Rhum. Soon after his inspection he went on leave to Europe. Two or three weeks later a postcard arrived from Como: while at Wadi Rhum the Pasha had noticed that *Jundi* Mahommed Qasim needed a new greatcoat. Would Armitage kindly see that he was given one.

Glubb did not like rows. This led him on occasions to deliver rebukes in writing when they might have been better delivered verbally. He was also reluctant to criticize anyone who had served under him. One student in search of enlightenment came away frustrated after a lengthy interview with him. 'He talked away happily about his days in the desert,' she said, 'but the moment I got on to personalities, he shut up like a clam. See no evil, hear no evil and speak no evil must be his motto!'[18]

He was a very private person. His formative years in Arabia had been spent among a people who attached great importance to dignity but virtually none to privacy. Living as he had to do among bedouins who will gossip far into the night, and in a tent which was open to every passing wayfarer, Glubb constructed round himself a kind of carapace inside which he could retain his privacy, while outwardly he would be sitting there patient and calm. Moreover, in Iraq, and during the early years in Transjordan, he had to do almost everything himself. He therefore became supremely self-reliant, sharing his inner thoughts with virtually no one until his marriage. Although never an unsociable man, he learnt to be self-sufficient.

His loyalty was absolute – to Jordan as much as to Great Britain. For more than a quarter of a century he maintained this dual loyalty which must have been a strain at times. The Arab Legion, long regarded as an élite force by friend and foe alike, owed more to Glubb Pasha than to any other man. It set a standard which is gratefully acknowledged in the Jordanian Armed Forces today. More than anything else he was the catalyst that brought together the bedouins and the settled Arabs as citizens of the same country. No one before him had attempted to do this. Few other men could have succeeded.

[18]Interview, 1981.

235

Appendix

Glubb Pasha's Orders and Decorations

British

Knight Commander of the Most Honourable Order of the Bath (K.C.B.)
Companion of the Most Distinguished Order of St Michael and St George (C.M.G.)
Distinguished Service Order (D.S.O.)
Officer of the Most Excellent Order of the British Empire (O.B.E.)
Military Cross (M.C.)
King's Police Medal

Jordanian

Wisam al Nahda Grade 3
Wisam al Istaqlal Grade 1
Wisam al Nahda Grade 1

Iraqi

Order of the Rafidain, Grade 4

Sir John Glubb was also a Knight of the Holy Sepulchre and the first recipient of the Lawrence Gold Medal established by the Royal Central Asian Society.

Acknowledgements

In the course of my research into Glubb Pasha's life I have been helped by a great many people, most of whom are listed below, I trust. If anyone has been omitted, I apologize. First I must thank His Majesty King Husain of Jordan for so graciously receiving me in audience during my visit to Jordan early in 1982 and for sparing the time to talk with me about the Pasha. Then I must thank General Zeid bin Shakir, Commander-in-Chief of the Jordan Armed Forces, for arranging the visit and for giving freely of his time to talk with me. While in Jordan I had the opportunity to discuss the Pasha with many old friends, such as Generals Mashour Haditha el Jazy, Suleiman Irtemeh and Motloq Ead, with whom I had soldiered in the same regiment twenty-five years before. It was heart-warming to meet them again. In London I have been given much help by General Shefiq Jumean and by the Defence Attaché at the Jordanian Embassy, Brigadier Mahmud Salem.

Miss Alexandra Ward, Head of the Army Historical Branch, has, as always, been of great assistance, as has Clive Hughes of the Imperial War Museum. Steven Stacey of Wadham College, Oxford, did some useful work for me in the P.R.O. and I am also grateful to my secretary, Mildred Fairclough, for her help. Among the many individuals who have helped I must thank the following:

The Earl of Oxford and Asquith, Sir Gawain Bell, Sir Geoffrey Furlonge, Colonel Nigel Bromage, Colonel Rodney Parsons, Brigadier Tim Hope-Thomson, Colonel Charles Coaker, General Rea Leakey, Brigadier Peter Young, Mrs Edith Gray, Miss Mollie White, the late Brigadier Robert Elliot, the late Colonel 'Rocky' Walsh, Colonel Charles Chaplin, St John Armitage, Michael Hankin-Turvin, Colonel Kenneth Heisch, Major Bob Young and Mrs Ruth Young, Colonel Desmond Goldie, Colonel John Branford, Dr Margaret McLeod, Mrs Thelma Kaiser, Mrs Denys Edwyn-Jones, The Regimental Colonel of the Royal Engineers, Colonel Bob Melville, Colonel James Pooley-Davis, the Bursar of Marlborough College, General Sir Christopher Welby-Everard, Colonel Alec Salmon, the Bursar of Cheltenham College, Professor Albert Hourani, the late Sir Patrick Coghill and Gillian Grant of St Antony's College, Oxford.

Sir John Glubb has been of immense help. I have visited him often and we have corresponded regularly. I am much in his debt, and in Lady Glubb's for her hospitality.

I have to thank Brigadier Peter Young for permission to quote from *Bedouin Command*; Jan Morris for a quotation from *Sultan in Oman*; Wilfred Thesiger from *Desert, Marsh and Mountain*; and the Pasha from his many books. I am indebted to Bob and Ruth Young for the illustrations selected from the many beautiful photographs they took during Bob's service in Jordan.

Last, but in no way least, I must thank my wife who shares my love for Jordan and its people, who often accompanied me on my journeys there, and who has borne patiently with me during the writing of this book.

Bibliography

Private Papers:

Sir John Glubb has written a great deal during his life, beginning with his First World War Diaries. He wrote voluminous reports and commentaries on his work and the contemporary situation in Iraq, Transjordan and Palestine. He also wrote reports on the campaigns in Iraq and Syria in 1941. Throughout his time as Commander of the Desert Area in Transjordan he wrote a Monthly Report for Headquarters Arab Legion; as Commander of the Arab Legion from 1939 onwards he wrote Periodic Reports. He has kept most of the letters written to him by his mother and father and also many letters received from other correspondents. Most of these papers are to be deposited in St Antony's College, Oxford. Many extracts from them are quoted in this biography, some previously unpublished.

Published sources:

J. B. Glubb *The Story of the Arab Legion* (Hodder & Stoughton, 1948)
    A Soldier with the Arabs (Hodder & Stoughton, 1957)
    Britain and the Arabs (Hodder & Stoughton, 1959)
    War in the Desert (Hodder & Stoughton, 1960)
    The Empire of the Arabs (Hodder & Stoughton, 1963)
    The Great Arab Conquests (Hodder & Stoughton, 1963)
    The Course of Empire (Hodder & Stoughton, 1965)
    The Lost Centuries, 1145–1453 (Hodder & Stoughton, 1967)
    The Middle East Crisis: A Personal Interpretation (Hodder & Stoughton, 1967; new edition 1969)
    The Mixture of Races in the Eastern Arab Countries (Blackwell, 1967)
    Syria, Lebanon and Jordan (Thames & Hudson, 1967)

A Short History of the Arab Peoples (Hodder & Stoughton, 1969 – new edition Quartet, 1978)

The Life and Times of Muhammad (Hodder & Stoughton, 1970)

Peace in the Holy Land: An Historical Analysis of the Palestine Problem (Hodder & Stoughton, 1971)

Soldiers of Fortune: The Story of the Mamlukes (Hodder & Stoughton, 1973)

The Way of Love: Lessons from a Long Life (Hodder & Stoughton, 1974)

Haroon Al Rasheed and the Great Abbasids (Hodder & Stoughton, 1976)

Arabian Adventures: Ten Joyful Years of Service (Cassell, 1978)

Into Battle: A Soldier's Diary of the Great War (Cassell, 1978)

The Fate of Empires and *Search for Survival* (Blackwood, 1978)

The Changing Scenes of Life (Quartet, 1983)

A Short History of the Glubb Family (privately printed in 1983)

King Abdullah   *My Memoirs Completed* (Longmans, 1978)

Sir Gawain Bell   *Shadows on the Sand* (C. Hurst & Co., 1983)

Folke Bernadotte   *To Jerusalem* (Hodder & Stoughton, 1951)

W. S. Churchill   *The Second World War, Vol. III* (Cassell, 1950)

L. Collins & D. Lapierre   *O Jerusalem* (Weidenfeld & Nicolson, 1972)

Ann Dearden   *Jordan* (Robert Hale, 1958)

Somerset de Chair   *The Golden Carpet* (Faber & Faber, 1944)

H. R. P. Dickson   *The Arab of the Desert* (Allen & Unwin, 1949)

C. S. Doughty   *Travels in Arabia Deserta* (Jonathan Cape, 1926)

G. S. Dragnich   *The Bedouin Warrior Ethic* etc. (Georgetown University, 1975)

Anthony Eden   *Full Circle* (Cassell, 1960)

S. A. El-Edroos   *The Hashemite Arab Army* (Publishing Committee in Amman, 1980)

Hugh Foot   *A Start in Freedom* (Hodder & Stoughton, 1966)

Geoffrey Furlonge   *Palestine is my Country* (John Murray, 1969)

Brian Gardner   *Allenby* (Cassell, 1965)

Helga Graham   *Arabian Time Machine* (Heinemann, 1978)

Philip Graves (Ed.)   *Memoirs of King Abdullah* (Jonathan Cape, 1950)

A. Hamilton (Lord Belhaven)   *The Uneven Road* (John Murray, 1955)

Chaim Herzog   *The Arab/Israeli Wars* (Arms & Armour Press, 1981)

King Husain   *Uneasy Lies the Head* (Heinemann, 1978)

Julian Huxley   *From an Antique Land* (Parrish Rogers, 1954)

C. S. Jarvis   *Desert and Delta* (John Murray, 1947)

George Kirk   *The Middle East 1945–50* (Royal Institute of International Affairs and OUP, 1954)

Alec Kirkbride   *A Crackle of Thorns* (John Murray, 1956)
   An Awakening (University Press of Arabia, 1971)

Robert Lacey   *The Kingdom* (Hutchinson, 1981)

Harry Levin   *Jerusalem Embattled* (Gollancz, 1950)

Godfrey Lias   *Glubb's Legion* (Evans, 1956)

James Lunt   *Imperial Sunset* (Macdonald, 1981)

Robin Maugham   *Nomad* (Viking Press, N.Y., 1948)

Richard Meinertzhagen   *Middle East Diary* (Yoselof, 1960)

Anthony Mockler   *Our Enemies The French* (Leo Cooper, 1976)

James Morris   *Sultan in Oman* (Faber & Faber, 1967)

Anthony Nutting   *No End of a Lesson* (Constable, 1967)

Edgar O'Ballance   *The Arab–Israeli War* (Faber & Faber, 1948)

F. G. Peake   *History of Jordan and its Tribes* (Miami, 1958)

I. S. O. Playfair   *The Mediterranean and the Middle East, Vols I & II* (HMSO, 1954 and 1956)

C. Raswan   *The Black Tents of Arabia* (Hutchinson, 1935)

Gerald Sparrow   *Husain of Jordan* (Harrap, 1960)

Freya Stark   *East is West* (John Murray, 1945)
   Dust in the Lion's Paw (John Murray, 1961)

Wilfred Thesiger   *Arabian Sands* (Collins, 1983 (revised edtn.))
    Desert, Marsh and Mountain (Collins, 1979)
Humphrey Trevelyan   *The Middle East in Revolution* (Macmillan, 1970)
P. J. Vatikiotis   *Politics and the Military in Jordan* (Cassell, 1967)
Geoffrey Warner   *Iraq and Syria 1941* (Davis-Poynter, 1974)
Peter Young   *Bedouin Command* (Kimber, 1956)
    The Arab Legion (Osprey, 1972)